Educational Sovereignty and Transnational Exchanges in Post-Secondary Indonesian Education

Anita Abbott

Educational Sovereignty and Transnational Exchanges in Post-Secondary Indonesian Education

palgrave
macmillan

Anita Abbott
School of Business
Charisma University
Providenciales, Turks and Caicos Islands
New Zealand

ISBN 978-3-319-85290-4   ISBN 978-3-319-53985-0 (eBook)
DOI 10.1007/978-3-319-53985-0

© The Editor(s) (if applicable) and The Author(s) 2017
Softcover reprint of the hardcover 1st edition 2017
This work is subject to copyright. All rights are solely and exclusively licensed by the Publisher, whether the whole or part of the material is concerned, specifically the rights of translation, reprinting, reuse of illustrations, recitation, broadcasting, reproduction on microfilms or in any other physical way, and transmission or information storage and retrieval, electronic adaptation, computer software, or by similar or dissimilar methodology now known or hereafter developed.
The use of general descriptive names, registered names, trademarks, service marks, etc. in this publication does not imply, even in the absence of a specific statement, that such names are exempt from the relevant protective laws and regulations and therefore free for general use.
The publisher, the authors and the editors are safe to assume that the advice and information in this book are believed to be true and accurate at the date of publication. Neither the publisher nor the authors or the editors give a warranty, express or implied, with respect to the material contained herein or for any errors or omissions that may have been made. The publisher remains neutral with regard to jurisdictional claims in published maps and institutional affiliations.

Cover image © dieKleinert / Alamy Stock Photo

Printed on acid-free paper

This Palgrave Macmillan imprint is published by Springer Nature
The registered company is Springer International Publishing AG
The registered company address is: Gewerbestrasse 11, 6330 Cham, Switzerland

Acknowledgements

There are many people whose assistance has been invaluable and without whose assistance, it would not have been possible for me to write this book:

Special thanks to my husband Maxwell, who has been very supportive. Words are not adequate to express my gratitude and appreciation to you. Thank you. Thank you for your love and patience. Thank you for being with me in good and bad times. I love you so much.

Sincere thanks to my mentors, Dr Alan Simpson and Dr Patrick Barrett of the University of Waikato, who have supported and encouraged me. They have been one of the sources of my inspiration. I really value not only their knowledge but also their wisdom.

Sincere thanks to Dr Teri McClleland and Dr Joanne Whittle of Southern Institute of Technology who have also supported me.

Last, but not the least, I am very grateful to my children Isaac and Jacob for their love and patience.

December 5, 2016   Hamilton

Contents

1 Introduction   1

2 Transnational Education and Educational Sovereignty:
   A Framework for Analysis   9
   Definitions of Transnational Education   9
   The Prevalence of Transnational Education   13
   Transnational Education and Parties Involved   15
   Summary   16
   Educational Sovereignty   17
      The Concept of Educational Sovereignty   17
      Perspectives on Educational Sovereignty   18
      Transnational Education and Homogenisation Processes   21
      Transnational Education and the New Imperialism   22
   Alternative Perspectives on Education Sovereignty   24
      Transnational Education and Hybridisation Processes   24
      Transnational Education and the Development of LDSs   26
   Educational Sovereignty Revisited   27
   *The Links Between Transnational Education and Educational
   Sovereignty*   28
      Homogenisation and Hybridisation of Education and Culture   29
      Development and the New Imperialism   31

The Importance of Sovereignty in Education and the Potential for Diminished Sovereignty   33
   Authority, Control, Autonomy, and the Resilience of Sovereignty in Education   37
   Understanding Transnational Education and Its Impact   38
   Features of Educational Sovereignty   39
   Concluding Remarks   42

3 Indonesian Post-Secondary Education and the Presence of Foreign Education   57
   Indonesia's Post-Secondary Education System, Its Development, and Policies from 1999 to the Present   57
      The Development of Indonesian Post-Secondary Education Institutions   57
      The Provision of Education Legislation   59
      Curriculum Development of Indonesian Post-Secondary Education   64
   Transnational Education in Indonesia   65
   Foreign Education and Indonesian Education Law   72
   Foreign Education Presence and National Education Law: Future Hope   74
   Concluding Remarks   75

4 Nature of Indonesian Transnational Education   81
   Knowledge Dependency: One-Way Transfer of Knowledge, Technology, and Research Projects   81
      Indonesia–US Education Relations   81
      Indonesia–New Zealand Education Relations   85
   Indonesian Education Relations with Other Developed States   87
   Prominence of Expatriates Among Academic Staff   88
      Indonesia–US Education Relations   88
   The Education Exchange and Learning About Each Other   94
      Indonesia–US Education Relations   94
      Indonesia–Australia Education Relations   102
   Concluding Remarks   103

5	**Equality in the Indonesia–US Relations**	107
	Why Equality?	108
	Impact on Indonesia's Educational Sovereignty	111
	American Financial Assistance in Education	119
	Concluding Remarks	127
6	**Indonesian Identity and Cultural Values**	135
	Indonesia's Identity and Cultural Values	135
	The Influence of Cultural Values on Indonesian Education	136
	Transnational Education and Homogenisation Processes	138
	Indonesia–US Relations and Homogenisation Process	140
	Hybridisation of Culture and Education	147
	Concluding Remarks	155
7	**Normative and Non-normative Discourses in Indonesia–New Zealand Relationship in Education**	163
	Indonesia–New Zealand Post-Secondary Education Relations	164
	Indonesia–New Zealand Post-Secondary Education Relations from 1945 to 1970	164
	Indonesia–New Zealand Post-Secondary Education Relations from 1970 to 1997	165
	Indonesia–New Zealand Post-Secondary Education Relations from 1999 to the Present	166
	Education Partnership	167
	Non-normative Discourse of Educational Partnership	167
	Normative Discourse of Educational Partnership	168
	Indonesia–New Zealand Education Collaboration: A Closer Look at Negotiators' Experiences	170
	Towards a Successful Indonesia–New Zealand Education Collaboration	175
	Concluding Remarks	177

8 Conclusion 181
   Evaluating Transnational Education in Indonesia 182
   Transnational Education and Indonesia's Educational Sovereignty 184
   *Does Transnational Education Involving a Developed State
   and a LDS Diminish the Educational Sovereignty of the Latter?* 186
   *Does Transnational Education Advance Learning About Other
   States and Has the Potential to Improve Relationships and Promote
   International Understanding?* 188
   *Does Foreign Financial Assistance in Education Threaten
   the Educational Sovereignty of Indonesia?* 189
   *Does the Indonesian Government Retain Sufficient Control Over
   Its National Education Curriculum?* 191
   *Does the Creation of Hybrid Education Programmes Diminish
   Indonesia's Educational Sovereignty?* 192
   Towards a Successful Education Partnership 193
   Final Remarks 194

Bibliography 195

Index 215

LIST OF FIGURES AND TABLES

Fig. 2.1	The process of hybridisation	25
Table 2.1	Modes of education delivery	12
Table 2.2	Forms and conditions of transnational education	39
Table 2.3	Understanding the forms of transnational education and their impacts	40
Table 2.4	Features of educational sovereignty	42
Table 3.1	Schedule of Indonesia's commitments to education services under the GATS	60
Table 3.2	Schedules of Indonesia's horizontal commitments	62
Table 3.3	US financial assistance to Indonesia in the period 2004–2007	67

CHAPTER 1

Introduction

Transnational education is not a new phenomenon. Colonialism was a significant historical factor in establishing transnational education. During the colonial period in Indonesia, for example, there was a lack of trained engineers, so the Dutch opened various professional colleges in which Dutch experts played significant roles in training Indonesians. From one perspective, this arrangement reflected a view that education is a foundation of economic development, as it improves the economic status of the individual and hence addresses the issues of a nation's rates of poverty and illiteracy. In Indonesia, education has been the cornerstone of the nation's economic development initiatives.[1] While transnational education is not new, the growing awareness of questions around educational sovereignty is new. Debate on the merits and threats associated with transnational education, particularly in terms of its potential impact on less-developed states (LDSs), has emerged in the literature (see Chap. 2). As the World Trade Organization's (WTO's) General Agreement on Trade in Services (GATS) has facilitated greater cross-border flow of education services, educational sovereignty has become a critical issue in the LDS.

During the Suharto era, education played a defining role in Indonesia's economic development and growing political stability. More recently, in the current surge of globalisation, education has become even more important to the process of development, equipping citizens to participate in a rapidly changing world. In the area of government policy, it has grown in importance, as it is recognised as playing an important role in developing a resilient economy by producing a more highly skilled labour force.

Suharto accepted foreign aid and loans as being necessary to promote development. He re-established relationships with the Western world (relationships which had suffered during Sukarno's presidency) and welcomed foreign aid to Indonesia, such as that from the World Bank, the US Agency for International Development (USAID), and the Harvard Institute for International Development (HIID).

Today, education is emphasised in Indonesia's strategic planning or *RENSTRA* and plays an important role in reaching development goals. Indonesia aims to achieve Education for All (EFA), and this aspiration is stated in the Millennium Development Goals (MDG).[2] Through USAID, support for improving the quality of education comes not only from improving education infrastructure but also through training educators and increasing access to higher-education opportunities for the wider communities. Today, USAID also provides grants to support activities that expand access to quality education services in remote areas.[3] USAID has also sponsored cluster-based in-service training, training in education performance assessment, training in the use of information and communication technology, Partnerships for Enhanced Engagement in Research (PEER), and Programmes to Extend Scholarships and Training to Achieve Sustainable Impacts (PRESTASI).

Since 2010, the US has also committed itself to invest $165 million over five years in education programmes through educational exchanges with Indonesia.[4] Post-secondary education programmes in Indonesia involving studying abroad for dual degrees[5] include academic and research collaboration between Indonesian and American universities, and invitations for young Indonesians to study in US community colleges in the areas of agriculture, business, engineering, information technology, and health.[6] To equip these students with the language skills for such study, the US has established a large English Language Fellow Programme (ELFP) in Indonesia, offering joint degrees, joint research projects, technical assistance, and scholarships.[7] The extent of US involvement in the provision of education services in Indonesia is, therefore, significant.

The growth in the prevalence and importance of transnational education leads to questions about the impact on Indonesia. Critical education theorists such as Huang, Albatch, Nguyen, Elliot, Terlouw, and Pilot argue that transnational education is a vehicle through which Western education influences affect both the cultures and the educational systems of non-Western states through one-way transfer of knowledge, and thus higher-education systems adopted in Asian states are made to conform to Western academic patterns.[8] Other authors such as Tikly and Pennycook argue that educational institutions are sites of cultural struggle for peripheral states, as their governments seek to negotiate pathways to modernity while remaining true to their distinctive histories and sustaining their cultures.[9] Authors such as Siqueira, Verger, and Bonal draw attention to the threat of the WTO's GATS regulations on most favoured nations and national treatment. These forbid differential treatment for national and foreign education providers, and limit government control over courses to ensure they include the local language and cultural values.[10] Indeed, there are concerns about retaining national cultures and the loss of educational sovereignty as a result of transnational education.

In contrast to the perspectives of critical education theorists, transnational and interdependence theorists laud transnational education for enabling development of new skills, attitudes, and knowledge in students. Knight, for example, concludes that international academic exchanges and programmes that are a part of development projects and technical assistance programmes have been an important source of knowledge and skill for emerging states.[11] Naidoo observes that many LDSs lack academic resources and have such a small number of skilled academics that the provision of post-secondary education by foreign providers becomes an attractive solution.[12] Krasner argues that as international agreements are based on mutual recognition of equal and independent states, parties can choose those agreements they consider to be beneficial for them. In this context, sovereignty in education is both a product of the relationship between the advanced state and the LDS, and the recipient state's political will, based on the benefits for them.

This book aims to make both theoretical and empirical advances in the study of transnational education and educational sovereignty. At the theoretical level, it explores the defining features of educational sovereignty and thus offers a framework for the analysis and assessment of whether a loss of sovereignty has occurred as a consequence of transnational education exchanges. Empirically, the study is aimed at providing an understanding of the complexity of the relationship between LDSs and developed states.

The term transnational education is often used interchangeably with cross-border education, international education, borderless education, or offshore education. The notion of educational sovereignty essentially concerns the control over the design and delivery of education programmes. The evaluation of transnational education and its implication for education sovereignty in Indonesia involved the collection and analysis of primary data (interviews and reports from institutions) and secondary data, such as newspaper articles, related publications, and journal articles. This book is based on the empirical–inductive approach through which facts from the literature reviews were observed. Data analysis was based on the identification of the patterns or emerging themes and interpretations from the raw data.

In-depth interviews with key actors in the negotiation of Indonesia–US and Indonesia–New Zealand education agreements were conducted, as they relate to matters of authority and control in education policy and its implementation.[13] Interviews are also an important way of gaining access to information that is not publicly available, especially information pertaining to the negotiation process.

A total of 30 participants were chosen from the following organisations:

1. State actors including the Indonesian Ministry of Education, the Coordinating Ministry of Welfare and Religion, the Indonesian Directorate General of Higher Education, and the National Education Standardisation Body;
2. Non-state actors including the representatives from Indonesia's education providers partnering with New Zealand education providers, and from Indonesia's education providers partnering with American education providers and public–private providers.

The Indonesian government ministries include the Ministry of National Education, Ministry of Religious Affairs, and Ministry of Coordination of the People's Welfare. Examples of Indonesian post-secondary education institutions involved in the transactions are the University of Diponegoro, Bogor Institute of Agriculture, and other post-secondary education institutions that have education transactions with American post-secondary education institutions. Examples of the American post-secondary education institutions involved in the transactions are the University of Ohio and Portland State University. Indonesian public–private partnership providers include the Sampoerna Foundation, which works together with an American aid agency.[14] Examples of American public–private partnership providers involved in the transactions are the ExxonMobil and USAID partnership, ExxonMobil and the US–Indonesia Society (USINDO), and the USAID and Ford Foundation partnership. USINDO is an example of an Indonesian–American non-governmental organisation. New Zealand participants include those who have been involved in the negotiations.

This book has eight chapters. Chapter 2 reviews the theory relevant to this book. It defines clearly what is meant by the term *transnational education* and the concept of educational sovereignty. It outlines the increased activity in the various forms of transnational education and examines the assumptions and arguments that underlie transnational education. It also critically reviews and appraises the key debates over sovereignty in education. This chapter develops a framework of criteria to be used for assessing the established theories surrounding transnational education and educational sovereignty.

Indonesian education presence and foreign education presence are set out in Chap. 3. The history of Indonesia's dominance by private post-secondary institutions despite the strong standing of the state post-secondary institutions is explored, which explains why the government ultimately opened Indonesia's education market to foreign providers. This chapter also provides the background to understanding the implications of national education regulations and practice for transnational education and educational sovereignty.

Chapter 4 discusses the nature of academic exchanges between Indonesia and developed states, particularly the US and New Zealand. Critics argue that transnational education about the development of a new imperialism is by perpetuating knowledge and financial dependency through the transfer of knowledge and aid in education. Yet supporters assert that transnational education advances global, cross-cultural learning about other states and peoples and has the potential to improve relationships and promote international understanding. This tension is addressed by analysing the extent to which transnational education leads to one-way transfers of knowledge, technology, and research projects—a process by which transnational education would lead to dependency on American financial assistance.

Chapter 5 discusses the meaning of equality in these bilateral relationships, the extent to which equality can function in the relationship with Indonesia's developed-state counterparts, and the implications of the function of equality on Indonesia's educational sovereignty. This chapter investigates whether Indonesia is free to endorse any contract it finds attractive or if it is coerced into accepting agreements.

Chapter 6 examines the extent to which Indonesia can preserve its identity and cultural values—its cultural sovereignty and integrity. This chapter explores whether Indonesia still has the authority to regulate its education in the face of globalising pressures and international laws favouring transnational educational processes.

Chapter 7 discusses the normative and non-normative discourses of partnership in education. Gerring and Yesnowitz argue that "empirical study in the social sciences is meaningless if it has no normative import. It simply does not matter."[15] To them, bringing an empirical approach to normative questions would render political science a much more relevant area. Chapter 7 discusses non-normative and normative framework of the transnational education partnership and thus offers an indicator of whether transnational education negotiations will advance to a sustained collaboration.

The conclusions are set out in Chap. 8, which demonstrates the emerging importance of the educational relationship between developed states and LDSs. Significant issues arising in this research, the limitation of the research design, and future research avenues are outlined in this chapter.

Notes

1. See Mochtar Buchori and Abdul Malik, "The Evolution of Higher Education in Indonesia," in *Asian Universities: Historical Perspectives and Contemporary Challenges*, eds. Philip Albatch and Toru Umakoshi (Baltimore, ML: The John Hopkins University Press, 2004): 249–277; Dewi Fortuna Anwar, "Human Security: An Intractable Problem in Asia," In *Asian Security Order: Instrumental and Normative Features*, ed. Muthiah Alagappa (Stanford, CA: Stanford University Press, 2003).
2. UNESCO. "Millennium Development Programmes." http://www.unesco.org/new/en/education
3. USAID, "About SERASI," last modified May 20, 2013, http://www.serasoi-ird.org/index.php
4. Cameron Hume, "Number of Indonesian Students in US Doubled," *Jakarta Post*, Friday 13, November 2009; The US made a commitment to grant Indonesia $301 million for environment and climate change research, development, and education. See *Jakarta Post*, "US Puts up $301 Million for Partnership with RI," http://thejakartapost.com; US Embassy in Indonesia, "Ambassador Marciel's Visit to Eastern Indonesia," http://www.jakarta.usembassy.gov; USAID, "Fact Sheet: Higher Education Partnership with Indonesia," http://www.indonesia.usaid.gov

5. See Chap. 2 for modes of education delivery.
6. US Department of State, "Background Note: Indonesia," last modified February 20, 2013, http://www.state.gov; USAID, "Comprehensive Partnership," http://www.indonesia.usaid.gov; Maureen McClure, "Sustainable University Partnerships: National Education Reform Challenges in Decentralizing Indonesia," *International Studies in Education*, 8, (2007): 5–6; US Department of State, "United States-Indonesia Education Cooperation," Bureau of Educational and Cultural Affairs, http://www.exchanges.state.gov; The White House, "Fact Sheet: Higher Education Partnership with Indonesia," last modified February 10, 2013, http://www.whitehouse.gov/sites/defaultfiles/us-indonesia_higher_education_partnership
7. US Department of State, "United States-Indonesia Education Cooperation," Bureau of Educational and Cultural Affairs, last modified August 10, 2012, http://www.exchanges.state.gov; The White House, "Fact Sheet: Higher Education Partnership with Indonesia," http://www.whitehouse.gov/sites/default/files/us-indonesia_higher_education_partnership; Alan Dessoff, "Building Partnerships: Indonesia and the United States," *Embassy of Indonesia*, http://www.embassyofindonesia.org/education.docpdf/building_partnerships_indonesia_us
8. Phuong-Mai Nguyen, Julian Elliot, Cees Terlouw, and Albert Pilot, "Neocolonialism in Education: Cooperative Learning in an Asian Context," *Comparative Education*, 45, (2009): 109–130.
9. Leon Tikly, "Education and the New Imperialism," *Comparative Education*, 40, (2004): 173–198; Alastair Pennycook, *The Cultural Politics of English as an International Language* (Harlow, Essex: Longman Group Limited, 1994).
10. Angela Siqueira, "The Regulation of Education through the WTO/GATS," *Journal for Critical Education Policy Studies*, 3, (2005): 1–16; Anthony Verger and Xavier Bonal, "Against GATS: The Sense of a Global Struggle," *Journal for Critical Education Policy Studies*, 4, (2006): 1–27.
11. Jane Knight, "Internationalization Remodelled: Definition, Approaches, and Rationales," *Journal of Studies in International Education*, 8, (2004): 5–31.
12. Rajani Naidoo, "Higher Education as a Global Commodity: The Perils and Promises for Developing Countries," *The Observatory on Borderless Higher Education*, February 2007: 1–19.
13. Norman Denzin and Yvonna Lincoln, *Strategies of Qualitative Inquiry* (Thousand Oaks, California: Sage Publications, 2003).
14. Public–private partnership (PPP) providers are government education services or private enterprise partnerships, which are funded and operated

through a partnership of government and one or more private-sector education institutions or enterprises.
15. John Gerring and Joshua Yesnowitz, "A Normative Turn in Political Science?" *Polity*, 38, (2006): 101–33.

CHAPTER 2

Transnational Education and Educational Sovereignty: A Framework for Analysis

DEFINITIONS OF TRANSNATIONAL EDUCATION

The Council of Europe's Code of Good Practice in the Provision of Transnational Education defines transnational education as "all types of higher education study programmes or set of courses of study, or educational services ... in which the learners are located in a country different from the one where the awarding institution is based."[1] The Global Alliance for Transnational Education defines it as "any teaching or learning activity in which the students are in a different country (the host country) to that in which the institution providing the education is based (the home country)."[2]

The definition of transnational education proposed by the Council of Europe draws attention to the mobility of educational programmes, services, and learners, but fails to refer to different and extensive modes of education delivery such as joint awards and franchising. Transnational education includes education that can be delivered in any of the following four ways: (a) cross-border supply, (b) consumption abroad, (c) commercial presence, and (d) the presence of foreign experts to provide education services.[3]

Knight refers to the cross-border supply mode (mode 1) as the provision of education services that does not require physical movement of students.[4]

© The Author(s) 2017
A. Abbott, *Educational Sovereignty and Transnational Exchanges in Post-Secondary Indonesian Education*, DOI 10.1007/978-3-319-53985-0_2

Consumption abroad mode (mode 2) refers to the provision of education services that involves physical movement of students to the country of the education providers. Commercial presence mode (mode 3) refers to education service providers establishing education institutions in another country. The presence of natural persons (mode 4) refers to educators or scholars travelling to another country for the purposes of providing education services.

McBurnie and Ziguras point to the existence of wider forms of education delivery such as franchising, twinning arrangements, branch campuses, and corporate programmes, in addition to study abroad and distance education.[5] The movement of education services may take the forms of (a) branch campuses, (b) mergers, (c) affiliations or networks, (d) independent educational institutions, (e) virtual universities, (f) franchising, (g) programme articulations, (h) double or joint degrees, and (i) twinning.

Branch campuses involve an education provider from state A establishing a campus in state B that offers its own educational programmes, qualifications, or both. The qualification awarded is from the education provider in state A. Branch campuses are also known as offshore campuses. Mergers are situations in which an education provider from state A purchases a part or all of a local post-secondary education provider in state B. This arrangement is also called offshore mobility.[6]

Affiliations or networks are situations in which public education providers enter into partnerships with private education providers, including either foreign or local education providers or both, to establish networks and institutions that deliver courses or educational programmes locally, in foreign states, or both, through distance or face-to-face modes. Independent educational institutions involve an education provider from state A establishing a campus in state B to offer its own educational programmes, qualifications, or both. These partnership arrangements are like branch campuses, but are independent institutions due to the absence of a home institution in state A. Virtual universities are institutions that provide students with course material via postal correspondence or the Internet.[7]

Massive open online courses (MOOCs) are important developments in transnational education and are an extension of open educational resources (OERs) through which universities around the world provide teaching materials freely and openly.[8] MOOCs were introduced in 2008 by Canadian researchers, Dave Cormier and Bryan Alexander, in response to a course called Connectivism and Connective Knowledge (CCK08).[9]

MOOCs have forced their way into the range and scope of transnational education. Nathan Harden argues:

> In fifty years, if not much sooner, half of the roughly 4,500 colleges and universities now operating in the United States will have ceased to exist. The technology driving this change is already at work, and nothing can stop it. The future looks like this: access to college-level education will be free for everyone; the residential college campus will become largely obsolete; tens of thousands of professors will lose their jobs; the bachelor's degree will become increasingly irrelevant; and ten years from now Harvard will enrol ten million students.[10]

MOOCs, through their access, have the potential to provide the opportunities for local students to free or low-cost courses from foreign university providers, without going overseas. They also provide the opportunity for foreign university providers to expand their courses. As Harden notes, the development of MOOCs has the potential to reduce the job opportunities for educators, result in job losses for professors, and threaten the incomes of education providers that charge fees for their courses. The development of MOOCs demands a profound redefinition of transnational education by including MOOCs in the discussion and analysis of transnational education.[11]

Franchising involves an educational institution in one state authorising another institution from the same or another state to provide its educational programmes. Programme articulations are inter-institutional arrangements through which two or more institutions agree to define jointly a study programme in terms of study credits and credit transfers. Twinning occurs when an education provider in state A collaborates with an education provider in state B to develop an articulated system that allows students to take course credits in one or both states. The arrangements for twinning programmes and awarding degrees usually comply with the national regulations of provider A. Double or joint degrees involve collaboration between states to offer programmes for which students receive a qualification from each provider or a joint award from the collaborating partner. These arrangements usually comply with national regulations in both states. Validation occurs when an education provider in state A can award the qualifications of an education institution in state B.[12] As the arrangements for twinning programmes allow students to take course credits in one or both states, the definition of cross-border mode is no longer limited to distance

Table 2.1 Modes of education delivery

Modes of delivery	Definition	Examples
Cross-border supply (mode 1)	The provision of education services that does not require physical movement of students	Distance education Virtual education Twinning Joint degree Double degree
Consumption abroad (mode 2)	The provision of education services that involve physical movement of students to the country of the education providers	Full degree Internship Sabbatical
Commercial presence (mode 3)	Education service providers establish education institutions in another country	Branch campuses, independent educational institutions
Presence of natural persons (mode 4)	Educators or scholars travelling to another country for purposes of providing education service	Professors, researchers, and educators working in another country

and virtual education. The movement of education services under commercial presence mode may take the forms of branch campuses and independent educational institutions. The modes of education delivery and the movement of education services are summarised in Table 2.1.

Educational services can refer to primary, secondary, higher, or tertiary, and adult education. The World Trade Organization (WTO) states that, "while these categories are based on the traditional structure of the sector, rapid changes taking place in higher education—which normally refers to post-secondary education at sub degree and university degree level—may be significantly affecting the scope and concept of education."[13]

Even though primary education and secondary education are in the category of education services covered by the WTO's GATS, in practice, they are outside the scope of the GATS. Sauve, the trade directorate of the Organisation for Economic Cooperation and Development (OECD), asserts, "ask any negotiator in Geneva, and she/he would be prone to regard primary and secondary schooling, so called basic/compulsory education, as lying outside the scope of the GATS."[14] International education scholars such as Pereira and Adlung note that basic education is the responsibility of the state.[15] The public sector, however, is unable to keep up with the growing demand for higher education, thereby creating a lucrative market for the private sector.[16] This book is concerned only with post-secondary education.

Overall, transnational education encompasses all types of post-secondary education study programmes, courses of study, and educational services delivered across borders through any of the varied modes described earlier.

THE PREVALENCE OF TRANSNATIONAL EDUCATION

Transnational education is a long-established phenomenon. International academic mobility can be traced back to about 569–445 BC.[17] The sophists of early Greece, for example, were professional educators who travelled around the Greek-speaking world, teaching children.[18]

Colonialism was a significant historical factor in establishing transnational education.[19] During the colonial period in Indonesia, for example, there was a lack of trained engineers, so the Dutch opened various professional colleges in which Dutch experts played significant roles in training Indonesians.[20] This mode of education delivery is currently known as mode 4, or the presence of foreign experts to provide education services. Another instance of colonialism being a significant historical factor in establishing transnational education is the phenomenon of students in colonised states completing their studies in Europe and the US.[21] This mode of education delivery is currently known as mode 2, or consumption abroad.

Development has also been a significant factor in the expansion of transnational education. After the Meiji Restoration, for example, the Japanese needed a large amount of Western technical knowledge. The Japanese government responded by both hiring Western experts and sending Japanese students to the West,[22] using mode 2 and mode 4 approaches, respectively.

Before and immediately after World War II, scholarships for foreign students, study-abroad programmes, international studies, foreign language training, and scientific and cultural agreements between states marked the development of transnational education. The agencies and organisations involved included the Institute of International Education (IIE), established in the aftermath of World War I; the *Deutscher Akademischer Austauschdienst* (DAAD), established in 1925; the British Council, established in 1934; and, more recently, the European Action Scheme for the Mobility of University Students (ERASMUS), established in 1987,[23] all of which have promoted international academic mobility and cooperation. The US, in particular, has played a dominant role in the LDSs since the 1940s, by including educational assistance in its development aid packages as part of its post-war foreign policy.[24]

International academic mobility and cooperation has continued to expand. In the 1950s, the Colombo Plan was developed by the founding states—Australia, Canada, India, Sri Lanka, New Zealand, United Kingdom, and Pakistan—to provide educational programmes, such as those in administration, advanced training, and science, that were not yet available within the newly independent states. Strategic, political, and cultural objectives also lay behind the Colombo Plan, as the provision of such aid was grounded in the assumption that the newly independent states would not embrace communism.[25]

The flow of students from newly independent states to developed ones has continued to expand since the 1950s through development aid and cooperation. Foreign assistance programmes that have sponsored students from the LDSs in pursuing their education overseas include the Colombo Plan Awards, the British Council Fellowships, the Fulbright Commission Scholarships, the Commonwealth Scholarship and Fellowship Plan, the Ford and Rockefeller Foundations, the Carnegie Corporation Awards, and the British Technical Cooperation Training Programme Awards.[26]

In the late 1960s, however, the developed states began to provide less aid.[27] As the World Bank Commission on International Development's 1969 Pearson Report noted, "The climate surrounding foreign aid programmes is heavy with disillusion and distrust. This is not true everywhere. Indeed, there are countries where the opposite is true. Nevertheless, we have reached a point of crisis."[28]

Although the amount of international aid was in decline, the demand for foreign post-secondary education continued to increase. Since the 1990s, educational institutions in Asia have begun to respond to the demand for post-secondary education through its commercialisation.[29] A 2005 UNESCO report estimated that two million students around the world were pursuing higher education outside their home countries. This number had increased to 3.45 million in 2009.[30]

These forms of transnational education were an aspect of globalisation, set within the framework of the GATS. Since 1995, the removal of trade barriers in education under the GATS has enabled the expansion of numerous forms of transnational education, thereby generating financial profits for advanced states.[31] Education is the US's third largest export-service sector, for example, generating more than US$17.6 billion in export earnings in 2008–2009.[32]

Although the provision of international aid has been in decline while demand for post-secondary educational assistance has simultaneously continued to expand through commercialisation, education is still part of the current development aid packages under such new arrangements as partnerships. Much debate has surrounded the use of the term partnership. As a result of corruption and weak government, donors have emphasised the term as a means of holding such governments accountable.[33]

The studies of Daniel, Crawford, Albatch, and Kelly, for example, have argued that the partnering of LDSs with developed states in itself establishes inequality, as developed states set the terms of such partnerships due to their technological superiority and the LDSs' aid dependency.[34] In this way, according to Abrahamsen, developed states retain the power to impose their values and solutions on LDSs.[35]

Both advanced and less advanced states tend to favour the term *education partnership*: for LDSs, the term implies equality in the relationship,[36] and for advanced states, it means likelihood of successful negotiations. Much debate, therefore, surrounds the meaning of partnership, but rather than discussing the concept in detail, this book acknowledges that the demand for post-secondary education continues to expand both because of the commercialisation of education and because of the existence of a new type of relationship in which educational aid or assistance is part of the package.

Overall, transnational education has become broader and has extended beyond the mobility of students and educational materials. Transnational education now implies both the commercialisation of education and the presence of a platform for partnership through franchising and twinning arrangements, branch campuses, and corporate programmes.

Transnational Education and Parties Involved

Both state and non-state actors are involved in transnational education. The relationships between state actors involve foreign development agencies and the recipient states. Those relationships between non-state actors involve foreign education providers and recipient education institutions and their roles in transnational education negotiations. Transnational education also involves relationships between non-state and state actors. Such examples include USAID providing grants and technical assistance by partnering with such firms as ExxonMobil and ConocoPhillips. The actors involved in transnational education vary, as do their interests. Non-state actors at the university level, for example, have an interest in the profits that the commercialisation of education generates, whereas state actors have both political and cultural interests.

The parties involved usually sign a memorandum of agreement (MoA) or a memorandum of understanding (MoU), which sets out the mutual benefits and agreements for initiating exchanges of teaching materials and literature, research collaboration, exchanges of scholars, and the conducting of joint workshops.[37] An MoU confirms the institutions' willingness to collaborate.[38] In international public law, these memoranda are often confined to the parties involved, do not need ratification, and can be kept confidential.[39] At the university level, both memoranda must be signed and finalised by the chancellor, the associate provost for international affairs, and the rectors.[40] MoUs depend on each state's constitution, laws, and practices and are, therefore, subject to domestic law. However, international standards do exist for transnational education, for example, the Guidelines for Quality Provision in Cross Border Higher Education established by UNESCO and the OECD in 2005. Although not legally binding, these are crucial for protecting students and other stakeholders involved in transnational education, and many states have adopted them as their guiding principles for transnational educational transactions.

MoAs specify how transnational education programmes operate. Parties frequently prefer MoUs to MoAs because the former lack formalities, are easier to amend, and ensure confidentiality.[41] Both MoAs and MoUs are important for clarifying the responsibilities of the parties involved in education exchanges.

Even though the actors involved in transnational education and their interests are varied, the basic aspects of their agreements, however, are the same, in that they are governed by domestic law and often use international standards as guidelines.

Summary

Transnational education encompasses two basic aspects: (a) all of the types of higher education study programmes or courses of study and educational services delivered across borders, and (b) the mode of educational delivery, such as distance education, partner-supported delivery, franchising, joint awards, Internet delivery, and offshore campuses.

Before World War II, and immediately afterwards, transnational education was typically characterised by education aid initiatives for LDSs. In the late 1960s, a decline in aid donations by developed states corresponded with increasing demand for transnational post-secondary education, facilitated by the GATS framework for the removal of trade barriers to education.

Transnational education has since become broader with the introduction of new delivery models beyond the mobility of students and educational materials. In addition to the commercialisation of education, these models also present a platform for such relationship arrangements as franchising, twinning, branch campuses, and corporate programmes. As the demand for transnational post-secondary education has continued to expand, the actors involved in transnational education and their interests have become more varied. This situation has drawn attention to the implications of transnational education on educational sovereignty.

EDUCATIONAL SOVEREIGNTY

This section defines educational sovereignty, based on a literature review, which is used in this book. This section also reviews key normative arguments associated with the concept of educational sovereignty within international relations, from contrasting perspectives. These arguments are important to the assessment of the impact of transnational education and whether or not it diminishes educational sovereignty. These arguments have been the subject of considerable debate, particularly in regard to the relationship between developed states and LDSs.

The Concept of Educational Sovereignty

Article 1 of the 1933 Montevideo Convention on the Rights and Duties of States asserts: "The state as a person of international law should possess the following qualifications: (a) a permanent population; (b) a defined territory; (c) government; and (d) capacity to enter into relations with other states."[42] This article extols the primacy of states and asserts that states have authority and control over all issues of domestic politics and should, therefore, be free to determine their own fate.[43] Such authority must be rooted in law.[44] Sovereignty is, therefore, the final legal authority within a territory. It follows from this statement that states have legal authority over education within their territories.[45]

Educational sovereignty is closely linked to state sovereignty for several reasons. First, policymaking in education is an essential element of the state's sovereignty as an important means of integrating society through culture and state ideology. Second, the supreme political power of the state and the supremacy of the state over citizens have been the bases for coining a definition of state sovereignty.[46] Third, transnational education transactions are formulated through the negotiation of agreements. Fourth, the state, as Morrow and Torres argues, acts as an alliance or "a pact of domination."[47] Thus, the notion that the state exercises power when entering international agreements in education is pertinent. Accordingly, this book emphasises the formal exercise of power by nation-states in entering international agreements. To overcome the emphasis of the formal exercise of power, which would result in a somewhat limited concept of educational sovereignty, two complementary theoretical perspectives must be integrated: the transnational and inter-dependent theorists, and the critical education theorists. Although the works of most critical education theorists are informed and shaped by post-colonial and dependency theories (which are of considerable importance to transnational education and educational sovereignty), critical education theorists challenge the existing social and political order. The perspectives of critical education theorists need to be included to understand the interaction and role of social agencies in transnational education—both state and non-state actors. Accordingly, in developing the conceptual framework of educational sovereignty, state actors, together with non-state actors, are playing an important role in the maintenance or loss of educational sovereignty.

Although no clear and established definition of educational sovereignty exists, there is growing concern among critical education theorists such as Moll, Carnoy, Tikly, Huang, Selvaratnam, and Albatch in regard to the loss, or potential loss, of state sovereignty in education.[48] In response to this concern, Moll argued that sovereignty in education was linked with the protection and maintenance of the cultural values of minority groups.[49] However, Moll's definition of educational sovereignty is restricted to the protection and maintenance of such values in education. Therefore, the term's meaning must be conceptualised before determining whether transnational education is diminishing or otherwise modifying educational sovereignty. Before doing so, it is necessary to understand the contrasting arguments surrounding the critical education theorists.

Perspectives on Educational Sovereignty

Critical education theorists such as Naidoo, Verger, Bonal, and Pennycook offer a deeper insight for analysis of the ramifications of the relationship between developed and the LDSs, for education of the latter.[50] For critical education theorists, the central issues are culture and the capacity to remain in control of it. Critical education theorists such as Kuehn and Fox argue that education is a cultural and social process.[51] Education has influenced the ways people construct their cultural identity, and how others construct their identity for them.[52] Cultures provide people with their primary sense of belonging and exert a powerful influence on education systems.[53] Globalisation, the driver of transnational education, to some theorists such as Albatch, poses a challenge to the preservation of national cultural autonomy and identity.[54] To Albatch, the spread of English as a global language threatens local cultures and identities.[55] Thus, the relationships between education, culture, and transnationalism are closely intertwined.

Critical education theorists emphasise the importance of culture and learning for empowerment, and it is expected that culture is central to their arguments. However, cultures are changing constantly in response to all manner of pressures and developments, and, at times, states are in more control, while at other times, they are short of control.[56]

New imperialism theorists such as Tikly, Furedi, and Munck argue that education and the so-called development in the LDSs is a new attempt to serve the hegemonic interests of the US and its Western allies.[57] Post-colonial theory is noticeable in the works of these authors. The proponents of dependency theories, such as Frank, assess the power relationships between developed states and the LDSs by viewing them within social, historical, and economic contexts. The works on dependency and imperialism by theorists such as Frank, Dos Santos, Memmi, Fanon, and Raskin have influenced the works of prominent scholars such as Carnoy, who argues that education is a tool of domination used by developed states, and that it perpetuates the financial and knowledge dependency of LDSs on developed states.[58] Whether dependency, new imperialism, or critical education theories are considered, they agree in their assessments of power relationships, which are viewed in social, historical, and economic contexts.

Such analysis offers valuable insights into the role of social agencies that must be considered in any analysis of transnationalism. Of considerable importance to transnational education and sovereignty in education is that the structuralism evident in the dependency, new imperialism, world system, and post-colonialism theories acknowledges the form of domination by the dominant groups or advanced states, which is discussed further in the chapter. Although this school of thought informs the work of critical education theorists, theorists such as Moll, Fox, Huang, Albatch, Selvaratnam, Stromquist, Torres, and Burbules offer critical perspectives that adapt, challenge, or even reject existing social and political orders. Moll, for instance, challenges the arbitrary authority of power structures in determining the essence of the educational experience. Moll is underscoring the need for educational sovereignty.[59]

The limits of state sovereignty and autonomy are acknowledged by critical education theorists such as Torres and Morrow. To Torres, those limits are manifested in the tensions between global and local dynamics in social, economic, cultural, and political domains,[60] meaning that the nation-state has lost its ability to cope with its own economic and political tensions. What is important in Torres's analysis is that he has captured the essence of critical education theories, in which global and local dynamics exist, both between state actors and non-state actors.[61]

At a broad level, critical theorists themselves share some common concerns about educational sovereignty. They share a concern for the inequality of power between states and within society and are concerned with the subjugation knowledge through the unequal relationship between developed states and LDSs; thus, the importance of challenging the existing power structure is imperative. This study does not seek to undermine either the views of critical education theorists on educational sovereignty or the complexity of the relationship between developed states and LDSs. Instead, it notes three key factors in assessing the exercise of educational sovereignty: dependency (foreign knowledge and financial assistance dependencies), the inequality of academic relationships between developed states and LDSs, and culture and the capacity to remain in control of it.[62] Within this framework, it is possible to comprehend the relationship between transnational education and educational sovereignty and their interactions. These factors interact, while state and non-state actors remain in control of knowledge and culture as they deal with transnational education.

Central to the theoretical endeavour of critical education theorists are critical views that challenge the present circumstances of education, and the analysis of the complex relationship between developed states and LDSs, and between transnational education and educational sovereignty. Theory and action, as Robert Cox puts it, are, nevertheless, both complex, and thus the task of theorising can never be finished but must continually be begun anew.[63] Thus, the framework developed in this book is used to open up further analytical research possibilities, such as research on foreign aid in education, and international educational partnerships.

Transnational Education and Homogenisation Processes

Critical education theorists who see education as a social and cultural process also see foreign-controlled education as presenting a risk to a recipient nation's cultural identity. Westernisation and Americanisation, Gargano argues, highlight the homogenising effects of global flows and processes on states' cultures because, as Albatch argues, transnational education is "dominated by the North in terms of curriculum, orientation and sometimes the teaching staff... frequently the language of instruction is the language of the dominant partner, very often English."[64] Huang points to a perception of transnational education as being one way to export Western ideas and cultures and thereby maintain colonial legacies.[65] According to Albatch and Selvaratnam, the importance of language for inculcating the values of the former colonial powers expresses a clear colonialist impact.[66] Huang, Albatch, and Selvaratnam argue that domination by developed states through the language of instruction, the presence of expatriates among academic staff, and the dependence of the LDSs on institutions located in the developed states is necessary for maintaining colonial links.[67] This line of thinking means that to Westernise and Americanise an education system, it is necessary to use the English language, ensure the presence of foreign experts, and maintain the dependence of the LDSs on institutions located in the developed states.

Globalisation discourses clarify the link between foreign education and homogenisation. Tomlinson uses homogenisation and Westernisation synonymously.[68] Waters refers to globalisation as "the direct consequence of the expansion of European cultures across the world via settlement, colonialisation and cultural mimesis."[69] Similarly, Zajda argues that globalisation displays the domination of cultures and is particularly unfavourable to weak cultures or societies.[70] Drawing on Tomlinson, Waters, and Zajda, homogenisation occurs as a result of the global extension of Western cultures. The freer movement of students, educational institutions, and educational resources across borders signifies the engagement of education within the process of globalisation. Critical education theorists such as Nguyen, Elliot, Terlouw, and Pilot argue that Western education has ways to influence both the cultures and educational systems of non-Western states through the one-way transfer of knowledge.[71] Huang, Albatch, Nguyen, Elliott, Terlouw, and Pilot see the conforming of educational systems in Asia to foreign academic patterns as one way of exporting Western ideas and cultural values. These authors argue that higher-education systems adopted in Asian states have conformed to foreign academic patterns.[72]

The struggle against Western domination has often involved the rejection of Western educational patterns. Critical education theorists often regard educational institutions as the sites of cultural struggles for the periphery. Tikly, for example, argues that in many previously colonised states, the governments are still struggling to develop educational curricula suited to their cultures and histories.[73] Pennycook recommends attempting initiatives to develop educational curricula, arguing that previously colonised states need to express their own cultural values through education.[74]

Critical education theorists are concerned that the GATS facilitates the process of the homogenisation of education and, therefore, creates the potential for the loss of local cultures. Siqueira, Verger, and Bonal argue that GATS regulations addressing Most Favoured Nations and National Treatment forbid differential treatment for national and foreign education providers without regard to whether the foreign education providers develop courses that include the local language and cultural values.[75] It is important to note, however, that some writers, such as Pierre Bourdieu and Anthony Giddens, emphasise hybridisation instead of homogenisation.

Transnational Education and the New Imperialism

Carnoy argues that the practice of advanced states and international institutions imposing conditions on another state could be a form of indirect control.[76] The core of contemporary discussions addressing imperialism is that indirect control reinforces what is called the *new imperialism.*[77] For their part, Tikly and Carnoy view the new imperialism as the continuation of the past Western imperialism and characterise it as being composed of knowledge dependency, financial dependency, cultural dependency, and cultural imperialism.[78] Tikly refers to the role of international education as the part of the new imperialism that integrates low-income states into the world economic system, thereby functioning to serve the interests of the US and its Western allies.[79] The analysis of a new imperialism is taken further by Samoff who argues that through the global flow of Western ideas, education has been dominated by a set of imperial assumptions concerning human capital and development.[80]

The new imperialism has consisted of two waves, the first of which has been related to the commercialisation of education. Advanced states are exporters of post-secondary education, and the GATS facilitates market access to post-secondary education, as it involves an agreement to open up education markets to more powerful education providers. Collins and Santos argue that the opening of education markets has created opportunities for developed states to achieve economic gains.[81] Said refers to these opportunities as a scheme of the new imperialists, in which "the powerful are likely to get more powerful and richer, the weak less powerful and poorer."[82] This analysis considers the GATS to be a threat to sovereignty in education because it ensures that the market, rather than the state, is what responds to the increasing demand for education.[83]

Critical education theorists consider foreign experts, as well as foreign education institutions, to be important for enforcing the new imperialism,[84] as they increase the LDSs' dependence on foreign knowledge, technology transfer, and scientific application. According to this view, transnational education has the potential to create knowledge dependency, which then significantly facilitates cultural imperialism.[85]

The second wave of the new imperialism is related to foreign aid for education. Carnoy, Brock-Utne, and Frank argue that the historical process remains active because LDSs have had their economies conditioned by the development and expansion of advanced states' economies. These theorists express concerns about foreign aid in education.[86] To these authors, financial assistance from developed states leads to financial dependency, which puts the LDSs in a position in which they are vulnerable to exploitation.

Brock-Utne and Carnoy adopt a post-colonial approach by arguing that having relationships with the LDSs helps advanced states to grow richer. Carnoy and Brock-Utne conclude that providing educational aid is a way for advanced states to exploit LDSs, their funding of educational institutions serving their own needs.[87] The crux of these arguments is that advanced states dominate the recipient states' educational institutions and economic, political, and social structures in order to meet their own power needs and to impose conditions on the LDSs' policy frameworks for their own benefit. On this account, transnational education may threaten educational sovereignty, as it reinforces the new imperialism through which advanced states are likely to become more powerful and the LDSs weaker.

ALTERNATIVE PERSPECTIVES ON EDUCATION SOVEREIGNTY

Transnational and inter-dependence theorists take a rather different view and do not emphasise the role of agency in international affairs. As such, the state is considered to exercise power, but it does not facilitate the exercise of power by agents. Further, they argue that cooperation between developed and LDSs is likely to be beneficial not only for the former but also for the latter.

Transnational Education and Hybridisation Processes

Although critical education theorists dismiss the internationalisation of curricula as the Americanisation of knowledge and values, transnationalist and inter-dependence theorists laud it as enabling the development of new skills, attitudes, and knowledge among students. For the former, the entrenchment of the maintenance of a native identity and cultural sensitivity has resonated as a critical feature of transnational education.[88]

As with the homogenisation of education, hybridisation is a pertinent term for discussions addressing the export and adoption of Western ideas. As a process, hybridisation refers to "the ways in which forms become separated from existing practices and recombine with new forms in new practices."[89] Figure 2.1 illustrates this process.

Such transnational and inter-dependence theorists have characterised the processes of hybridisation as a way to learn from each other. Between states, such learning from each other is possible due to what Pieterse calls "cultural interpenetration."[90] As a corollary of the cross-permeation of the two states' cultures, culture becomes translocal rather than territorial.[91] Pieterse depicts translocal culture as a culture based on "an outward looking sense of place [or a] global sense of place." Unlike the process of homogenisation, in which resemblance is completely absent, in the process of hybridization, local cultures survive by making the dominant cultural traits the new practice and new set of values.[92]

Transnational education is one of the driving forces behind hybridisation. Its transactions are characterised by the processes involved in sharing values, customs, and traditions through education as well as by the forms of educational delivery, resulting in hybridisation, or the combination of foreign and local cultural values in regard to education. Educational

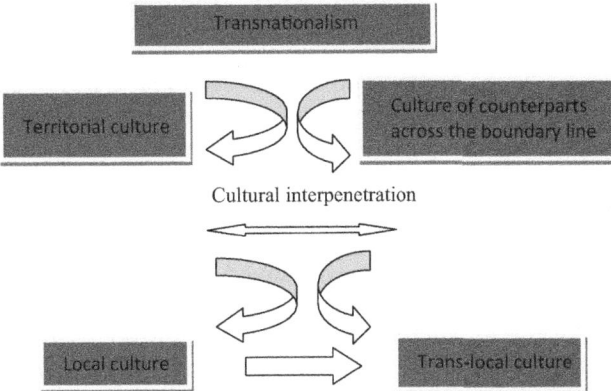

Fig. 2.1 The process of hybridisation

hybridisation is not inevitable—it requires the adoption of new practices and learning experiences as well as the selection of culturally relevant values for inclusion in the curriculum, thereby combining the existing educational curriculum with new practices and learning experiences. The hybridisation of education also refers to the combination of different educational methods. Shale and Cookson regard the adoption of new ways of delivering education, such as distance education, as examples of educational hybridisation.[93] Writers such as Thompson and Knight, Rizvi, Schwindt, and Hayden consider learning from each other to have the potential to promote international understanding.[94] As Knight noted, "scholarships for foreign students who are seen as promising future leaders are considered to be an effective way of developing an understanding of and perhaps affinity for the sponsoring country. This affinity may prove to be beneficial in future years in terms of diplomatic or business relations."[95]

These scholars clearly consider that transnational education results in hybridisation rather than homogenisation, visualising the former as a process of learning from each other in order to promote international understanding—a process that transnational education facilitates. In this context, the hybridisation of education refers to the process and function of combining foreign and local cultural values regarding education for the purpose of promoting international understanding. As a form, hybridisation refers to the combination of educational methods.

Transnational Education and the Development of LDSs

For Anwar, education is necessary for development, as it enables people to use educational attainment to improve their economic status by addressing the problems of poverty and illiteracy; low education attainment has trapped millions in Asia in a vicious cycle of misery and despair.[96] Anwar argues that the main hindrance to fulfilling the educational needs of many millions is state incapacity.[97] Bauer argues that it is impossible to overcome poverty without foreign financial assistance.[98]

Tilak's study on knowledge-based aid marked the importance of foreign financial assistance in education.[99] According to Tilak, development is related to knowledge—knowledge of one's own history of socio-political, cultural, and economic development policies, and current situation. Higher education is an important aspect of the knowledge society in creating and rediscovering knowledge. According to Tilak, ensuring the higher education system is of high quality is necessary for the effective creation and application of knowledge. In this context, foreign financial assistance in education plays an indirect, yet important, role in knowledge development of LDSs. For Tilak, in order for knowledge-based aid to be effective, both donor and recipient states have to work together. The donor state should learn about the recipient state, and the necessity of knowledge sharing should be taken into consideration. In this context, the donor is also able to learn whether or not the aid is effective. For the recipient, Tilak argues that the recipients "should make serious efforts at developing and strengthening their own research."[100]

Unlike Tilak, who is optimistic about the potency of foreign financial assistance on LDSs' development, Bauer is pessimistic regarding the benefits of foreign financial assistance. For Bauer, foreign financial assistance is an ineffective instrument for development because of the attitudes and conduct of the people of the recipient state whose interpretations of economic advance differ from people of the donor state.[101] Nevertheless, Bauer argues that without foreign financial assistance, it is impossible for poorer states to develop.

The recent work by Knight and Naidoo on transnational education provides an example of the benefits of foreign assistance for what they call "capacity building," as it has the potential to improve the development of LDSs with inadequate financial resources and physical and human infrastructure. King provides a salutary example of the role of development assistance in India, provided by the UK, the US, Russia, and Germany in the post-war period, which had an impact on the establishment of strong science- and technology-based development.[102] Naidoo argues, however, that the priority given to trade in higher education may erode the political will to offer aid to LDSs.[103]

Educational Sovereignty Revisited

The critical education theorists consider transnational education to have caused dependence in LDSs and cultural domination and control of LDSs by advanced states. The crux of their argument is that donor states dominate curricula, experts, and the choice of language of instruction, thereby making the recipient states' educational systems conform to foreign academic patterns. To some, the GATS rules are threats to the LDSs' educational sovereignty by facilitating educational homogenisation, with the important corollary of the loss of local cultures. In this context, educational sovereignty is related to the ability of states to maintain cultural values through transnational education.

To some critical education theorists, transnational education is perceived as threatening the loss of educational sovereignty through the new imperialism, in which the market, rather than the state, responds to the increasing demand for education, thereby enabling advanced states to become richer and more powerful at the expense of LDSs. From this approach, foreign educational assistance is likely to be the subject of criticism because of its perceived potential for control over the imposition of conditions favourable to the donors over the recipient's policy framework. In this context, educational sovereignty is related to the ability of states to regulate the flow of educational activities across their borders and to respond to the increasing demand for education without the imposition of foreign control, and to the ability to choose foreign involvement in education. As transnational education is delivered through such varied modes as distance education and offshore campuses, educational sovereignty is also related to the ability of states to regulate the flow of educational materials, students, educators, and practitioners across their borders.

Educational sovereignty also means the ability of states to maintain local cultural values through education, to regulate the flow of educational institutions, materials, students, and practitioners across their borders, and to respond to the increasing demand for education without onerous impositions by foreign powers. Those taking a contrasting stance to critical education theorists tend to conclude that transnational education does not result in homogenisation, because the process of hybridisation preserves local cultural traits despite the presence of dominant Western ones, and that this process of cultural preservation protects educational sovereignty. The hybridisation process is the means whereby transnational education offers the potential to promote international understanding.

Further, such a contrasting stance tends to view transnational education as having the potential to improve the development of states with inadequate financial resources and physical and human infrastructure. This perspective sees educational sovereignty as attainable because, although a state may seek foreign involvement in education through financial aid, it retains the ability to accept or to reject such involvement. Educational sovereignty does not, furthermore, mean the isolation of a state from other states.

The two major perspectives have arisen on the cultural influences of transnational education: critical education theorists highlight the importance of sovereignty as representative of the primacy of the people, while others stress sovereignty as representative of the primacy of the state. Both, however, enrich the overall understanding of educational sovereignty. The approaches of the critical education theorists are based on considerations of dependency and post-colonial theories.[104] Although their case studies are dissimilar, these two types of theories have similar views on the importance of sovereignty in education. They have enriched the understanding of the relationship between LDSs and advanced states, the normative value of educational sovereignty, and its capacity to protect a state from control by other states. Deeper discussion of both perspectives bears further exploration, as it will clarify the links between transnational education and educational sovereignty.

The Links Between Transnational Education and Educational Sovereignty

This section discusses the contrasting perspectives presented by the critical education theorists and other scholars on transnational education and educational sovereignty, and it then identifies the importance of educational sovereignty, how it might be lost, and its resilience against loss. Educational sovereignty's key features can then be discussed.

Homogenisation and Hybridisation of Education and Culture

As noted earlier, the terms *Americanisation* and *homogenisation* have been used synonymously by authors such as Rizvi and Lingard in reference to transnational education. The same holds true for the terms *Westernisation* and *homogenisation* (despite significant differences between American and Western *writ large* educational standards and practices). As this study includes the Indonesia–US education relationship as a case study, the terms *Americanisation* and *homogenisation* are used interchangeably.[105] Spilimbergo refers to the term *Westernisation* as the transfer of cultural influences generated through cultural contact with the West.[106] In this context, the term *Americanisation* can also be referred to the transfer of influences, such as cultural values in support of liberal democracy, generated through cultural contact with America.[107] Several authors, such as Nye and Huntington, have associated American cultural values and identity with US foreign policy.[108] Nye argues that American values in support of liberal democracy and human rights can be promoted and transferred through higher education.[109] Conversi defines homogenisation as a purposeful process of change, such as change in the less dominant culture to mirror the culture of the dominant culture, in order to achieve uniformity.[110] By drawing on Spilimbergo's and Conversi's definitions, and on Nye's argument, homogenisation is both the transfer of American values as a result of contact with Americans, and a purposeful process of change to reflect American values.

Like homogenisation, hybridisation is a process in which new cultural forms and practices occur as a result of the combination of existing and new practices.[111] Unlike homogenisation, hybridisation, Pieterse argues, is "the making of global culture as a global mélange."[112] In this context, hybridisation is also a purposeful attempt to adapt the culture of the dominant, meaning that LDSs have the ability to receive, adapt, modify, or reject the culture of the developed states.

As noted earlier, for those who conclude that transnational education encourages learning about other states, thereby promoting international understanding, the result is hybridisation rather than homogenisation. The critical education theorists, in contrast, tend to emphasise the advanced states' prestige and power due to their domination of the curriculum.[113]

The homogenisation of education is, however, more than just Americanisation or Westernisation, because, although some have linked transnational education to the expansion of European and American cultures, this link does not imply that the entire globe has become or must become Westernised Americanised.[114] Educational exchanges have consequences, including cultural influence. Lingard and Rizvi argue that although the argument suggests all spheres of social life "must establish their position in relation to the capitalist West," this assertion does not mean that the entire globe has become Westernised.[115] Indeed, educational sovereignty continues to be associated with homogenisation as advanced states maintain their relationships with LDSs.

The critical education theorists see transnational education as a threat to sovereignty and, consequently, local cultures.[116] Tikly argues that in many parts of the previously colonised world, governments are still working on developing curricula that suit their cultures and histories,[117] noting that, "The cultural element looks at the emergence of the borderless world where national cultures are transformed by global communications and cultural hybridisation."[118] He goes on to assert that "the subsequent interpretation and hybridisation of cultural forms (processes in which education systems have been so deeply implicated) have made it increasingly difficult to define what a more culturally 'relevant' curriculum might entail."[119] As such, cultural hybridisation both accentuates the previously colonised world's struggle to reconstruct its educational curricula and diminishes its ability to develop curricula that suit its cultures and histories. Robertson, Bonal, and Dale, among others, use the term *cultural imperialism* to explain cultural hybridisation,[120] which they perceive to be a form of cultural imposition, asserting that, "language and national identity are vulnerable social functions in a global marketplace dominated by multinational educational corporations."[121]

Whether educational relationships between advanced and less-advanced states have the potential to homogenise education, however, needs further examination. Transnational education has long existed across civilisations, cultures, and religions, and educational exchanges result in a range of consequences, including cultural influence. Cultures may be conceptualised as "products of past human behaviour and as shapers of future human behaviour."[122] As such, humans are producers and consumers of culture, and culture influences human behaviour. Furthermore, people have control over their culture, and can choose to combine aspects of foreign cultures with their local ones. Transnational education is far broader than a Western or American model of education and has a long tradition, with religious institutions frequently providing education at the tertiary level. It did not take long for many other political and non-political organisations to embark on their own educational provision.

Development and the New Imperialism

Scholars such as Crawford and Abrahamsen argue that placing LDSs in the role of primary actors in their development and education is a strategy for strengthening donors' effective influence in making important development choices as well as one for countering critics of their activities both at home and abroad.[123] Abrahamsen explained that:

> the discourse of partnership places developing countries in the driver's seat, assigning them prime responsibility for their own development strategies. This reconfiguration of the subject of government confers obligations and duties, at the same time as it opens up new possibilities for decision and action. To a significant extent, development aid as a principle of international solidarity gives way to an obligation on the part of the developing country to manage its own underdevelopment wisely. Only then will development assistance be forthcoming, as the language of partnership emphasises again and again.[124]

Abrahamsen highlights the importance of ensuring that conditions or obligations be addressed in order to enable development assistance to be forthcoming. Nevertheless, it is not mutually beneficial if the state that gives financial assistance is unable to impose obligations that will ensure mutual benefit. Furthermore, the effectiveness of financial assistance must be questioned if the recipient accepts no accountability.

Carnoy and Brock-Utne, among others, consider foreign assistance to be a threat to LDSs' educational sovereignty due to the advanced states and international institutions imposing conditions formulated to benefit only themselves. Critical education theorists charge advanced states' educational aid with creating a new imperialism by perpetuating the recipient states' financial dependence. Carnoy and Tikly argue that advanced states grow richer from such relationships. Carnoy adopts the arguments of Frank and Wallerstein, among others, that the historical process remains active because the development and expansion of advanced states' economies has conditioned the nature of the LDSs' economies.

Critical education theorists express concerns about foreign aid to education, the mobility of educational institutions, and the transfer of educational materials across borders. Carnoy concludes that providing aid in education is one method that advanced states employ to exploit LDSs, and that the funding for educational institutions primarily serves their own needs.[125] The crux of these arguments is that donor states dominate the institutions of education and use the others' economic, political, and social structures to satisfy their own needs, while imposing conditions on the others' policy frameworks that primarily benefit themselves.[126]

Like Crawford and Abrahamsen, however, Carnoy and Tikly fail to recognise that in an increasingly inter-dependent world economy, advanced states and international institutions cannot impose conditions on LDSs but rather can only suggest practices of mutual benefit. Instead, as Tilak succinctly asserts, "in a growing interdependent world economy, it becomes the responsibility of the rich to assist the development of poor countries."[127]

Criticism of the critical education theorists also lies in its lack of empiricism. Drysdale, for example, points out that even though Carnoy's argument is convincing in the sense that the poverty of education in LDSs is a human disgrace, the same could be said for Boston, Massachusetts, which fails to provide higher education for most of its African-American and other poor citizens, despite being home to Harvard, MIT, and several other elite universities.[128] Similarly, Tikly bases his arguments on education in African states. While his studies enrich the understanding of the exercise of control through education by advanced states, they are not necessarily applicable to non-African developing states elsewhere such as those in Asia.

The extent to which international institutions impose conditions on LDSs requires further examination. International agencies such as USAID have the potential to influence the policies of aid-recipient governments, which raises the question of whether the conditions for aid are often in direct conflict with the recipients' sovereignty.[129]

Accepting the critical education theorists' argument that advanced states exploit LDSs recognises the lack of enforcement of international legal regulations. International legal regulations, therefore, provide a promising basis for a framework analysis of educational sovereignty. This study advances educational sovereignty as a concept clustered around the educational transactions between two states along with the externalities of international legal regulations and foreign educational aid.

Identifying the role of education in facilitating development is a good starting point for assessing the benefits and risks of foreign financial assistance in education. This role involves education's links to political, social, and economic factors. Foster observes that, "The effect of enhanced educational inputs upon economic outputs must be seen within a broader historical and sociological perspective which attempts to examine the problematic relationship between education and development in the widest sense."[130]

Education facilitates the stabilisation of internal factions and the unification of diverse ethnic groups within a state by using the curriculum to promote and emphasise a sense of national identity. This stability has been particularly important for such multi-ethnic states as Indonesia and Singapore.

Education plays an important role in developing a strong economy by producing a highly skilled labour force to advance development and generate economic returns.[131] The limitations of LDSs in their ability to educate their citizens and thereby produce a high-quality workforce have often been a major obstacle to economic growth and development. This situation means that foreign financial assistance for education is likely to be beneficial to its recipients, although it is necessary to acknowledge the risk of financial dependence.

The concern that foreign financial assistance is a threat to educational sovereignty has yet to be examined. In Asia, Taiwan, South Korea, and Singapore, for example, have intervened strongly and directly in both the international education market and in financing and planning education. In this context, it cannot be argued that foreign financial assistance has been a threat to educational sovereignty.

Education also has an important role in consolidating cultural values by promoting them in the curriculum. Foreign financial assistance to education may indeed be a threat to its recipients, as the critical education theorists claim, when donors use it as a tool for homogenising education or impose conditions on its recipients for their own benefit. Instead of focusing solely on whether foreign financial assistance is a threat, it is necessary to consider the extent to which foreign financial assistance is effective and can be beneficial for both recipients and donors.

The Importance of Sovereignty in Education and the Potential for Diminished Sovereignty

This section discusses the link between transnational education and educational sovereignty. It considers the extent to which transnational education may be considered to have an impact on educational sovereignty, whether it diminishes it, and, if so, how it does so.

Critical education theorists stress that transnational education involves the LDS being in a commercially and politically weaker position than the donor and, consequently, vulnerable to exploitation, regardless of whether the objective of the donor is the commercialisation of education or the promotion of mutual understanding. Huang contends that in most Asian states, education across borders still maintains its "basic character of a process of catching up with advanced countries and approaching the levels and provisions of the current centres of learning, mostly identified with the English-speaking countries in Europe and especially the United States."[132]

Critical education theorists, therefore, tend to challenge the role of educational sovereignty in international relations, arguing that the delivery of education tends to be tailored to the needs of international institutions and international education providers, both of which are likely to diminish educational sovereignty. Scholars such as Tomplinson, Burbules, and Torres argue that states have lost power, influence, and even sovereignty as they choose to tailor their policies to fit the needs of international market mobility.[133] One of the aims of this research is to explore the extent to which states seek to tailor their national policies in response to the demands of other states. It assesses this process by exploring and identifying the demands and responses between states in bilateral agreements.

Unlike the critical education theorists, Krasner argues that international agreements are based on the mutual recognition of states as being equal and independent. This recognition, Krasner concludes, is accorded to juridically sovereign territorial entities, which have the ability to enter into voluntary contractual agreements.[134] Exercising their educational sovereignty, states are free to endorse any contract they find attractive.[135] When this happens, educational sovereignty is both a product of the relationships between advanced states and LDSs and a product of the recipient states' political will based on the agreements' benefits for them.

Krasner's argument stresses that LDSs can choose those international agreements that they consider to be beneficial for them. Krasner, however, fails to assess how international agreements can be beneficial for both donor and recipient states. This study seeks to explore the extent to which education agreements between advanced states and LDSs can benefit both, and to what extent recipient states concede their educational sovereignty in order to achieve these benefits.[136]

The principle of the equality of sovereign states is fundamental to international law, which recognises that sovereign states are not subject to any superior external authority.[137] The International Court of Justice (ICJ) has also confirmed the equality of states.[138] Some, however, have disputed whether sovereign states are indeed equal under international law. Henkin argues that although "almost all nations observe almost all principles of international law and almost all of their obligations almost all of the time," international law is not enforceable.[139] It is important to recognise that although states may be guaranteed equality in law, political inequality persists. Henkin argues, however, that states usually abide by international law and recognise the principles of international legal sovereignty and the equality of states.

The critical education theorists perceive the demise of sovereignty to be a corollary of increasingly porous international borders and the loss of authority, both of which affect education in a myriad of ways. Verger and Bonal argue that the loss of educational sovereignty is a consequence of its ongoing violation resulting from state commitments under the GATS and the public administration controls and plans for state educational systems per such agreements.[140] This perspective, therefore, sees transnational education as having the potential to diminish a state's educational sovereignty. This study assesses this conclusion. Unlike Verger and Bonal, Carnoy argues that while overall sovereignty is diminished, some aspects of it remain unaffected. Hybridisation diminishes it because that compels states to adapt their policies to suit international institutions' needs, but states still retain influence over education within their territorial boundaries.[141] Carnoy's analysis captures both the limitations and the supremacy of the state.

Whether LDSs still have the capacity to regulate their national education systems despite extensive flows of foreign education across their borders requires further examination in the light of the existence of cultural hybridisation.[142] The nature of the educational transactions between donor and recipient states, therefore, strongly influences their effects on educational sovereignty.

The attraction of the critical education theorists' ideas lies in the importance of educational sovereignty. There is, however, a danger in assuming its primacy. Authoritarian Asian states, for example, have used education as a tool for achieving political gains by maintaining passivity among the learners and inhibiting critical thinking.[143]

Educational sovereignty is particularly valuable for protecting a state from control by others, which raises the question of the nature of such control. Critical education theorists argue that three main factors determine the level of educational sovereignty's importance for states, particularly LDSs, in regard to protecting it from others.

The first of these factors concerns whether donor states impose conditions on the recipients. For example, Carnoy, Tikly, and Ferudi argue that the ability of advanced states and international institutions to impose conditions can be seen to be a form of indirect control. Although they do not consider whether states are free to endorse any contract they find attractive, this study acknowledges their concerns by including their argument in its investigation of the extent to which an LDS tailors its national policies to suit the demands of a prospective donor, the extent to which such educational agreements are mutually beneficial, and the extent to which the recipient state sacrifices its educational sovereignty to achieve such benefits.

The second factor influencing the level of importance of educational sovereignty is whether transnational education agreements are tailored to the needs of international institutions and international education providers. The concept of the homogenisation of education is pertinent, as LDSs establish their positions in relation to the West. Sovereignty in education has, therefore, become a salient value through which LDSs endeavour to protect themselves from Western cultural domination. This study, therefore, considers the extent to which LDSs are able to regulate their national educational systems, enforce education law within their territory, and still be able to use education to preserve their cultural values.

The third factor influencing educational sovereignty's level of importance is whether foreign aid for education benefits only the donors. The LDSs' task of achieving economic development entails the employment of education, which often requires foreign assistance, as it is one of the available options for meeting the educational needs of a large population. This circumstance raises the question of whether the conditions attached to aid are in conflict with and in opposition to the LDSs' sovereignty. This book addresses such questions by examining the extent to which recipient states retain and exercise educational sovereignty.

Critical education theorists who associate transnational education with transactions between LDSs and advanced states have addressed the issue of whether it diminishes educational sovereignty by imposing conditions for those accepting it and tailoring its curriculum content to suit the donors' needs.[144] Robertson, Bonal, and Dale consider the GATS as a source of diminished educational sovereignty by encouraging the commercialisation of education through a focus on economic policies that advance global competitiveness at the expense of national consciousness.[145]

Other writers, such as Krasner, however, argue that LDSs' authority to govern themselves and to regulate their own domestic affairs is ensured despite their limited power in negotiations with donors.[146] The supremacy of sovereignty, according to Krasner, and the non-binding nature of commitment in education under the GATS challenge the arguments that violations of educational sovereignty result from any commitments a state makes under the GATS.

Clearly, these critical education theorists' perspectives on sovereignty in education point to the potential for loss of educational sovereignty, its importance, and the advanced states' dominant role in their relationships with LDSs. This book elaborates upon this initial assessment further in order to establish the situation in regard to educational sovereignty with a focus on Indonesia's current and future agreements.

AUTHORITY, CONTROL, AUTONOMY, AND THE RESILIENCE OF SOVEREIGNTY IN EDUCATION

Foreign education providers rely on the willingness of client states to open up their markets to them. The nature of these relationships in this regard is one of mutual cooperation, as each party relies on the other for commitment to the arrangement. When such relationships are aimed at promoting understanding between two states, the LDSs can respond to proposals from advanced states by rejecting or accepting any offer of a bilateral relationship.[147]

Since advanced states' education programmes penetrate into LDSs, which can reject or accept them, the nature of the relationship is, therefore, mutually beneficial. Arrangements between states, as reflected in such documents as MoUs and MoAs, are governed by domestic law. This backing in domestic law means that the LDSs are not disadvantaged, as the critical education theorists have argued.

The measurement of sovereignty is indeed a difficult task. As Thomson argues, the central problem is misunderstanding the relationship between authority and control, with authority concerning rule-making, and control concerning rule enforcement.[148] Autonomy also constitutes a fundamental principle of sovereignty and is essential to the practices of the LDSs as it is a means of safeguarding against the negative effects of the international system.[149] Autonomy functions to control the activities of transnational actors, to enhance international negotiating capacities, to uphold state interests, and to effectively direct domestic affairs.[150] This book acknowledges that the defining features of educational sovereignty include autonomy, the making of regulations by the LDSs (authority), and the enforcement of education law within their territory (control).

While states have the authority and control over education within and across their territories, whether a state's ability to make authoritative political decisions becomes eroded depends on how adaptable and resilient it is to such changes as the removal of trade barriers. Krasner argues that states can never isolate themselves from their external environment, as represented by other states.[151] States have always struggled to control the flow of people or services. Krasner argues that loss of control can precipitate a crisis of authority, but that the condition is insufficiently serious to warrant the development of new authority structures.[152]

Understanding Transnational Education and Its Impact

As argued earlier, transnational education is often associated with LDSs' economic development, trade in education, and the promotion of understanding between states. LDSs' use of transnational education for their economic development involves meeting their objectives to increase their capacities. The aim of promoting understanding between states also involves striving to achieve academic, cultural, and political objectives.[153] Table 2.2 summarises the aims and conditions of transnational education and the forms it takes.

There are impacts of transnational education on enrolled students in a recipient state, foreign education provider institutions, and education institutions in a recipient state. Table 2.3 explains this point graphically.

Table 2.3 shows two important aspects of the relationship in education between the developed states and the LDSs. Firstly, the relationships with foreign education providers can be either competitive or collaborative. Secondly, there are advantages and disadvantages of transnational education. Table 2.3 shows the advantages and disadvantages of transnational education for enrolled students in a recipient state, foreign education provider institutions, and education institutions in a recipient state. For instance, enrolled students in a recipient state benefit from virtual and distance education because it is less expensive than the consumption abroad mode, and the students gain foreign education qualifications without leaving home. The disadvantage is, however, they are vulnerable to poor-quality education. For education institutions in a recipient state, the relationship

Table 2.2 Forms and conditions of transnational education

Forms	Conditions of transnational education		
	Development (capacity-building objectives)	Academic, cultural, and political objectives	Commercial/ trade (trade objectives)
Mode 1 Programme articulation, twinning, double or joint degrees, validation, virtual universities	Delivery of the program is often done through partnership arrangements or can be an independent initiative by a foreign provider		
Mode 2 Full degree, fieldwork, educational exchanges, internships	The funding for these forms of transnational education can be from scholarships from government, exchange agreements, public-private sources, and self-funding		
Mode 3 Branch, mergers, virtual universities, affiliations and networks, independent institutions	The emphasis is on the establishment of foreign education providers in a receiving state		
Mode 4 Education consultancy, professional development, research, joint curriculum development, technical assistance	The projects and services can be undertaken as part of development, cultural and educational, and commercial objectives		

with foreign education can be collaborative or competitive. Nonetheless, incomes of local education providers can decrease as affluent local students may prefer foreign educational institutions. Although the importer or recipient state has the benefits of transnational education, it is exposed to more risks than the exporter states. It is expected, therefore, that there are concerns surrounding the impact of transnational education on LDSs. This study then explores and examines the impact of transnational education on the recipient/importer state.

FEATURES OF EDUCATIONAL SOVEREIGNTY

Educational sovereignty involves both the maintenance and development of local cultural values through education and state authority to control the movement of people, educational materials, and institutions within and across borders. Educational sovereignty also refers to a state's refusal to

Table 2.3 Understanding the forms of transnational education and their impacts

Forms of transnational education	Influencing factors	Impacts		
		Enrolled students in a recipient state	Foreign education provider institutions	Education institutions (recipient state)
Virtual education, distance education	High technology, removal of restrictions on imports of education materials, elimination of non-recognition of degrees obtained through distance and virtual education	Gaining foreign education qualifications without leaving home Less expensive Students may be exposed to low quality foreign education	Low cost for the establishment of education programmes as distance and virtual education require less investment and infrastructure than educational institutions that require buildings and campuses	Relationships with foreign education providers can be competitive Incomes of local education providers can be decreased
Full degree, fieldwork, educational exchanges, internships	Removal or reduction of restriction on foreign travel based on disciplines, areas of study, or both; removal or reduction of quotas on the number of students proceeding to a state or institution	Expensive. Although students receive scholarships, consumption abroad is an expensive option, as it involves the high cost of living in a foreign state	Fees could be high for students from client states. This form generates profits	Incomes of local education providers can decrease as affluent local students may prefer foreign educational institutions
Branch campuses, independent institutions	Removal or reduction of restrictions on certain disciplines or programmes; restrictions on Foreign Direct Investment (FDI) by education providers; removal or reduction of such barriers on	Gaining foreign educational qualifications without leaving home. This can be beneficial for students who have family or work commitments. This option is also less expensive	Relationship with foreign education providers can be either competitive or collaborative	Relationship with foreign education providers can be either competitive or collaborative Incomes of local education providers can decrease as affluent local

(*continued*)

Table 2.3 (continued)

Forms of transnational education	Influencing factors	Impacts		
		Enrolled students in a recipient state	Foreign education provider institutions	Education institutions (recipient state)
	commercial presence as insistence on equal academic qualifications and disapproval of franchise operations			students may prefer foreign educational institutions.
Professors, researchers, and educators working in another country	Removal or reduction of visa and entry restriction; removal or reduction of nationality or residence requirements; elimination or reduction of restrictions on repatriation of earnings	New knowledge and skills	The opportunity to maintain relationship with education institutions in a recipient state	New knowledge and skills

Adapted from Knight (2010). Also see McBurnie and Ziguras (2007)

accept foreign intervention in education unless it has sought and agreed to that intervention.

What is missing, however, is the role of territoriality, or the physical extent of a state's exclusive sovereign jurisdiction, in the preservation of educational sovereignty.[154] As transnational education involves the intrusion of each other's territories, territoriality is salient in the discussion of transnational education. The salience of territoriality influences domestic policymaking in the areas among others, education, foreign relations, and defence to establish their "state-centred forms of territoriality,"[155] which other states recognise. Recognition by foreign authorities is, therefore, an important feature of educational sovereignty. Consequently, the loss of educational sovereignty can be determined by reference to its criteria. Table 2.4 illustrates this point.

Table 2.4 Features of educational sovereignty

Educational sovereignty
1. Autonomy to regulate national education and control over national educational law without intervention from foreign authorities
2. Authority and control over educational materials and programmes, and educational institutions across borders and within the state's territory
3. The ability to refuse intervention in education from outside the state unless the state has sought that intervention
4. State retention of the ability to maintain local cultural values through education
5. Recognition of independent entities, that include territorial jurisdiction, by other states
6. The need and ability of non-state actors to challenge the arbitrary authority of power structures to determine the essence of individuals' educational experience

Table 2.4 illustrates the criteria for measuring the maintenance of the presence of education sovereignty. To claim sovereignty, the state maintains autonomy over national laws regulating education. The state has authority over educational activities within its border, and it can allow transnational education intervention, provided intervention has been sought. State also promotes cultural values through education and requires that state entities are accorded due respect by others.

Table 2.3 and the preceding discussion provide the following framework for analysing the extent of educational sovereignty. This framework offers the criteria for this study to use in assessing the following question associated with educational sovereignty: Does transnational education involving a developed state and an LDS diminish the education sovereignty of the latter?

Concluding Remarks

This chapter has defined transnational education as the mobility of educational materials, people including students, and foreign educational service providers across borders. It refers to all types of post-secondary educational study programmes or courses of study and educational services, which are delivered through various modes, including distance education and partner-supported delivery, franchising, joint awards, Internet delivery, and offshore campuses.

Transnational education has become broader as new delivery models beyond the mobility of students and the mobility of educational materials have emerged. In addition to providing for the commercialisation of education, transnational education also presents a platform for partnership through franchising, twinning arrangements, branch campuses, and corporate programmes. The relationship with foreign education providers can, therefore, be either competitive or collaborative, a point that both perspectives outlined and discussed in this chapter fail to address. This book, therefore, addresses transnational education's impact on the relationship between donor and recipient states.

Educational sovereignty is a state's ability to maintain local cultural values through education, to regulate the flow of educational institutions, materials, and students and practitioners across its borders, and to respond to the increasing demand for education without accepting unwanted impositions from foreign states. It also refers to the ability to choose which foreign involvements in education to accept and which to reject.

Of considerable significance to transnational education and educational sovereignty is the complexity of the relationship between developed states and LDSs, and between transnational education and educational sovereignty, and the role of social agencies, both state and non-state actors. Central to the endeavours of critical education theorists are their critical perspectives that challenge the existing social and political order and the state autonomy in resisting being an alliance or a pact of domination. Thus, within the context of transnational education, complex questions are raised about the reconstruction of the meaning of educational sovereignty. Educational sovereignty then also refers to the need to determine the essence of the educational experience and the ability of non-state actors to challenge capricious authority of power structure in determining individuals' educational experience.

This book begins its assessment of educational sovereignty by establishing its position within current agreements, with particular reference to Indonesia. It presents educational sovereignty as a concept through the example of the educational transactions between Indonesia and the US, including both those with trade and development objectives and those with the objective of promoting understanding between the states involved.

Whether transnational education diminishes educational sovereignty has been the subject of prolonged discussions. The critical education theorists argue that the developed states' dominance in curriculum, language, and expertise, and their indirect control through educational aid money, reduces the recipient states' sovereignty through retaining superior knowledge and expertise, creating financial dependence, and through the homogenisation of education and culture.

The opposing view is that transnational education has the potential to promote understanding between states through the process of hybridisation, which is visualised as a process of learning from each other. This view, furthermore, holds that transnational education does not diminish educational sovereignty because the recipient states have the capacity to control their national education systems.

The extent to which recipient states have lost sovereignty, if at all, will be determined by their political will to consider all the benefits from the contracts and to agree only to those they find attractive, rather than merely tailoring their educational policies to suit the needs of international institutions and international education providers. A state's ability to make authoritative decisions or policies regarding education depends on how adaptable and resilient it is to such changes as the removal of trade barriers. Rule-making and rule enforcement, therefore, have important roles in maintaining educational sovereignty. This book acknowledges that the retention of sovereignty in education requires that the recipient states need to be both making regulations and enforcing education law within their territories.

Notes

1. UNESCO, *Council of Europe's Code of Good Practice in the Provision of Transnational Education*, 2001.
2. Global Alliance for TNE, "Certification manual," last modified July 28, 2012, http://www.edugate.org
3. Grant McBurnie and Christopher Ziguras, *Transnational Education: Issues and Trends in Offshore Higher Education.* (New York: Routledge, 2007); Jane Knight, "Higher Education Crossing Borders: A Guide to the Implications of the General Agreements on Trade in Services (GATS) for Cross-border Education," A report prepared for the Commonwealth of Learning and UNESCO, 2006; Grant McBurnie and Christopher Ziguras, "The Regulation of Transnational Higher Education in Southeast Asia: Case Studies of Hong Kong, Malaysia and Australia," *Higher Education*, 42, (2001): 85–105.
4. Jane Knight, "Higher Education Crossing Borders: Programmes and Providers on the Move," in Higher Education in a Global Society, eds. D. Bruce Johnston, Madeleine D'Ambrosia, and Paul Yakoboski (Massachusetts: Edward Elgar Publishing, 2010). Also see OECD, "Current

Commitments under the GATS in Educational Services," Forum on Trade in Educational Services, Washington, DC, 23–24 May 2002.
5. McBurnie and Ziguras (2001, 2007). Also see Futao Huang, "Internationalization of Higher Education in the Developing and Emerging Countries: A Focus on Transnational Higher Education in Asia," *Journal of Studies in International Education*, 11, (2007): 421–432; Terra Gargano, "(Re)conceptualizing International Student Mobility: The Potential of Transnational Social Fields," *Journal of Studies in International Education*, 13, (2009): 331–346.
6. Ibid.
7. Ibid.
8. Karen Fasimpaur, "Massive and Open MOOCs," last modified June 27, 2014, http://www.files.eric.ed.gov/fulltext/EJ1015163.pdf. Also see Muralee Thummarukudy, "Transnational Education: Global Challenges, Local Opportunities," prepared for International Meet on Transnational Education organised by the Kerala State Higher Education Council, 3–5 January 2014, last modified June 28, 2014, http://www.kshec.kerala.gov.in/images/documents
9. Ibid.
10. Nathan Harden, "The End of University as We Know It," *The American Interests*, December 11, 2012.
11. MOOCs are a relatively new concept and virtually unknown when this book was conceived. This book uses the Indonesia–US education relationship as the case study. MOOCs are a relatively, and rather limited, new phenomenon in Indonesia and outside the scope of this book. [Since Nathan Harden's study in 2012, there may be evidence that free MOOCs will not be used as much as previously believed.]
12. Harden (2012).
13. WTO, "Education Services—WTO," Council for Trade in Services, last modified December 23, 1998, http://www.wto.org. Also see WTO, "Education Services—WTO," (2011), http://www.wto.org/
14. Pierre Sauve, "Trade, Education and the GATS: What's in, What's out, What's all the Fuss About?" Prepared for the OECD/US Forum on Trade in Services (Washington, DC: 2002).
15. Ana Pereira, "The Liberalization of Education under the WTO Services Agreement (GATS): A Threat to Public Education Policy," *Journal of International Economy*, 2005: 1–40; Rudolf Adlung, "Public Services and the GATS," *Journal of International Economic Law*, 2006: 1–29.
16. Adlung (2006); Pereira (2005).
17. This chapter, however, only briefly discusses the history of transnational education.

18. Welsh cited in Kemal Gürüz, *Higher Education Student Mobility in the Global Knowledge Economy* (New York: State University of New York Press, 2008).
19. Religions had long been operating such education programmes during the colonial era.
20. Justus Van Det Kroef, "Higher Education in Indonesia," *The Journal of Higher Education*, 26, (1955): 366–377.
21. Melanie Walker and Pat Thomson, eds, *The Routledge Doctoral Supervisor's Companion: Supporting Effective Research in Education and Social Sciences* (New York: Routledge, 2010).
22. Richard Easterlin, "Why Isn't the Whole World Developed?" *The Journal of Economic History*, 41, (1981): 1–19. Also see Masaru Saito, "Introduction of Foreign Technology in the Industrialization Processes: Japanese Experience since the Meiji Restoration," *Journal of Developing Economies*, 13, (1975): 1–19.
23. Kemal Gürüz, *Higher Education Student Mobility in the Global Knowledge Economy* (New York: State University of New York Press, 2008).
24. In the late 1940s, the US shared among some 30 countries $50 billion in assistance. It established USAID, an agency that assists other countries' development efforts, in 1961. See USAID, last modified July 30, 2012, http://www.transition.usaid.gov/about_usaid. Also see Robert E Wood, *From Marshall Plan to Debt Crisis: Foreign Assistance and Development Choices in the World Economy* (London: University of California Press, 1986); Andrew Natsios, "Five Debates on International Development: The US Perspective," *Development Policy Review*, 24, (2006): 131–139.
25. Daphne Keats, *Back in Asia* (Canberra: Research School of Pacific Studies, The Australian National University, 1969). Also see Viswanathan Selvaratnam, "Higher Education and Cooperation and Western Dominance of Knowledge Creation and Flows in Third World Countries," *Higher Education*, 17, (1988): 48.
26. Gürüz (2008).
27. Cited in Gürüz (2008). The Pearson Commission on International Development was established in August 1968 by World Bank president, Robert McNamara, to investigate the effectiveness of the World Bank development assistance. See the World Bank, "Pages from World Bank History: The Pearson Commission," last modified August 20, 2012, http://www.web.worldbank.org
28. Cited in *Reforming the United Nations: New Initiatives and Past Efforts*, Volume 1, ed. Joachim Muller (The Hague: Kluwer Law International, 1997): 16.
29. Factors influencing this demand include increased numbers of secondary-school students, low-quality local post-secondary education, the desire to

increase personal incomes, and the emergence of interest in lifelong learning by mature adult students. See Gu Jian Jing, "Transnational Education: Current Developments and Policy Implications," *Front Education China*, 4, (2009); Huang (2007).
30. UNESCO, *OECD Indicators* (Paris: Organisation for Economic Cooperation and Development, 2005); UNESCO, "Trends in Global Higher Education", last modified July 30, 2012, http://www.unesdoc.unesco.org
31. Making sense of these earnings, however, requires more information in regard to the returns and costs for many different parties, changes over time, and comparison with other earnings, which is beyond the scope of this book.
32. David Riker and Brandon Turner, "Manufacturing and Services: Economics Brief," *US Department of Commerce*, last modified September 12, 2012, http://www.trade.gov/mas
33. James Wolfensohn, "A Partnership for Development and Peace," last modified August 10, 2012, http://www.worldenergysource.com; Jennifer Brinkerhoff, "Choosing the Right Partners for the Right Reasons," in *Partnership for International Development: Rhetoric or Results?* (Boulder, Colorado: Lynne Rienner Publishers, 2002): 47–56.
34. Gordon Crawford, *Foreign Aid and Political Reform: A Comparative Analysis of Democracy Assistance and Political Conditionality* (Basingstoke: Palgrave, 2001); Phillip and G.P. Kelly, *Education and Colonialism* (New York: Longman, 1978).
35. Crawford (2001); Rita Abrahamsen, "The Power of Partnerships in Global Governance," *Third World Quarterly*, 25, (2004); Isabel Canto and Janet Hannah, "A Partnership of Equals? Academic Collaboration between the United Kingdom and Brazil," *Journal of Studies in International Education*, 5, (2001).
36. Ibid.
37. Both MoUs and MoAs commonly contain such provisions. For instance, see MoU of Ohio University, last modified June 20, 2012, http://www.oia.osu.edu/pdf/MoU
38. Ibid.
39. See United Nations, *Treaty Handbook* (New York: Treaty Section of the Office of Legal Affairs, 2006).
40. http://www.ilint.illinois.edu/partnerships/agreements
41. Anthony Aust, *Handbook in International Law*, 2nd edition (Cambridge: Cambridge University Press, 2010).
42. Signed December 26, 1933. Also see http://www.molossia.org/montevideo
43. Bodin developed what is commonly regarded as the first statement of a modern theory of sovereignty. See David Held, "Law of States, Law of

Peoples: Three Models of Sovereignty," *Legal Theory*, 8 (2002). Jean Bodin, *The Six Books of a Commonwealth*, ed. and trans. Michael Tooley (Oxford: Blackwell, 1967); Francis Harry Hinsley, *Sovereignty*, 2nd edition (Cambridge: Cambridge University Press, 1986).
44. See H. L. A. Hart, *Concept of Law* (Oxford: Oxford University Press, 2012): 50–60. Hart developed what is regarded as the definitive defense of legal authority and positive law (or legal positivism).
45. This statement, however, relies heavily on legal notions of sovereignty. This book comprises both state and non-state actors in conceptualising educational sovereignty.
46. Aristotle, Jean Bodin, and Hugo Grotius all emphasised the supremacy of the state in their legal theories.
47. Raymond Morrow and Carlos Torres, "The States, Social Movements, and Educational Reforms," In *Comparative Education: The Dialectics of the Global and the Local*, eds. Robert Arnov and Carlos Torres (Maryland: Rowman and Littlefield Publishers, 2007): 93.
48. All three theories—critical education, new imperialism, and dependency theories—and their intertwined nature are usually understood in the context of structuralism. This book, however, uses critical-theory-based perspectives, as they focus on education. The terms *critical education theorists* and *critical educationalists* are used interchangeably in this book.
49. Luis Moll, "The Concept of Educational Sovereignty," *Penn GSE Perspectives on Urban Education*, 1, (2002).
50. Alastair Pennycook, *The Cultural Politics of English as an International Language* (Harlow, Essex: Longman Group Limited, 1994); Anthony Verger and Xavier Bonal, "Against GATS: The Sense of a Global Struggle," *Journal for Critical Education Policy Studies*, 4, (2006): 1–27; Rajani Naidoo, "Higher Education as a Global Commodity: The Perils and Promises for Developing Countries," *The Observatory on Borderless Higher Education*, February 2007: 1–19.
51. Christina Fox, "The Questions of Identity from A Comparative Education Perspective," in *Comparative Education: The Dialectic of the Global and the Local*, eds. Robert Arnove and Carlos Torres (Maryland: Rowman and Littlefield Publishers, 2007): 134–138.
52. Ibid.
53. Graham Pike, "Global Education and National Identity: In Pursuit of Meaning," *Theory in Practice*, 39, (2000): 64–73.
54. Albatch (2004b): 3–25.
55. Philip Albatch, "Globalisation and the University: Myths and Realities in an Unequal World," *Tertiary Education and Management*, 10, (2004): 3–25.
56. This argument has been one of the underlying points surrounding economic arguments about imperialism.

57. Leon Tikly, "Postcolonialism and Comparative Education," *International Review of Education*, 45, (1999): 603–621; Leon Tikly, "Education and the New Imperialism," *Comparative Education*, 40, (2004): 173–198; Ronaldo Munck, "Dependency and Imperialism in Latin America: New Horizons," in *The Political Economy of Imperialism: Critical Appraisals*, ed. Ronald Chilcote (Lanham, Maryland: Rowman and Littlefield Publishers Inc., 2000); Frank Furedi, *The New Ideology of Imperialism* (London: Pluto Press, 1994).
58. Martin Carnoy, *Education as Cultural Imperialism* (New York: David McKay, 1975).
59. Luis Moll (2002).
60. Carlos Alberto Torres, "Globalization, Education, and Citizenship: Solidarity Versus Markets?" *American Educational Research Journal*, 39, (2002): 363–378.
61. Dynamic interactions in transnational education occur not only between state actors but also between non-state actors, affecting people in a myriad of ways, particularly in economics and culture. See Nelly Stromquist and Karen Monkman (eds), "Defining Globalization and Assessing its Implications for Knowledge and Education, Revisited," in *Globalization and Education* (Maryland: Rowman and Littlefield Education, 2014): 1–19.
62. Carlos Alberto Torres (2002): 363–378; Leon Tikly (1999): 603–621; Leon Tikly (2004): 173–198; Ronaldo Munck (2000); Frank Furedi (1994); Martin Carnoy (1975).
63. Robert Cox, "Social Forces, States, and World Orders: Beyond International Relations Theory". *Millennium: Journal of International Studies*, 10, (1981): 135.
64. Gargano (2009); Phillip Albatch, "Higher Education Crosses Borders," *Change*, 36, (2004): 5.
65. Huang (2007): 421–432.
66. Albatch and Selvaratnam (1989).
67. Phillip Albatch, "The University as Centre and Periphery," *Teachers College Record*, 4, (1981): 601–621; Albatch and Selvaratnam (1989); Huang (2007).
68. John Tomlinson, "Cultural Globalisation: Placing and Displacing the West," *European Journal of Development Research*, 8, (1996): 22–35.
69. Malcolm Waters, *Globalisation* (New York: Routledge, 1995): 3.
70. Joseph Zajda, "Globalising Education: Designing a Renewed Agenda for Teacher Education," *Education and Society*, 16, (1998): 90.
71. Phuong-Mai Nguyen, Julian Elliot, Cees Terlouw, and Albert Pilot, "Neo-colonialism in Education: Cooperative Learning in an Asian context," *Comparative Education*, 45, (2009): 109–130.

72. Huang (2007): 421–432; Albatch and Selvaratnam (1989); Phuong-Mai Nguyen et al. (2009).
73. Tikly (2004): 173–198.
74. Pennycook (1994).
75. Angela Siqueira, "The Regulation of Education Through the WTO/GATS," *Journal for Critical Education Policy Studies*, 3, (2005): 1–16; Verger and Bonal, "Against GATS: The Sense of a Global Struggle," *Journal for Critical Education Policy Studies*, 1–27.
76. Martin Carnoy and Diana Rhoten, "What Does Globalization Mean for Educational Change? A Comparative Approach," *Comparative Education Review*, 46, (2002): 1–10; Carnoy, *Education as Cultural Imperialism*. Also see Philip Albatch, "Higher Education Crosses Borders: Can the United States Remain the Top Destination for Foreign Students?" *Change*, 36, (2004): 18–25; Albatch and Nathan (1989); Tikly (2004).
77. *Imperialism* is the policy of extending a country's power and influence through colonialism, the use of military force, or other means. *Colonialism* is the policy or practice of acquiring full or partial political control over another country, occupying it with settlers, and exploiting it economically. See Oxford dictionary, http://www.oxforddictionaries.com
78. Tikly (1996); Carnoy and Rhoten (2002); Carnoy (1975).
79. Tikly (2004).
80. Joel Samoff, "International Influence," in *Comparative Education: The Dialectic of the Global and Local*, eds Robert Arnove and Carlos Torres (Lanham, Maryland: Rowman and Littlefield Publisher, 1999).
81. Christopher Collins, "A General Agreement on Higher Education: GATS, Globalization, and Imperialism," *Research in Comparative and International Education*, 2, (2007): 1–14; Boaventura de Sousa Santos, "The University in the 21st Century: Toward a Democratic and Emancipatory University Reform," in *The University, States, and Market: The Political Economy of Globalization in the Americas*, eds Robert Rhoads and Carlos Torres (Stanford, CA: Stanford University Press, 2006).
82. Edward Said, *Culture and Imperialism* (New York: Vintage Books, 1993): 284.
83. Siqueira (2005); Verger and Bonal (2006).
84. Albatch and Selvaratnam (1989); Tikly (2004).
85. Ronaldo Munck, "Dependency and Imperialism in Latin America: New Horizons," in *The Political Economy of Imperialism: Critical Appraisals*, ed. Ronald Chilcote (Lanham, Maryland: Rowman and Littlefield Publishers Inc., 2000); Albatch and Selvaratnam (1989); Carnoy (1975); Said (1993).
86. Carnoy (1974); Andre Gunder Frank, "The Development of Underdevelopment," *The Political Economy of Development and Underdevelopment*,

3rd edition (New York: Random House, 1984); Brigit Brock-Utne, Education *for All: The Recolonialization of the African Mind* (New York: Falmer Press, 2000).
87. Carnoy (1975).
88. An emerging argument amongst international education scholars emphasises the neutrality of transnational education and argues that ideally students should be able to look at the evidence and make informed decisions. See John Daniel, "Building Capacity in Open and Distance Learning," *Presentation at OECD/UNESCO Australia Forum on Trade in Education Services*, October 12, Sydney.
89. William Rowe and Vivian Schelling, *Memory and Modernity: Popular Culture in Latin America* (London: Verso, 1991): 231.
90. Jan Nederveen Pieterse, *Globalization and Culture: Global Melange* (Lanham, Maryland: Rowman and Littlefield Publisher, 2009).
91. Ibid., 65–83.
92. Ibid., 65–83.
93. See Douglas Shale, "The Hybridisation of Higher Education in Canada," *The International Review of Research in Open Distance Learning*, 2002: 1–5; Peter Cookson, "The Hybridisation of Higher Education in Canada: Cross National Perspectives," *The International Review of Research in Open Distance Learning*, 2002: 1–2.
94. Jane Knight, "Internationalization of Higher Education: A Conceptual Framework," in *Internationalization of Higher Education in Asia Pacific Countries*, eds. Jane Knight and Hans De Wit (Amsterdam: European Association for International Education, 1997). Fazal Rizvi, "International Education and the Production of Globalization Imagination," in *Globalization and Education: Critical Perspectives*, eds. NC Burbles and CA Torres (London: Routledge, 2000); Erika Schwindt, "The Development of a Model for International Education with Specific Reference to the Role of Host Country Nationals," *Journals of Research in International Education*, 2, (2003): 67–81; Jeff Thompson and Mary Hayden, "International Schools and International Education: A Relationship Reviewed," *Oxford Review of Education*, 21, (1995): 327–45; JJ Hayden Thompson and MC Williams, "The Crossing Frontiers," *International Schools Journal*, 15, (1995): 13–20.
95. Knight (1997): 9.
96. Dewi Fortuna Anwar, "Human Security: An Intractable Problem in Asia," *Asian security order: Instrumental and Normative Features*, ed. Muthiah Alagappa (California: Stanford University Press, 2003).
97. Ibid.
98. Peter Bauer, "Dissent on Development," *Scottish Journal of Political Economy*, 16, (1969): 75–94.

99. Jandhyala Tilak, "Knowledge society, education and aid," *Compare*, 32, (2002): 298–308.
100. Tilak (2002): 308.
101. Bauer (1969).
102. David King, "The Scientific Impact of Nations: What Different Countries Get for Their Research Spending," *Nature*, 430, (2004): 311–316.
103. Rajani Naidoo, "Higher education as a global commodity: The perils and promises for developing countries," *The Observatory on Borderless Higher Education*, (London: OBHE, 2001): 1–19.
104. Dependency theory attempts to explain situations in which advanced states exercise control through education and the growing international economy to maintain the dependence of such LDSs as former colonies, colonies, and other third-world countries, upon themselves in general and former colonisers in particular. Dependency theorists include Andre Gunder Frank, Dos Santos, and Samir Amin. This book refers to the contemporary manifestation of Western capitalist colonialism as post-colonialism.
105. John Tomlinson, "Cultural Globalisation: Placing and Displacing the West," *European Journal of Development Research*, 8, (1996): 22–35.
106. Antonio Spilimbergo, "Democracy and Foreign Education," *The American Economic Review*, 99, (2009). Also see Joseph Heath, "Liberalization, Modernization, Westernization," *Philosophy and Social Criticism*, 30, (2004): 665.
107. Some authors such as Rizvi and Lingard have used the term *Americanisation* synonymously with *homogenisation*. Bob Lingard and Fazal Rizvi, "Globalisation and the fear of Homogenisation in Education," *Change: Transformation in Education*, 1, (1998): 62–71.
108. Samuel Huntington, "American Ideals versus American Institutions," *Political Science Quarterly*, 97, (1982): 1–37. Joseph Nye, "The Decline of America's Soft Power: Why Washington Should Worry," *Foreign Affairs*, 83, (2004): 16–20; Joseph Nye, "Soft Power and Higher Education," The Internet and University Forum, last modified September 8, 2013, http://www.net.educause.Edu.ir/library
109. Nye (2013).
110. Daniele Conversi, "Homogenisation, Nationalism and War: Should We Still Read Ernest Gellner?" *Nations and Nationalism*, 13, (2007): 371–394.
111. Rowe and Schelling, *Memory and Modernity: Popular Culture in Latin America*.
112. Jan Nederveen Pieterse, "Globalisation as hybridisation," *International Sociology*, 9, (1994): 175.
113. Nicholas Burbules and Carlos Torres, *Globalization and Education: Critical Perspectives* (New York: Routledge, 2000); Carlos Torres,

"Globalization, Education, and Citizenship: Solidarity versus Markets," *American Educational Research Journal*, 39, (2002): 363–378; Gargano (2009); Albatch (2004a, b). Albatch and Selvaratnam (1989); Tikly (1999); Carnoy and Rhoten (2002); Carnoy (1975).
114. Burbules and Torres (2000); Torres (2002); Gargano (2009); Albatch (2004a, b). Also see Bob Lingard and Fazal Rizvi, "Globalisation and the Fear of Homogenisation in Education," *Change: Transformation in Education*, 1(1998): 62–71.
115. Lingard and Rizvi (1998). Also see Waters (1995).
116. Hastings Donnans and Thomas Wilson, *Borders: Frontiers of Identity, Nation, and State* (Oxford and New York: Berg, 1999).
117. Tikly (1996).
118. Tikly (1996): 616; Bray, "Education and the Vestiges of Colonialism: Self-determination, Neo- colonialism and Dependency in the South Pacific," *Comparative Education*, 29(1993): 333–348.
119. Tikly (1996): 613.
120. Susan Robertson, Xavier Bona, and Roger Dale, "GATS and the Education Service Industry: The Politics of Scale and Global Territorialization," *Comparative Education Review*, 46(2002): 472–495.
121. Ibid., 494.
122. Marshall Segall, PR Dasen, John Berry, and Ype Poortinga, *Human Behaviour in Global Perspective: An Introduction to Cross-cultural Psychology* (2nd ed.) (Boston, MA: Allyn and Bacon, 1999): 23.
123. Gordon Crawford, "Partnership or Power?: Deconstructing the 'Partnership for Governance Reform' in Indonesia," *Third World Quarterly*, 24, (2003): 139–159; Abrahamsen (2004): 1453–1467.
124. Abrahamsen (2004): 1460.
125. Carnoy (1975).
126. Tikly (1996); Carnoy and Rhoten (2002); Carnoy (1975); Albatch (2004a, b); Albatch and Nathan (1989); Tikly (2004).
127. Jandhyala Tilak, "Foreign Aid for Education," *International Review of Education*, 34, (1988): 318.
128. Robert Drysdale, "Education as a Cultural Imperialism: Book Review," *School of Review*, 84 (1975).
129. See Christopher Kilby, "Aid and Sovereignty," *Social Theory and Practice*, 25, (1999): 79–92.
130. Cited in Paul Morris, "Asia's Four Little Tigers: A Comparison of the Role of Education in their Development," *Comparative Education*, 32, (1996): 96.
131. Morris (1996): 95–110.
132. Huang (2007).
133. Burbules and Torres (2000). Also see Torres (2002).

134. Stephen Krasner, "Sovereignty," *Foreign Policy,* 122, (2001a): 20–28.
135. Ibid., 21.
136. This book uses the term LDS to distinguish states that have high rates of population growth and debt, high infant mortality, and low levels of literacy and per capita income, in comparison with those of advanced states. LDSs include mainly Africa, Asia, and Latin America. See Alfonso Gonzales and Jim Norwine (eds), *The New Third World* (Boulder, Colorado: West View Press, 1998); Less Developed Countries, "Dictionary of Finance and Investment Terms," http://www.credoreference.com.ezproxy.waikato.ac.nz; Philip's Encyclopaedia, "Less Developed Countries," http://www.credoreference.com.ezproxy.waikato.ac.nz
137. Martin Loughlin, "Ten Tenets of Sovereignty," in *Sovereignty in Transition,* ed. Neil Walker (Oregon: Hart Publishing, 2003).
138. Ibid., 183–205.
139. Louise Henkin, *How Nations Behave,* 2nd ed., New York: Columbia UP, 1979.
140. Anthony Verger and Xavier Bonal (2006); Angela de-Siquieira (2005).
141. Carnoy and Rhoten (2002). Also see Sini Sanou, "Critical Transnational Education," *Western Humanities Review,* 60, (2004). Hybridisation is defined by Rowe and Shelling as "the ways in which forms become separated from existing practices and recombine with new forms in new practice." W. Rowe and V. Shelling, *Memory and Modernity: Popular Culture in Latin America* (London: Verso, 1991).
142. See Lingard and Rizvi (2000); Christian Maroy, "Converges and Hybridization of Educational Policies around 'post-bureaucratic' models of regulation," *Compare: A Journal of Comparative and International Education,* 39, (2009): 71–84.
143. See Ballard, "Some Issues in Teaching International Students," in *Reaching More Students,* eds L. Conrad and L. Phillips (Queensland: Griffith Institute for Higher Education, 1995): 107–114; Sandra Egege and Salah Kutieleh, "Critical Thinking: Teaching Foreign Notions to Foreign Students," *International Education Journal,* 4, (2004): 75–85.
144. Burbules and Torres (2000); Torres (2002); Gu Jian Jing (2009); Huang (2007): 421–432; Gargano (2009); Phuong-Mai Nguyen, Julian Elliot, Cees Terlouw, and Albert Pilot, "Neo-colonialism in Education: Cooperative Learning in an Asian context," *Comparative Education,* 45, (2009): 857–875; Luis Moll and Elizabeth Arnot-Hopffer, "Socio-cultural Competence in Teacher Education," *Journal of Teacher Education,* 56, (2005): 242–247; Carnoy and Rhoten (2002).
145. Robertson et al. (2002).
146. Stephen Krasner, "Abiding Sovereignty," *International Political Science Review,* 22, (2001b): 229–251. Sauve (2002); Pereira (2005).

147. Dean DeRosa, "US Free Trade Agreements with ASEAN," in *Free Trade Agreements: US Strategies and Priorities,* ed. Jeffrey Schott (Washington, DC: Institute for International Economics, 2004). Also see Krasner (2001b).
148. Janice Thomson, "State Sovereignty in International Relations: Bridging the Gap between Theory and Empirical Research," *International Studies Quarterly,* 39, (1995): 213–33.
149. Arlene Tickner, "Seeing IR Differently: Notes from the Third World," *Millennium Journal of International Studies,* 32, (2003): 318.
150. Ibid.
151. Krasner (2001a).
152. It cannot be assured, however, that any new authority structures will be effective.
153. See Simon Marginson and Grant McBurnie, "Cross-border post-secondary education in the Asia-Pacific region," *Internationalisation and trade in higher education: Opportunities and Challenges,* OECD 2004. Also see OECD, "Internationalisation of higher education," *Observer,* 2004.
154. John Agnew, "Sovereign Regimes: Territoriality and State Authority in Contemporary Politics," *Annals of the Association of American Geographers,* 95, (2005): 437.
155. Anssi Paasi, "Boundaries as Social Processes: Territoriality in the World of Flow," *Geopolitics,* 3, (1998): 73.

CHAPTER 3

Indonesian Post-Secondary Education and the Presence of Foreign Education

INDONESIA'S POST-SECONDARY EDUCATION SYSTEM, ITS DEVELOPMENT, AND POLICIES FROM 1999 TO THE PRESENT

The Development of Indonesian Post-Secondary Education Institutions

Currently, Indonesia has more than 3449 post-secondary education institutions.[1] This represents an increase from 2316 in 2004, when there were 2235 private and 81 state post-secondary education institutions (academies, institutes, universities, polytechnics, and advanced schools). Because Education Law 30 of 1990 recognised private post-secondary education, private education institutions expanded in number. Around 3,400,000 students enrolled in higher education in 2001, of which 1,900,000 were enrolled at private institutions. By 2005, the enrolments had reached 3,500,000, and by 2010, there were 5 million students enrolled, and about 60% of all students were enrolled at private institutions.[2]

Of the 3449 post-secondary education institutions, only 49 are state universities, of which 7 are regarded as "elite." Access to these seven universities demands exceptional scholarly merits of the students, and these universities boast international rank. These seven elite state universities are located in Java Island, where 60% of Indonesia's population lives. They include the following: University of Gadjah Mada in Yogyakarta,

© The Author(s) 2017
A. Abbott, *Educational Sovereignty and Transnational Exchanges in Post-Secondary Indonesian Education*, DOI 10.1007/978-3-319-53985-0_3

University of Indonesia in Jakarta, University of Airlangga in Surabaya, University of Diponegoro in Semarang, Bandung Institute of Technology (ITB), Bogor Institute of Agriculture, and University of Padjajaran. According to the latest world ranking of universities, published by Quacquarelli Symonds (QS), the ITB is ranked 82nd in the world, and 13th in Asia.[3] By subject, ITB ranks 109th in engineering and technology in the world.[4] The University of Indonesia is ranked 273rd in the world, and 37th in Asia. By subject, the University of Indonesia is ranked number 122 in social sciences, 142 in arts and humanities, and 162 in medicine and life sciences. The University of Gadjah Mada is ranked 69th in Asia.

Unlike state post-secondary education institutions, which are highly esteemed, many Indonesians consider private post-secondary education to be academically weak, as many of those who fail to gain entry to state institutions subsequently enter private post-secondary education. Yet, private post-secondary education continues to dominate the post-secondary education market. Hardihardaja has stated that the government's reason for expanding private post-secondary education institutions was:

> the result of an overflow of high school graduates who could not be accommodated in the existing public higher educational institutes. ... [T]he government needs to boost the private sector's participation in the development of the country's education as part of an effort to cover the limited education funds.[5]

Unlike private education institutions, state post-secondary education institutions are funded for the most part by government subsidies. They are also financed from student fees, collaboration with the private sector, and support from donors and charities. Although private post-secondary education institutions also receive support from donors and charities, they are funded mainly through student tuition fees.[6]

The number of post-secondary education institutions has increased significantly from 1999 to the present, and private institutions have dominated the tertiary education sector. The growth in the private post-secondary education institutions, nonetheless, is due significantly to the government's recognition of them through education, law, and the need to accommodate an overflow of high school graduates.

The Provision of Education Legislation

Despite the growing number of post-secondary education institutions, particularly private institutions, in 2003, the government of Indonesia agreed to open Indonesia's post-secondary education market to foreign providers. The government accordingly enacted new legislation during the Hong Kong round of the WTO and agreed that Indonesia would offer access to its education market but would restrict the commercial presence of foreign providers.[7] Since the enactment of Law number 20 of 2003, regulating the National Education System, Indonesia has allowed foreign education providers to operate in Indonesia subject to several requirements. Not only must foreign providers partner with Indonesian education providers and Indonesian educators, they are also required to provide courses in religion and Indonesian citizenship responsibility presented by Indonesian educators. Education services are included in the GATS under the heading of public services, which means that governments are within their rights to regulate domestic policy and are bound only by specific commitments. Foreign education providers are obligated to seek prior permission from the Indonesian Ministry of Education and the Ministry of Manpower for the operation of their services. Foreign education providers are also required to apply for a licence from the Indonesian Directorate General of Higher Education within the Ministry of Education. According to Presidential Regulation Number 77 of 2007, not only must foreign education providers established in Indonesia work in conjunction with Indonesian education providers but both must also be approved by the Ministry of Education.[8]

Being accredited by the Ministry of Education requires that both Indonesian and foreign providers comply with Indonesian customary laws. Both Indonesian and foreign providers also need to frame and ratify an MoU. Indonesia's commitment to market access and to national treatment according to education modes is summarised in Table 3.1.

This schedule of Indonesia's commitments refers to Indonesia's specific commitment to provide market access (foreign access to Indonesia's market) and national treatment (treating foreign and local suppliers equally) for the services listed in the schedule. Table 3.1 shows that there is no limitation on market access and national treatment for cross-border supply (the movement of education materials) and consumption abroad (the movement of people/students) modes for courses and training in language, machinery and electrical, electronics and automotive, and football and chess. The

Table 3.1 Schedule of Indonesia's commitments to education services under the GATS

Sub-sector	Limitations on market access	Limitations on national treatment
A. Technical and vocational secondary education services (electronics, automotive)	1. None 2. None 3. As indicated in the horizontal section 4. Unbound except as indicated in the horizontal section	1. None 2. None 3. Unbound 4. As indicated in the horizontal section
B. Post-secondary technical and vocational education services (polytechnic machine and electrical)	1. None 2. None 3. As indicated in the horizontal section 4. Unbound except as indicated in the horizontal section	1. None 2. None 3. Unbound 4. Unbound
C. Adult education (language courses and training)	1. None 2. None 3. As indicated in the horizontal section 4. Unbound except as indicated in the horizontal section	1. None 2. None 3. Unbound 4. Unbound

Source: ASEAN Framework Agreement on Services (AFAS)
Note: 1. Cross-border supply (mode 1). 2. Consumption abroad (mode 2). 3. Commercial presence (mode 3). 4. Presence of natural persons (mode 4)

significance of this commitment is that Indonesia's service market is wide open to these courses. Table 3.1 also shows that Indonesia's commitment to national treatment for commercial presence mode (the presence of foreign education service providers in another state) and the presence of natural persons mode (the presence of foreign experts to provide education services) for the aforementioned courses is unbound, which means that Indonesia can impose limitations on foreign suppliers with respect to commercial presence (mode 3) and the presence of natural persons (mode 4). The significance of this commitment is that, while Indonesia can introduce or maintain commitments to national treatment for commercial presence and the presence of natural persons modes for the aforementioned courses, it is still able to declare an area exempt from some rules stipulated in the GATS. Such safeguards include barring the presence of foreign education institutions in Indonesia unless in cooperation with local institutions. The implication of this safeguard is that local education institutions are protected from competition with foreign education institutions.

Limitations on market access for commercial presence mode (mode 3) are emphasised in the schedule, as this mode has the potential to compete with local providers. The horizontal section, which establishes limitations on market access for commercial presence and the presence of natural persons modes, is shown in Table 3.2.

Table 3.2 shows that Indonesia's horizontal commitments are subject to several laws, like Indonesian labour law, investment law, immigration laws and regulations, land law, and income tax law, and are also subject to the authority of the Ministry of Manpower. Previously, Indonesian investment law had restricted the presence of foreign companies operating in Indonesia, that is, foreign companies that had the potential to support Indonesian education institutions financially had been discouraged. With the Presidential Regulation 111 of 2007, however, foreign companies are allowed, with a 49% equity limit. Under Presidential Regulation 36 of 2010, foreign investment in education is permissible, and foreign equity limits on investment in education were also removed, though foreign operators remain subject to Indonesia's education laws.[9] This means that although Indonesia's horizontal commitment prescribes that commercial presence is not allowed, foreign investment in education is permissible in other forms, subject to Indonesia's education laws. One implication of the restriction of the commercial presence mode in education is that Indonesia is still able to protect its local education institutions from competing foreign education institutions.

An important shift from the Suharto era (New Order Era) to the post-Suharto era (Reformation Era) has been the restructuring of Indonesia's legislative provision. In the New Order Era, education policies were controlled by the central government, whereas in the Reformation era, under the provision of Law 25 of 1999 on decentralisation, district governments and regional post-secondary education institutions have had the responsibility for financing education.[10]

Another important shift has been the change in the status of post-secondary education. The status in law of the university is now *Badan Hukum Milik Negara* (BHMN), or State Legal Entity, which has given post-secondary education institutions greater autonomy and public

Table 3.2 Schedules of Indonesia's horizontal commitments

Sub-sector	Limitations on market access	Limitations on national treatment
Horizontal commitments		
All sub-sectors in education included in this section	(3) Commercial presence of the foreign service providers may be in the form of joint venture and/or representative office, unless mentioned otherwise. Joint venture should meet the following requirements: (a) should be in the form of limited liability enterprise (Perseroan Terbatas/PT); (b) not more than 49 percent of the capital share of the limited liability enterprise (Perseroan Terbatas/PT) may be owned by foreign partner(s). (4) Subject to Indonesian Labour and Immigration Laws and Regulations, only directors, managers, and technical experts/advisors, unless mentioned otherwise, are allowed to stay for two years, which may be extended for a maximum two times subject to two years' extension each time. Manager and technical experts (intra corporate transfer) are allowed based on an economic needs test. The entry and temporary stay of business visitor(s) is (are) permitted for a period of 60 days and may be extended for a maximum of 120 days	(3) The Income Tax Law provides that non-resident taxpayers will be subject to withholding tax of 20 percent if they derive the following income from Indonesian sources: interest, royalties, dividends, and fees from services performed in Indonesia. Land Law number 5 of 1960 stipulates that no foreigners are allowed to own land. However, a joint venture enterprise may have the right to land use (Hak Guna Usaha) and building rights (Hak Guna Bangunan, and they may rent/lease land and property Any juridical and natural persons should meet professional qualification requirements (4) Any expatriates employed by a joint-venture enterprise, representative's office, and/or other types of juridical person and/or an individual service provider must hold a valid work permit issued by the Ministry of Manpower and Transmigration

Source: ASEAN, "Indonesia: Schedule of specific commitment," last modified 20 November 2012, http://www.aseansec.org
Note: (3) Commercial presence (mode 3). (4) Presence of natural persons (mode 4)

accountability than they had earlier when they were answerable to the government only. This is to say that universities are required to be more transparent to public enquiry. Universities with BHMN status are no longer responsible to the Ministry of National Education, but to a board of trustees. Unlike universities without BHMN status, rectors of universities with BHMN are no longer appointed by the president of the Republic of Indonesia, but by a board of trustees. Additionally, universities with BHMN status are more accountable for their own revenue-generating activities such as through commercialising courses.

Under the presidential decree on higher education, number 60 of 1999, the status of private post-secondary education institutions was regulated. Unlike state post-secondary education that is regulated under the jurisdiction of the state treasury law, private post-secondary education is regulated under the foundation law. The foundation law controls the commercial aspects of post-secondary education in Indonesia, and the commercialisation of post-secondary education occurs, for the most part, in the private sector.

With the expansion of post-secondary education institutions, *Badan Akreditasi Nasional Perguruan Tinggi* (BAN-PT), or the Accreditation Board of National Higher Education, was established in 1994.[11] A ministerial decree of 1998 and the National Education Act of 1989 are now the basis of BAN-PT. BAN-PT, however, took effect in 1999 when all post-secondary education programmes had to be accredited for the purpose of maintaining education standards. New autonomy for post-secondary education institutions, however, means that the institutions often have financial responsibilities, which restrict the ability of the institutions to maintain the quality of education. For instance, as reported in a study by Buchori and Malik, many post-secondary education institutions provide engineering courses without sufficient equipment. Thus, when BAN-PT conducted inspections, those institutions compromised their integrity by using the deceitful strategy of borrowing equipment from local companies and returning the equipment once the evaluation from BAN-PT was conducted.[12]

In 2009, *Badan Hukum Pendidikan* (BHP), or Education Legal Body legislation, established the independent legal status of all post-secondary education institutions, with the BHP board to oversee them.[13] BHP then was necessary as a form of legal entity in education and was the basis for commercialisation of education, and thus profit. Ministry of National Education (MONE) aimed to grant BHP status to at least 50% of state post-secondary education institutions and 40% of private institutions.[14] The World Bank supported the draft of BHP.[15] The draft of BHP, however, ignited controversies, as it was seen to violate the constitution, which stated that all citizens have the right to education, which is not for commercialisation and privatisation.[16] Consequently, on March 31, 2010, the Constitutional Court abolished BHP.

As already discussed, the expansion of private post-secondary education was stimulated by the government prioritising economic development and attempting to boost the role of the private education sector in that development. BHP, on the contrary, was introduced to promote the commercialisation of education, a move supported by the World Bank. It is not surprising then that the present phenomenon of commercialisation of education, which has resulted in the growing number of private education institutions, and legislation that enabled the expansion of private post-secondary education institutions such as the National Education Law of 1990 and BHMN status, did not spark controversies, whereas the drafting of BHP did.

Overall, there have been several changes in legal provisions. First, post-secondary education institutions have become more independent and autonomous in their academic and financial management. Second, the elite universities became state legal entities, which means they are more responsible to the public than to the government.

Third, all post-secondary education programmes have to be accredited to ensure education quality and standards are maintained. Fourth, Indonesia continues to allow foreign education providers to operate in Indonesia, subject to stipulations.

Curriculum Development of Indonesian Post-Secondary Education

The post-secondary education curriculum has been developed with the aim of preparing students to be competitive and to develop character with the aim of edifying the nation's life. With these purposes foremost, the curriculum is competition- and character-oriented. The national post-secondary education curriculum, known as *Kurikulum Tingkat Satuan Pendidikan* (KTSP) or Education Unit Level Curriculum, was established in 2006/2007. KTSP is based on the National Education Law of 2003 and Government Regulation 19 of 2005.[17] KTSP is competition-oriented and student-centred. Since the regulation of education was no longer centralised, educators could develop curriculum based on the needs of the students.

National education ministerial decree number 232 of 2000 and decree number 45 of 2002 have encouraged the development of a curriculum based on developing competitiveness for the purpose of creating people who achieve at the international level.[18]

Tri Dharma Perguruan Tinggi (the three pillars of service of higher education comprising education, research, and community service, established in 1961) is still the foundation of post-secondary education institutions promoting research and community service for Indonesia's development.

Pancasila is no longer emphasised to the extent it was when used as a political instrument under the Suharto regime, although it is still considered necessary, according to ministerial decree 45 of 2002, as the document for the inspiration of character-based curriculum. According to the National Education Law of 2003, Chap. 3, national education must function to develop intellectual ability and to form personal character. From the National Education Law of 2003, the term 'character' refers to human beings devoted to Almighty God and who are noble, knowledgeable, creative, independent, democratic, and responsible. This character-based curriculum has been regarded as essential for preserving the Indonesian national identity.[19]

It is apparent that competition and the development of character have been encouraged and emphasised in the curriculum, as both are regarded as necessary, and it is perceived that there would be dire consequences were they to be lost from the society.

Transnational Education in Indonesia

The US is one of the Indonesian students' preferred destinations for study. The intentions of Indonesia and the US are strongly connected to the significant role each state has in the other's best national interests. Indonesia, for instance, regards the US as making an important contribution to Indonesia's economic development through its contributing role in education. To generate knowledge, skills, and scientific progress for development, the Indonesian government has attempted to address the nation's education needs through education expenditure, transnational education, education legislation, and transforming the quality of education. Several Indonesian observers of transnational education argue that Indonesia does not have the capacity to fulfil the demand for quality higher education. Indonesia's Constitution outlines that at least 20% of the federal budget must be allocated to education services.[20] Nonetheless, as stated by Indonesia's Vice-President Boediono in 2010, Indonesia does not have the capacity to address its education needs,[21] thus necessitating opening up its market to transnational education.

According to Totok Suprayitno of the Indonesian embassy in Washington, D.C., government spending in education is a low priority.[22] To meet the community's demand for quality higher education, Indonesia has also taken the initiative of partnering with other states, including the US. It is important to note, however, that although Indonesia has a "free and active" foreign policy, which means Indonesia is active in international affairs and is free to choose any state as its partner, post-secondary education from the US is regarded as credible and highly desirable by Indonesians.[23] Bambang Sudibyo, the Indonesian education minister, argued that the education exchange was crucial for strengthening the Indonesia–US relationship.[24] Thus, the Indonesian government is enthusiastic about this relationship and is actively building relationships with top-ranked universities in America.

Education exchange with Indonesia is also considered by the US to be crucial for improving relationships between the two countries. Karl Stoltz, the director of Public Diplomacy for the US State Department's Bureau of East Asian and Pacific Affairs, stated in September 2009 that a close relationship in education is a priority for both governments.[25] Educational exchanges and more people-to-people connections, Stoltz added, "will help educate Americans about Indonesia and Indonesians about America ... we hope more Americans will come to know and appreciate the value of an enhanced relationship with the world's largest Muslim nation and third largest democracy." The US government hoped that the numbers of Indonesian students studying in the US would double in the year ahead.[26]

In the Indonesia–US bilateral relationship, the US has played a significant role in assisting Indonesia's development and education. Table 3.3 shows US assistance (in thousands of dollars) to Indonesia from year 2004 to 2007.

In the area of education, under President George Bush, the US launched a $157 million education grant initiative. Bush's unpopular foreign policy, nevertheless, had weakened the Indonesia–US relationship.[27] However, on November 10, 2010, both Presidents Obama and Yudhoyono officially launched the Indonesia–US Comprehensive Partnership.[28] The Comprehensive Partnership was built on "a long-term commitment to elevate bilateral relations by intensifying consultations and developing habits of

Table 3.3 US financial assistance to Indonesia in the period 2004–2007

Account	2004	2005	2006	2007
Child survival and health	33,000	37,100	28,017	27,507
Development assistance	33,291	27,848	33,212	26,724
Economic support	49,705	68,480	69,480	80,000
Foreign military financing	0	0	90	6500
International military education and training	599	728	792	1285
International narcotics control and law enforcement	0	0	4950	4700
Non-proliferation, anti-terrorism, demining, and related programmes	5998	6262	6092	7771
Food aid (USAID Food Grant)	4115	10,489		24,000
Tsunami relief	–	400,000		

Source: US Department of State; USAID; US Department of Agriculture in Thomas Lum, "US Foreign Aid to East and South Asia: Selected Recipients." CRS Report for Congress. Last modified October 5, 2013, http://www.fpc.state.gov/documents

cooperation on key bilateral, regional, and global issues."[29] Included in the partnership are cooperation commitments in politics and security, economics and development, public health, marine biodiversity, technology cooperation, socio-cultural fields, and education and science.[30] It signifies that both Indonesia and the US were seeking to improve and edify the relationship. On September 17, 2010, Indonesia and the US inaugurated the US-Indonesia Joint Commission Meeting in Washington, D.C. It was led by the foreign ministers of both states.[31]

Clearly, the objectives of both Indonesia and the US are strongly related to the substantial role each state has in the other's national interests. There are ample claims of support for the relationship. It is sufficient to say that the US has played a significant role in Indonesian education.

Indonesia has also maintained the relationship in education with New Zealand. The diplomatic relationship between New Zealand and Indonesia started in 1953 when New Zealand assisted Indonesia through the Colombo Plan. This included the establishment of a technical trade training institution, English language teaching, and short-term courses in dentistry. By 1960, 99 Indonesians had been given scholarships to study in New Zealand, and 29 New Zealander expatriates had been sent to Indonesia.[32] In 1961, a Colombo Plan office was established in Jakarta. As part of the Colombo Plan, approximately 3500 Indonesian students came to

New Zealand during the 1960s and 1970s.[33] New Zealand also opened its embassy in Indonesia in 1968.

There were three main forms of relationship in education between New Zealand and Indonesia from the 1950s to the 1970s. English language teaching projects were the main forms of technical assistance in Indonesia. Other forms of exchange included New Zealand experts working in Indonesia, and Indonesian students training in New Zealand. Such technical assistance brought almost 900 trainees to Indonesia, particularly in engineering, agriculture, health, general education, and technical fields.[34] Another form of educational relationship was offshore study. For instance, Soedjati Djiwandono, an Indonesian student, studied education, politics, and language at Otago University.[35]

During the Suharto New Order Era, policies on development and modernisation were formulated in the endeavour to modernise Indonesia. Thus, the involvement of Indonesia on the international stage was emphasised during this era. As with many other southeast Asian states, Suharto emphasised the importance of human resources as a key factor to improving Indonesia's economy. As such, the government actively sought international collaboration in the form of consultation and assistance, particularly in higher education, and sought such collaboration with New Zealand institutions.

The New Zealand government paid greater attention to Indonesia during the 1970s and 1980s, more than any other period during the Suharto era. Michael Green stated, "The potential of the relationship was more fully realized in the Suharto era. The two governments forged a rounded relationship comprising political links, development assistance, trade and economic ties, diplomatic coordination on regional problems, defence coordination and a range of people-to-people contacts."[36] In development assistance, New Zealand, like other donors, had laid emphasis on good governance for its assistance programmes to Indonesia.[37] During the New Order Era, under Suharto's leadership in the early 1990s, the National Commission on Human Rights was established. To improve the Commission's research capabilities, New Zealand funded two senior Commission staff to study in New Zealand and provided fellowships of two years each to seven Indonesians.[38]

Enthusiasm for Indonesia, however, waned in the New Zealand public mind following the Indonesian military's atrocities in East Timor. New Zealand had helped the Indonesian military with officer training from 1973. Leadbeater, in *New Zealand International Review*, who criticised New Zealand's approach to assisting the Indonesian military, stated: "Most of the time, New Zealand's relations with Indonesia do not get onto the public radar. But in the 1990s, as news began to spread about atrocities in East Timor, the Foreign Affairs Ministry had to perfect a public relations strategy to account for the pro-Indonesia policy position."[39] The relationship in education between New Zealand and Indonesia, however, has continued since 1999.

In 2002, Prime Minister Helen Clark of New Zealand showed support for the relationship in a remark she made at a state dinner for Wahid's successor, President Susilo Bambang Yudhoyono, when he visited New Zealand in 2005. Clark stated:

> New Zealand is part of the Asia-Pacific and our closest neighbour in Asia is Indonesia. The dramatic political evolution means that there is much that it is positive to build on for the future, and we look forward to working with you and your government to strengthen our ties.[40]

New Zealand then began to improve its education ties with Indonesia by expanding cooperation in education. David Taylor, New Zealand ambassador to Indonesia and ASEAN, states that education is an area where New Zealand and Indonesia can work together very effectively.[41] Taylor also states that increased cooperation is reflected in the establishment of the bilateral Education Joint Working Group where both governments exchange best practices on education policy. What is more, scholarships are offered for Indonesian students. In 2011, according to Taylor, 50 scholarships were offered to postgraduate studies, an increase from 15 in 2010. David Treacher, who was a political counsellor at the New Zealand Embassy, states that New Zealand has made a commitment to offer up to NZ$6 million per year for the scholarship programme, which has led to the increased numbers of Indonesian students in New Zealand.

The opportunities in education relations also include joint research programmes and institutional links, teacher development training programmes, train-the-trainer programmes, cultural exchanges, onshore and offshore programmes, and government training programmes. According to Education New Zealand, there is also potential for collaboration in the areas of agriculture and food science, disaster risk management and planning, and geothermal energy and earth science.[42] Small grants in the four main areas—sustainable economic development, renewable energy, disaster risk management, and conflict prevention—are also included in the relationship.[43] There were 740 Indonesian students studying in New Zealand, and the year following, in 2014, that number increased to 865. New Zealand's stated objective is to increase the numbers of Indonesian students by 4000 in 2017.[44] Indonesia now has collaboration agreements with eight New Zealand universities for joint research, joint degrees, and pathways for Indonesian students to study in New Zealand.[45]

Both New Zealand and Indonesia consider the benefits of the collaboration. David Taylor, New Zealand's ambassador to Indonesia, stated:

> The reasons for getting closer to Indonesia have never been more compelling. It's a trillion-dollar economy now, and it will be a US$9 trillion economy by 2030, according to most estimates, which puts it in the top six economies in the world.... It's a no-brainer. It's so close to us geographically. There will be massive opportunities, and we have to work to get those opportunities. We have to build relationships and tend them well.[46]

A 2011 World Bank report states that the number of Indonesians who spend between US$2 and US$20 a day had increased by 50 million in seven years.[47] Amris Hassan, chairman of Indonesia–New Zealand Friendship Council, states, "There are so many trade areas to be explored with the growing middle class. For New Zealand, it is a missed opportunity."[48] It is clear that, like the US, economic gain is one of the benefits of education collaboration for New Zealand.

Besides New Zealand and American education providers, profit-making universities such as Limkokwing University for Creative Technology (Chinese education provider) and Gandhi Institute of Business and Technology (Indian education provider) are already operating in Indonesia, and Indonesia will open its borders to foreign universities from across ASEAN in the next few years. Indonesia and the National University of Laos have signed an education agreement and organised various training collaborations, student exchanges, and scholarships. The Indonesian government has also signed an agreement in education with the government of Japan. Likewise, Indonesia and Thailand have collaborated in the education sector. The University of Slamet Riyadi in Indonesia and Khon Kaen University in Thailand, for instance, signed an agreement on transnational education exchanges in such fields as joint research, internship programme exchanges, cultural exchanges, and language teaching programmes. Other universities, colleges, and foreign training providers that are recognised under Indonesian education law include All Asia

Aviation Academy (AAA Academy), backed by the Japanese cooperation, Swiss German University, International University, and Liaison Indonesia.

Indonesia and the UK have also maintained their relationship in education. In 2016, there were five agreements in the relationship: sport, culture, fisheries, maritime, and education. The government of Indonesia supports the study of Indonesian students in the UK through several scholarships, such as the Indonesian Directorate General of Higher Education (DIKTI) scholarships, Ministry of Religious Affairs scholarships, and the Indonesian Endowment Fund for Education (LPDP) scholarships. Several universities in the UK have also worked together with Indonesian universities. The Open University and Indonesian Open University, for instance, collaborate in quality assurance and curriculum development. Cranfield University and Bandung Technology Institute also have worked together on double degree masters programmes in engineering and technology. The University of Newcastle and the University of Indonesia have collaborated on the Doctoral Training Centre. The University of Oxford, together with the Indonesian Ministry of Education and Culture, has encouraged Indonesian students to study at University of Oxford. The current president, Joko Widodo or Jokowi, signed MOU in April 2016 for the relationship, particularly the relationship in education, to grow.

Australia has also maintained a relationship in education with Indonesia. Australian education providers have addressed Indonesia's needs for educating corporates. University of New South Wales (UNSW) Business School has partnered with Indonesian university, BINUS International, an Indonesian education institution, and with UNSW for educational exchanges.

There are several modes of transnational education delivery (see Chap. 2). Cross-border supply (mode 1) is one mode of education delivery that does not require physical movement of students. The delivery of the programmes through the cross-border supply mode is often achieved through partnership arrangements. Foreign education providers that operate in Indonesia under this mode of delivery include the Photography Institute operated by New Zealand and Australia, and the Interior Design Institute backed by Australian and Canada. University of Melbourne and the University of Indonesia collaborate in conducting seminars in leaderships, with focus on corruption and governance as another example of cross-border supply mode.

The delivery of the programmes through consumption abroad (mode 2) occurs through both partnership arrangements, independent initiative of Indonesian students who go overseas for study by self-funding. Commercial presence is another mode of delivering tertiary education. Australian universities, such as Monash University, RMIT University, University of Queensland, University of Melbourne, and Australian National University (ANU), have operated in Indonesia. Their operations, however, are restricted to research collaboration.

Eugene Sebastian, the director of global engagement in the vice-chancellor's office at Monash University, states, "No physical presence is planned for Indonesia. ... In a restrictive regulatory environment, more fluid, innovative, and 'win-win' partnership models are required. These include research partnerships and higher-degree research training."[49]

The Netherlands has also maintained a relationship in education with Indonesia. Like Indonesia–US relations, the Netherlands also considers cultural research, science, and technology to be essential aspects in the relationship. Netherlands Education Support Office (NESO) has encouraged the cooperation in cultural and science aspects in the relationship.

Education has been prioritised in Indonesia's bilateral relationships with its developed-states counterparts. Business, science, technology, and cultural exchange have been the focus of the relationships. With the growing interest of foreign education institutions in maintaining education relationships with Indonesia, Indonesian education law will need to be applied and enforced.

Foreign Education and Indonesian Education Law

Indonesian higher education adopted the Dutch education system for its programme structure. After 1979, the American semester credit system was adopted. Rapid economic development in Indonesia has created skills shortages, and this has compelled the government of Indonesia to open the doors of opportunity and for private education institutions to flourish. According to Corrs Chamber Westgarth, by 2030, Indonesia is projected to spend $42 billion educating its eligible 135 million people.[50] The skills shortage and the lack of academic research have encouraged foreign education institutions.

There are regulations for foreign education institutions in Indonesia. Under the law, foreign education institutions must obtain a permit to collaborate with Indonesian education institutions.

Foreign education institutions must also be able to demonstrate that they are reputable in their country of origin and they must employ Indonesian educators. Education and Culture Ministerial Decree No. 31/2014 stipulates that educators at international schools must be registered with the Manpower and Transmigration Ministry and the Education and Culture Ministry.[51] Foreign educators must also be proficient in the Indonesian national language. Curriculum must also be adjusted to national standards, and foreign students must be taught cultural studies. Educational institutions operating in Indonesia cannot be fully owned by foreign stakeholders. The law stipulates that foreigners can own just 49% of a school. Chapter 18 of Law number 20/2003 states that foreign entities are allowed to invest in Indonesia, albeit in conjunction with local institutions. Under Law number 20 (2003), a maximum of ten years' imprisonment and a Rp1 billion (approximately US$ 86,000) fine is to be applied for not complying with the law.[52] Other regulations governing foreign education institutions are also outlined in chapter 6 article 90, which states:

1. Foreign tertiary education institutions may provide higher education in the unitary state of the Republic of Indonesia under the laws and regulations.
2. Such foreign tertiary education institutions, as referred to in paragraph 1, must have been accredited and/or recognised in their countries.
3. The government shall determine regions and types of study programmes to be provided by such foreign tertiary education institutions as referred to in paragraph 1.
4. Such foreign tertiary education institutions, as referred to in paragraph 1, must: (a) obtain a licence from the government, (b) be based on non-profit principle, (c) cooperate with Indonesian tertiary institutions with the approval of the government, and (d) give priority to engaging Indonesian lecturers and teaching personnel.
5. Such foreign tertiary education institutions, as referred to in paragraph 1, must support the national interest.
6. Further provisions on foreign tertiary education institutions, as referred to in paragraph 2 to paragraph 5, shall be set out in a ministerial regulation.

Commercial presence (mode 3) is highly regulated in Indonesia with the delivery of programmes through the presence of natural persons (mode 4), and is typically achieved through partnership arrangements with organisations and through academic and research collaboration conducted through partnership agreements.

Inconsistencies have arisen between the rules governing the operation of foreign education providers and its practice. For instance, profit-making universities, such as Limkokwing University for Creative Technology and Gandhi Institute of Business and Technology, operate in Indonesia even though the national education law declares that foreign education institutions in Indonesia must be non–profit-making institutions.

The inconsistency between statute law governing the operation of foreign education providers and its application has resulted in confusion. According to some educational practitioners, government's lack of a global vision for the country's education system is one of the factors the confusion over education law has occurred.[53] Ng Eng Chin, the executive principal of Tiara Bangsa Anglo-Chinese School, said that despite complying with regulations, confusion arises when it comes to interpreting and implementing the regulation. Aileen Riady, the associate head of Pelita Harapan Foundation, states that confusion was borne out of a lack of understanding of the nation's education goals.[54] Both Chin and Riady have proposed that there should be firm and clear goals on what the nation wants to achieve in its education, and that the government should set up a think tank specifically to work on a blueprint for Indonesia's national education system, which would include goals and ways to achieve them.

The government of Indonesia endeavours to protect the autonomy and cultural values (see Chap. 7) on one hand, and foreign education institutions are valued and are considered to be beneficial for Indonesia's education needs (see Chap. 5) on the other hand. This partly contributes to the inconsistencies in the education regulations.

Although the government of Indonesia has laid out regulations concerning foreign education institutions, the government still has a task of addressing inconsistencies between rules governing the operation of foreign education providers and what is practiced.

Foreign Education Presence and National Education Law: Future Hope

The Boston Consulting Group reported in May 2013 that Indonesian companies will struggle to find qualified personnel due to the low rate of enrolment in secondary and tertiary education.[55] The field of engineering, according to the report, is expected to experience the worst shortages. English language skill is also in high demand as Indonesia participates in international trade. To address this issue, the government is focusing on expanding vocational programmes rather than traditional academic training. This presents the opportunity for foreign education institutions to meet the needs of Indonesia's skills shortages.

In 2012, the British Council predicted that the number of Indonesians participating in higher education will grow by a total of 2.3–7.8 million students by 2020, which will make Indonesia the fifth largest education market in the world after China, India, US, and Brazil.[56] The inability of the government to address Indonesia's current need for skills training means it will certainly not be able to meet the demand of industry for qualified personnel in the coming years. Thus, increasingly the growing, wealthy Indonesian middle class will be forced to select international education qualifications.

Concluding Remarks

A significant implication for present-day post-secondary education is the endorsement of new legislation for opening access to Indonesia's education market for foreign providers. This endorsement was in response to the growing demand for transnational post-secondary education. Nonetheless, Indonesia has applied horizontal commitment in its schedule of commitment in education. An important ramification of this application is that Indonesia is still able to protect its local education institutions from competition with foreign education institutions. What Indonesia has achieved is the change in its post-secondary education system, from being under total government control to being relatively autonomous, through the implementation of BHMN or State Legal Entity. Nonetheless, what the government of Indonesia has failed to achieve is the permanent installation of law of BHP, or the Education Legal Body, as part of its attempt to commercialise education to encourage financial autonomy of post-secondary education institutions.

Foreign institutions deliver education in four modes: cross-border supply, consumption abroad, commercial presence, and the presence of natural persons. The Indonesian government has laid out regulations concerning foreign education institutions. Nevertheless, confusion over the interpretation of the national education laws governing foreign educations, and inconsistencies between the laws governing the operation of foreign education providers and the application of the law, coupled with lack of a clear national vision for education, means that the government still has an important task it needs to address. For foreign education providers, however, the increasingly wealthy Indonesian middle class will be forced to select international education qualifications from foreign providers. This means, for foreign education providers, the prospects are optimistic for attracting Indonesian students. This will be explained further in the next chapters.

NOTES

1. Purwadi (2001); Buchori and Malik (2004); Welch, A. R. "Blurred Vision: Public and Private Higher Education in Indonesia." *Higher Education*, 54, (2007): 665–687.
2. See http://edukasi.kompas.com/inilah.lima.waja.indonesia. Also see Wicaksono, Teguh, and Deni Friawan. "Recent Development in Higher Education in Indonesia: Issues and Challenges." *Financing Higher Education and Economic Development in East Asia*, eds. Shiro Armstrong and Bruce Chapman (Canberra: ANU Press, 2011).
3. http://www.4icu.org
4. See http://www.qs.com. Also see Erwida Maulia, "MIT Tops Rankings for the First Time, Indonesia Universities' Positions Drop," http://www.thejakartaglobe.com
5. J. Hardihardaja, "Private Higher Education in Indonesia: Current Developments and Existing Problems," in *Private Higher Education in Asia and the Pacific*, eds. Wongsothorn Tong-In and Yibling Wang (Bangkok: UNESCO, PROAP and SEAMO RIHED, 1996): 31.
6. Welch (2007). Also see Teguh Wicaksono and Deni Friawan, "Recent Development in Higher Education in Indonesia: Issues and Challenges," in *Financing Higher Education and Economic Development in East Asia*, eds. Shiro Armstrong and Bruce Chapman (Canberra: ANU E Press, 2011); Satryo Brodjonegoro (n.d.) "Higher Education in Indonesia," http://www.worldedreform.com
7. There were, of course, opponents to the government's policy of opening up Indonesia's education market to foreign providers. A common perspective in academic communities has been that although foreign providers have contributed much to improving the quality of post-secondary education, agreeing with the WTO's GATS to liberalise education would have dire consequences on Indonesia's education system if the government did not implement regulations that would protect curriculum.
8. See http://www.bkpm.go.id
9. See President Regulations, last modified January 20, 2013, http://www.presidenri.go.id/documentuu.php

10. See Department of Finance, Indonesia, last modified January 20, 2013, http://www.depkeu.go.id
11. Wicaksono and Friawan (2011); Brodjonegoro (n.d.).
12. Buchori and Malik (2004): 262.
13. World Bank, *Indonesia Managing Higher Education for Relevancy and Efficiency*, April 12, 2011.
14. Department of National Education, *Strategic Plan of the Department of National Education 2005–2009* (Jakarta: Department of National Education, 2005): 63.
15. World Bank, *Indonesia Managing Higher Education for Relevancy and Efficiency*, April 12, 2011.
16. All post-secondary education programmes have to be accredited to ensure education quality and standards are maintained. Indonesia continues to allow foreign education providers to operate in Indonesia, subject to stipulations.
17. Indonesian Ministry of National Education and Culture, last modified January 15, 2013, http://www.paudni.kemedikbud.go.id; Directorate General of Higher Education, last modified January 20, 2013, http://www.inherent-dikti.net
18. See Directorate General of Higher Education, "Competition based curriculum development," last modified June 38, 2013, http://www.akademik.dikti.go.id
19. Indonesian Ministry of Education and Culture, last modified January 15, 2013, http://www.paudni.kemedikbud.go.id; Indonesian Ministry of National Education, "Character based Education," last modified January 10, 2013, http://www.perpustakaan.kemendiknas.go.id
20. The House of Representatives, Indonesia, "UUD 1945," last modified January 18, 2013, http://www.dpr.go.id/id/uu-dan-ruu; Directorate General of Budgeting, "Budget for Education in APBN (State Revenue and Expenditure)," last modified January 10, 2013, http://www.anggaran.depkeu.go.id
21. Boediono in Karin Fischer, *A New Start for US and Indonesian Higher Education* (Washington, DC: The Chronicle of Higher Education Inc., 2010).
22. Suprayitno in Karin Fischer, "Obama Begins Rebuilding Academic Ties to Indonesia," *The Chronicle of Higher Education*, last modified May 2012, http://www.chronicle.com/article
23. *Mendayung diantara dua karang* (Jakarta: Ministry of Information, 1951); Michael Leifer, *Indonesia's Foreign Policy* (London: Allen and Unwin, 1983).
24. Bambang Sudibyo, in Gatra, "Numbers of Indonesian Students Drop," last modified July 17, 2012, http://www.gatra.com/article.php/id

25. Karl Stoltz, in May Baptista, "Students Conduct Research and Study at the US Embassy's Information Resource Center in Jakarta, Indonesia," last modified January 20, 2013, http://www.america.govt
26. Charles Silver, in *Kompas*, "Let's Study in the US," last modified July 18, 2012, http://www.kompas.com
27. President Bush's foreign policies on war on terrorism and the war in Iraq were regarded as an attack on the Muslim world.
28. Ibid.
29. US Embassy, "White House Fact Sheet: US-Indonesia Comprehensive Partnership," last modified January 20, 2017, http://iipdigital.usembassy.gov/st/english/texttrans/2011
30. Ibid.
31. US Department of State, "US-Indonesian Joint Commission Meeting with Indonesian Foreign Minister," last modified December 16, 2016, http://www.state.gov/secretary/travel/rm
32. Mike Green, "Governance Issues in Post-Suharto Indonesia," last modified January 20, 2017, http://www.asiaforum.org/nz/wpcontent/uploads/governance-issues-in-postsoeharto. Paper was presented at Asia Forum, 12/02/2002.
33. Ibid.
34. Ibid.
35. Ibid.
36. Ibid. Also see Adam Schwarz, *A nation in waiting. Indonesia in the 1990s* (Sydney: Allen & Unwin, 1994). A detailed review of the New Zealand–Indonesia relationship in political links, and security and defence is largely beyond the scope of this book.
37. The Advisory Committee on External Aid and Development defined good governance as "the effective management of a country's resources in a manner that is participatory, transparent, and accountable." See Green (2002).
38. Ibid.
39. Maire Leadbeater, "New Zealand Aid Foster Impunity, Status Quo by Indonesian Security Forces," *New Zealand International Review*, 5, (35) September/October 2010.
40. Scoop, "PM Speech: State Dinner for Indonesian President," last modified August 30, 2016, http://www.schoop.co.nz/ stories/PA0504/S00128.htm
41. In Jakarta Post, "New Zealand Highlights Education Relations with RI," last modified July 26, 2016, http://www.thejakartapost.com/news/2013/03/16/new-zealand-highlights-education-relations-with-ri.html
42. ENZ, "Market Opportunities," last modified September 5, 2016, http://www.enz.govt.nz/markets/indonesia/opportunities

43. The grants are administered through the $3 million Community Resilience and Economic Development Partnership with the University of Gadjah Mada.
44. ENZ, "Market Opportunities," last modified September 5, 2016, http://www.enz.govt.nz/ markets/indonesia/opportunities
45. Ibid.
46. In The Listener, "Another Giant Awakes," last modified November 15, 2016, http://www.noted.co.nz/archive/listener-nz-2012/indonesia-another-giant-awakes
47. Ibid.
48. Ibid.
49. According to the Indonesian National Education Law, education institutions operating in Indonesia cannot be fully owned by foreign stakeholders. In addition, foreign education institutions in Indonesia must be non–profit-making institutions.
50. Corrs Chamber Westgarth, "Education in Indonesia: Opportunities Open for Australia," last modified October 5, 2016, http://www.corrs.com.au/thinking/insights/education-in-indonesia-opportunities-open-for-australia
51. See http://dikdas.kemdikbud.go.id/wp-content/uploads/2014/06/Permendikbud-No-31-Tahun- 2014.pdf
52. See Jakarta Post, "International School must comply with new ministerial decree," last modified August 20, 2016, http://www.thejakartapost.com/news/2014/05/23
53. Jakarta Globe, "With rules hazy, international school in Indonesia are left in confusion," last modified October 5, 2016, http://jakartaglobe.beritasatu.com/news/rules-hazy-international-schools-indonesia-left-confusion
54. Ibid.
55. In AE Kubo, 2013, "Indonesian education falls behind its economic growth," last modified September 20, 2016, http://thediplomat.com/2013/12/indonesian-education-falls-behind-its-economic-growth
56. British Council, "The shape of things to come: Higher Education Global Trends and Emerging Opportunities to 2020," http://ei.britishcouncil.org/sites/default/files/going_global

CHAPTER 4

Nature of Indonesian Transnational Education

What is the nature of the educational relationships between Indonesia and its developed state counterparts? Is transnational education about the development of a new imperialism by perpetuating knowledge and financial dependency through the transfer of knowledge and aid in education? Or does it advance learning about other states and has the potential to improve relationships and promote international understanding?

This chapter addresses these questions by analysing to what extent transnational education leads to one-way transfer of knowledge, technology, and research projects. This chapter also identifies whether expatriates are prominent among academic staff in Indonesia and analyses the extent to which transnational education leads to dependency on foreign assistance in education.

KNOWLEDGE DEPENDENCY: ONE-WAY TRANSFER OF KNOWLEDGE, TECHNOLOGY, AND RESEARCH PROJECTS

Indonesia–US Education Relations

In the Indonesia–US education relationship, the first apparent indicator of Indonesian knowledge dependency on the US is the one-way transfer of knowledge. Most Indonesian respondents regarded the US as important in terms of its knowledge. The following comment captures this:

© The Author(s) 2017
A. Abbott, *Educational Sovereignty and Transnational Exchanges in Post-Secondary Indonesian Education*, DOI 10.1007/978-3-319-53985-0_4

> In terms of knowledge, American education is superior. But we are rich in languages, cultures, tropical environment and natural resources. We are richer in these areas than America. (*Indonesian vice-rector negotiating and administering MoUs* (*Respondent 2*))

This respondent identified areas unique to Indonesia, which represent an advantage for leveraging beneficial exchanges. The comment also indicates that the education relationship is beneficial for Indonesia because of American superiority in education. Respondent 2 also commented that the US benefitted from the research collaboration with Indonesia because Indonesia provided access for American institutions to the vast, but under-researched, natural environment. The perceptions of Indonesian respondents on American education superiority and on Indonesia's lack of experts in conducting research and cultivating its rich natural environment show Indonesia's dependence on foreign experts and their knowledge.

In the US–Indonesia Comprehensive Partnership, science can be combined with education through research collaboration between Indonesian universities and American universities. The following respondent's comments point to the importance of the research component in the education relationship:

> We have participated and we have gained the benefits of international cooperation. The most beneficial cooperation is in research. (*Indonesian chair of international cooperation of a university in Indonesia* (*Respondent 18*))

This comment suggests, therefore, that collaboration is valued, which is evident in the joint research and combined student and researcher exchange arrangements. For this respondent, there were many benefits to be gained from including research in Indonesian higher education aspirations. This view was echoed by the following respondent:

> Universities, therefore, need to cooperate with foreign education institutions mainly in research. They [Americans] have accurate organisation and good management. (*Indonesian vice-rector negotiating and administering MoUs* (*Respondent 2*))

It was apparent, therefore, that these respondents saw the relationship, particularly in research collaboration, as advantageous for Indonesia.

The comments of most Indonesian respondents indicated that they are not coerced, as mentioned earlier, but rather are willing to learn and adopt new skills and knowledge in order to improve the quality of Indonesian education, graduates, educators, and researchers. Indonesians who studied at the University of California, Berkeley, and who applied their knowledge to bring Indonesia back from the brink of perilous economic circumstances, show that Indonesians have been willing to embrace knowledge.

Although transfer of knowledge is evident, it is an initial process used to strengthen Indonesian education and to reduce reliance on knowledge from developed states. The role of USAID in achieving Indonesia's Millennium Development Goals also provides a good example to illustrate that transfer of knowledge is an initial process to strengthen Indonesian education. According to USAID, Indonesia was at risk of not achieving its goal of EFA by 2015.[1] USAID has played a significant role in Indonesian education by encouraging changes in the way teachers communicate and students learn. Students were encouraged to change from being passive to active learners, and classrooms to transition from teacher-centred to student-centred. In this context, with critical thinking skills, there is potential to reduce reliance on knowledge from the US and other developed states. It is appropriate that Indonesian education institutions first seek to partner with American research initiatives in order to acquire research skills and enhance critical thinking. USAID has also played a significant role in Indonesian education by developing education programmes for Indonesia, encouraging public–private partnerships, and encouraging university-to-university (U-to-U) relations between Indonesia and the US.

Although one-way transfer of technology was evident, the comments from respondents suggested Indonesian institutions approached this transfer with a willingness to learn and adopt new skills and knowledge. One respondent commented:

> we need America because America is a developed country with high technology. Developed countries have higher technology and quality research development. I must admit that American books here are popular. (*Indonesian vice-rector negotiating and administering MoUs (Respondent 2)*)

This respondent clearly valued the advantages provided by the quality of research and technology of developed states. The comment illustrates that the respondent is not being coerced but rather is embracing the opportunities for learning and accepting technology from the US. This observation, however, does not particularly answer the question of why choose America. After all, Japan and several European countries also have education institutions to be envied. American education institutions clearly have a long relationship with Indonesia, which creates an advantage over other providers, an advantage from which Indonesians see themselves as benefitting.[2]

Although one-way transfer of technology was evident, Indonesia has endeavoured to be independent in conducting its research. Although the US grants $15 million through Fulbright Indonesia Research, Science, and Technology Programme (FIRST), Indonesia has made efforts to be less dependent on foreign researchers, as is evident in the strengthening of the role of the *Lembaga Ilmu Pengetahuan Indonesia* (LIPI), or Indonesian Institute of Sciences, which encourages Indonesian researchers to develop high-quality research through the Research Incentive Programme.[3]

This respondent identified areas unique to Indonesia, which represent an advantage for leveraging beneficial exchanges. The comment also indicates that the education relationship is beneficial for Indonesia because of American superiority in education. The respondent also commented that the US benefitted from the research collaboration with Indonesia because Indonesia provided access for American institutions to the vast, but under-researched, natural environment. The perceptions of Indonesian respondents on American education superiority, and on Indonesia's lack of experts in conducting research and cultivating its rich natural environment, show Indonesia's dependence on foreign experts and their knowledge.

The relationships with American education institutions are considered beneficial not only for enhancing Indonesian education quality and establishing credibility of Indonesian education institutions through double degrees but also in research. The following respondent commented:

> I can see, now the partnerships can be developed; from environment to bio-engineering to child protection, nanotechnology, etc. We have rich programmes that we can offer. I hope in the future, we can develop stronger relationships. Joint research, one semester in America and the rest in Indonesia, is a good start. (*Indonesian government official*)

In summary, academic and research collaboration was valued by the Indonesian respondents as there were many benefits to be gained from including research in Indonesian higher education aspirations. Although knowledge dependency is evident in the Indonesia–US education relationship, Indonesian respondents are willing to learn and adopt new skills and knowledge in order to improve the quality of Indonesian education, its graduates, educators, and researchers. Although transfer of knowledge is evident, it is an initial step to strengthen Indonesian education and to reduce reliance on knowledge from developed states. The one-way transfer of technology is also evident, but the comments from respondents suggested Indonesian institutions approached this transfer with a willingness to learn and adopt new skills and knowledge. What is more, to most respondents, the Indonesia–US relationship is based on recognition of the strengths and interests of both sides. For these reasons, although one-way transfer of knowledge and technology is evident, the Indonesia–US education relationship does not necessarily exist for maintaining knowledge dependency, but rather for strengthening Indonesian education quality and reducing reliance on knowledge from the US developed states. That is to say that the Indonesia–US education relationship does not necessarily perpetuate a new type of imperialism.

Indonesia–New Zealand Education Relations

As a neighbouring state, New Zealand is one of Indonesians' study destinations. At an early stage of the collaboration, most Indonesian respondents indicated that they do not see the reciprocal benefits and shared interests in the relationship. The reason for the absence of reciprocal benefits, pressing needs, and shared objectives is indicated by the following respondent:

> New Zealand doesn't seem to be very aggressive looking for opportunities to co-operate. Unfortunately, with the global image, Indonesians want to go to places like America, Australia, and in some cases Korea and Japan. ... With New Zealand, we just talked about our plan and the possibility of student exchanges or scholarship programmes. But we [both Indonesian and New Zealand parties] did not do anything. For us somehow there was no pressing need for it to happen. (*Head of International Relations and a negotiator at an Indonesian university* (*Respondent 22*))

> We have no relationship. We have had talks with Victoria University in Wellington but we don't have formal co-operation. They are not active but we also think that there are no pressing needs to connect with them! We

mainly have co-operation with American universities and Australian universities. (*Head of International Relations and negotiator at an Indonesian university* (*Respondent 29*))

The principle for the relationship should be based on mutual benefits but we do not see that. The relationship is not as strong as with other governments such as the US. New Zealand does not seem to be active. New Zealand does not have education fairs like those of Europe, Thailand, the US, India, and many other countries. New Zealand pays less attention and effort. Grants from the government of New Zealand are not as much as grants of other countries. New Zealand is also not a popular country like other countries. (*Head of International Relations and negotiator at an Indonesian university* (*Respondent 21*))

Unlike other countries such as Singapore, Thailand, and the US, according to Respondents 21, 22, and 29, New Zealand parties are not active in following up early discussions on the possibility to collaborate, or conducting education fairs. For these respondents, the failure to actively follow up earlier discussions or conduct education fairs, the fact that grants from the New Zealand government are less than grants of other countries, and the possibility of collaboration with credible world universities mean that many Indonesian students go to countries other than New Zealand.

Victoria University in Wellington has good programmes in business. Business papers are certainly attractive but New Zealand is a small country. New Zealand should be active and aggressive in maintaining a relationship with Indonesia. Many Indonesian students prefer to go to the US, the UK, Singapore, Japan, South Korea, and many other countries. (*Head of International Relations and negotiator at an Indonesian university* (*Respondent 21*))

The respondent does not explain what "good" programmes mean. Nonetheless, it is widely acknowledged that the Indonesian labour market requires more graduates with business qualifications and skills.[4]

The forms of delivery in the relationship vary. Consumption abroad (mode 2) is certainly the obvious delivery form, by which Indonesian students go to New Zealand to study. The presence of New Zealand experts in Indonesia (mode 4) is also another delivery form in the relationship. As in Indonesia–US education relations, one-way transfer of knowledge is evident in the Indonesia–New Zealand education relationship. The difference is many Indonesians prefer to go to the US to study. The credibility of US universities is one of the reasons Indonesians choose to study there. It is necessary to note that the proximity and cheaper tuition fees New Zealand institutions offer mean that New Zealand remains one of Indonesians' preferred study destinations.

INDONESIAN EDUCATION RELATIONS WITH OTHER DEVELOPED STATES

The UK and Indonesia have also developed a relationship in education. In 2016, President Joko Widodo signed a MoU in education.[5] Northumbria University and Bina Nusantara University have set up four new undergraduate and postgraduate programmes in media and interior design. The Department of Medicine at University of Oxford, in cooperation with the University of Indonesia, has established the Clinical Research Centre for health research at the University of Indonesia. Integrated Masters and PhD programmes in material design, in which Indonesian students study in Nottingham and students from Nottingham study in Indonesia, were initiated and developed by the University of Nottingham and the University of Muhammadiyah Surakarta. Further evidence of the relationship is the cooperation in teaching, research, and academic exchanges between the University of Southampton, England, and Sepuluh Nopember Institute of Technology.

The forms of delivery include not only consumption abroad (mode 2) and presence of natural persons (mode 4) but also cross-border supply (mode 1) such as online MBA degree programme offered by Edinburgh Business School. A branch campus of Edinburgh Business School is also located in Indonesia, so its form of delivery includes commercial presence (mode 3). It is important to note that although there are limitations on market access for commercial presence mode, business is one of the necessary areas for addressing the needs of Indonesia's markets and Indonesia's demands for experts in business. Therefore, commercial presence mode of delivery for business courses is approved.

Like New Zealand and the UK that offer courses in business programmes, Australia and Indonesia have cooperated in business studies. University of Bina Nusantara and University of New South Wales have cooperated in offering double-degree programmes in International Business. Several Australian universities have cooperated with Bina Nusantara University in business studies. Queensland University of Technology and Bina Nusantara University have developed double-degree programmes in

International Business. A further example is the developing of double programmes in business studies between Macquarie University and Bina Nusantara University.[6]

The Netherlands has also maintained a relationship in education with Indonesia. The historical ties between these two nations have seen them maintain close relations through cultural and education exchanges. In April 2016, President Joko Widodo showed the willingness and commitment of Indonesia to develop bilateral ties and signed a MoU on higher education and science.[7] Every year, approximately 1500 Indonesians study in the Netherlands.

From these examples and discussion, it is clear that types of education delivery vary. It is necessary to note, however, that the variety of education mode of delivery does not guarantee that one-way transfer of knowledge does not occur. Indonesian education is still left behind. According to Times Higher Education survey, University of Gadjah Mada, one of the best universities in Indonesia, is ranked 360 of 400.[8] Bandung Institute of Technology is ranked 369, and University of Indonesia is ranked 395. Yet there are demands for education as Indonesia's middle class is growing.[9] Thus, many Indonesians have sought opportunities to study overseas, gaining high-quality education.

Next, another apparent indicator of Indonesian knowledge dependency—the prominence of expatriates among academic staff—is examined.

PROMINENCE OF EXPATRIATES AMONG ACADEMIC STAFF

Indonesia–US Education Relations

The second apparent indicator of Indonesian knowledge dependency on the US is the prominence of expatriates among academic staff. The following respondent shared the experience:

> The US truly helps us by sending experts here. Without their [Americans] cooperation, there would not be MoUs and without MoUs we would not have the benefits that we do. (*Indonesian international office staff administering MoUs (Respondent 13)*)

This respondent clearly claimed the benefits of the relationship. The existence of MoU in the Indonesia–US education relationship is an outcome of the bilateral agreement between the Indonesian and American parties. Through MoUs, the terms that the parties have negotiated are implemented.[10] Thus, as the respondent indicated, the relationship benefits Indonesian parties.

The following comment from a respondent partly explains why Indonesia needs foreign experts:

> We need more people in vocational not academic areas because we are rich in natural resources. [Currently] we have more graduates in academic [areas]. As a result, their rate of unemployment is increasing. We still need experts from other countries in natural resources management because we simply do not have enough people [ourselves]. (*Indonesian government official dealing with standardisation of national education* (Respondent 4))

It is important to note that although experts are needed for the management of Indonesia's natural resources, the government of Indonesia has endeavoured to reduce its dependence on foreign experts. The ability to make independent decisions is one of the reasons why the government of Indonesia has endeavoured to reduce its dependence on foreign experts. One strategy has included an emphasis on vocational training in order to create the necessary human capital for natural resource management. It is also important to note that, although expatriates are able to work with Indonesian academic staff, the Indonesian government is determined that academic directors and executives must be Indonesian citizens unless the education providers are wholly owned by foreigners, in order to protect local institutions and to guard against any domination of expatriates among local academic staff.[11]

Although most Indonesian respondents claimed that the Indonesian government had regulated to minimise dependency on foreign experts and institutions, it is necessary to note that one of Indonesia's development goals has been to enhance international competitiveness by 2025, and the education relationship with the US is viewed by the authorities to be important in achieving this goal. As is indicated in Indonesia's development goal to become fully independent and develop, foreign involvement in education is necessary. Such involvement, in turn, gives rise to the question of whether being independent means not only being free from colonial rule and being able to preserve sovereignty, but also, as Weinstein argues, being able to reduce dependence on foreign states.[12]

To minimise the influence of foreign experts among local academic staff, Indonesian parties would require leverage in their relations with their American counterparts. Weinstein argues:

> The less developed countries are not wholly without leverage in their relations with more powerful nations. Under certain circumstances, underdevelopment can be advantageous. Could a modern state like Belgium have defied American military might as Vietnam did? North Vietnam's lack of a highly specialised economy undoubtedly helped to minimise the disruptive effects of American bombardments ... the Vietnamese tail wagged the American dog, the tail at least displayed a capacity to cause the dog to stumble when it ran in a displeasing direction.[13]

Similarly, being a weaker party in the relationship does not mean that Indonesia is in a disadvantaged position. Indonesia requires leverage in its relations with developed states like the US. In the past, Indonesia had successfully challenged foreign power in the form of the Dutch and the Americans.[14] Currently, foreign influence in policy making is a major concern for Indonesian foreign policymaking. The *Jakarta Post* reported that 63 Indonesian laws had been drafted by foreign consultants.[15] To gain leverage in its relations with the US, it is expected then that the Indonesian respondents would carefully assert that the relationship with the US is mutually beneficial, through research collaboration. It is necessary to note, however, the term "leverage" was not mentioned in the interviews. It was, however, implied throughout the interviews, in ways such as:

> We are rich in languages, culture, and natural resources. They often are interested in these areas. We also need the partnership for technology. They are also good in management. (*Indonesian vice-rector negotiating and administering MoUs (Respondent 2)*)

Respondent 2 saw the relationship as having the potential to benefit Indonesia, technologically. As a negotiator, he was also conscious of the richness of what the Indonesian parties could offer as a response in the bargaining. Bargains and agreements are different for Indonesians. It is considered indiscreet to enquire about what the other party might have to offer in the trade.[16] Here, even though neither the term "leverage" nor "bargaining power" is mentioned, bargaining is indicated through the offering of the richness in natural resources environment, languages, and cultures to the American parties. Leveraging is also indicated in the assertion of the Indonesian negotiators that the relationship is mutually beneficial and equal. In an extreme case, one Indonesian respondent, who dealt with Indonesian curriculum and international research collaboration, stated: "If we cannot agree with America and other Western countries, we can partner with Asian countries" (*Indonesian research manager* (*Respondent 3*)).

In summary, there is no evidence that transnational education constitutes a new type of imperialism by perpetuating knowledge dependency through foreign experts, as Indonesia has endeavoured to be less dependent on foreign experts. The government of Indonesia has endeavoured to reduce its dependence on foreign experts including American experts. The attempts of the government to reduce Indonesia's dependence on foreign experts include emphasising vocational training in order to create the necessary human capital for natural resources management, and regulating that academic directors and executives must be Indonesian citizens unless the education providers are wholly owned by foreigners, in order to protect local institutions and fend off domination of expatriates among local academic staff.

Dependency on Foreign Financial Assistance

In addition to the one-way transfer of technology and science, and the domination of expatriates among academic staff, theorists such as Carnoy, Tikly, and Crawford have argued that relying on financial assistance is one form of dependency.[17]

Foreign financial assistance is beneficial for Indonesia, and it is difficult to conceive of development without foreign assistance.[18] The financial aspects of education are a significant challenge for Indonesia. Indonesia has increased its budget for national education. President Yudhoyono initiated the plan to increase expenditure to Rp 331.8 trillion (US$34.9 billion) in 2013, up from Rp 310.8 trillion in 2012.[19] The Indonesian government scholarships include Ministry of Religious Affairs scholarship, and the Indonesian Directorate General of Higher Education and the Indonesian Endowment Fund for Education which has offered 6400 recipients going overseas. Weinstein argues that the dilemma is not one of aid or independence, but of how much dependence on foreign financial assistance should be accepted, and thus how much foreign control can be tolerated.[20] Although foreign assistance in education is welcomed, an increased budget for national education is necessary for reducing dependence on foreign financial assistance. Reducing this dependence, however, does not mean that Indonesia would refuse foreign financial assistance.

American Financial Assistance
Whether financial dependency is the consequence of American financial assistance, thus, requires further assessment. The following respondent commented:

> We learnt from a big mistake by having loans from the World Bank. Now we are gradually able to educate our students but we still need grants. Only grants. Not loans. Not even a soft loan. We do not want any kind of loan. That is why a grant from America is useful. (*Indonesian research manager (Respondent 3)*)

Indonesia has been on the top ten list of the World Bank's borrowers. In 2011, Indonesia's debt reached US$ 215.5 billion.[21] It is expected then that grants, not loans, were welcomed by the Indonesian respondents. Significant amounts of financial assistance from the US in particular are welcome. The following respondent stated:

> We mainly partner with ASEAN countries but America also has partnered with us. USAID is going to support us financially for our research project 900 million rupiah. (*Indonesian research manager (Respondent 3)*)

One might ask that if Indonesia only wants grants, not loans, does that stance mean that Indonesia is dependent financially on the US. USAID has played a significant role in Indonesia's education through its financial assistance since Indonesia gained independence. USAID also initiated an investment of US$19.7 million to support the Higher Education Leadership and Management (HELM) programme.[22]

At the post-secondary education level, Indonesia's attempt to be less dependent on foreign education aid is shown in the budget allocated to partnerships with foreign education providers. For instance, through the Directorate General of Higher Education, Indonesia allocated a budget for joint funding with its partner, the US. The following respondents also commented:

> In 2007/2008, we provided scholarships for faculty members to study abroad. For the first time in our history, we are able to send our faculty

members abroad fully funded by the government. (*Indonesian government official* (*Respondent 11*))

We have $195 million from the US. In addition to our own funding, we support Indonesians going to America and Americans coming here. (*Indonesian government official dealing with MoUs* (*Respondent 8*))

Both comments indicate the attempt of the government of Indonesia to contribute to the education relationship. This contribution, as illustrated by Respondent 8, is done through the financing of Indonesians going to the US and Americans coming to Indonesia. For Respondent 11, milestones have been reached as the Indonesian government has been able to fund university faculty with overseas travel grants.

New Zealand and Australia Financial Assistance

Developed states such as the US, Australia, and New Zealand have profited from the economic opportunities presented by Indonesia's growing middle class. New Zealand, for instance, despite a multi-million dollar export dispute with Indonesia, signed agreements on tourism, e-commerce, and renewable energy as part of the plan to double trade to $4 billion by 2025.[23] New Zealand gives Indonesia financial assistance of approximately $90 million a year, making Indonesia the biggest recipient of any country outside the Pacific. At least $7.1 million is allocated for education, of which $2.3 million goes towards short-term training scholarships, postgraduate scholarships, and English language training.

Like New Zealand, Australia has also given Indonesia financial assistance. Australia's official development assistance to Indonesia during 2015–2016 was $379.1 million. In that year, Australia awarded 866 scholarships to Indonesians.[24] Nonetheless, the government of Australia has announced it will cut its aid to Indonesia by 40%.[25] Like previous presidents, the cuts did not intimidate president Joko Widodo. Widodo stated, "Aid is in their interest, not ours."[26] Indonesia is careful not to enter agreements that lead to aid dependency. To avoid aid dependency, Indonesia not only has allocated finance for development projects, but also has improved cooperation with other states such as Korea, Japan, and China. For Indonesia, foreign financial assistance complements the national budget. It means, without foreign financial assistance, Indonesia's development projects will still continue within its national budget. Since 2003, the government of Indonesia had also passed a number of regulations that are aimed to prevent dependency on foreign states. These regulations include Law of Finance number 17/2003, Law of National Treasury number 1/2004, and the National Development Plan number 25/2004. These regulations limit the quota of foreign financial assistance to Indonesia and prevent foreign states dictating with regard to Indonesia's development policies.

The US, Australia, and New Zealand have taken advantage of the economic opportunities of Indonesia's growing middle class; thus, any disputes arising will not necessarily weaken the relationships. Indonesia has taken a clear stance that it does not depend on foreign financial assistance.

From these examples and discussion, it is safe to argue that transnational education does not necessarily constitute a new type of imperialism, perpetuating financial dependency through foreign aid in education, as Indonesia has endeavoured to be less dependent on foreign financial assistance. Although foreign assistance in education is welcomed, an increased budget for national education is necessary for reducing dependence on foreign financial assistance.

THE EDUCATION EXCHANGE AND LEARNING ABOUT EACH OTHER

Indonesia–US Education Relations

One study conducted by Novotny presents Indonesia's relationships with the US and with China as the major concerns of the Indonesian elite.[27] Both countries are perceived by the Indonesian elite to have the potential to jeopardise Indonesia's national security and interests, as they are major powers and both have political interests in Indonesia.[28] Nonetheless, in several MoUs and the interviews, it is often stated that the education relationship is for learning about each other and for improving understanding in the relationship. Typical comments from the respondents included:

> It [the political relationship with the US] is indeed emotional. Our sympathy is for Palestine and our standpoint is clear; we expect their freedom and we facilitate it. Americans and Israelis lobbies know about it. . . . I think we need to have this partnership in spite of political tension. A political relationship is up and down and sometimes emotional. But I am sure through this education partnership, people can build relationships people to people and be tolerant, accept other differences, and facilitate official diplomatic conflicts. (*Indonesian government official (Respondent 8)*)

This is [political relationship with the US] the political dynamic and it could change through time. Different political parties have different approaches and also political sensitivities can change in time. My kind of thinking is that we must overcome misunderstandings. (*Indonesian vice-president of an American company* (*Respondent 9*))

Both respondents, like other Indonesian respondents, were aware of the political tensions and dynamics with the US. These respondents, nevertheless, did not explain what they meant by political tensions and dynamics.[29] The American war with Iraq had an impact on Indonesia's relationship with the US. According to Budianta, the war showed the failure of US foreign policy to distinguish clearly, fundamentalism from terrorism, and this is an essential reason, "a great majority of Indonesians view the US government as an aggressive, militaristic danger to the world."[30] Nonetheless, all Indonesian respondents viewed that the relationship in education with the US had benefitted Indonesia. It is expected, therefore, by the Indonesian respondents that there must not be political agendas in education. It is also not surprising that the education relationship is emphasised and relied on to enhance understanding between Indonesia and the US. Typical comments from the respondents included:

The ultimate aim of the partnership is to improve understanding between the two countries. (*Indonesian official working in a US governmental agency* (*Respondent 6*))

Learning both sides; Indonesia learns by sending students to the US and they are not only learning science, technology or math but also learning the culture. By having this learning, misunderstanding would be eliminated or minimised. (*Indonesian vice-president of US company* (*Respondent 9*))

For these respondents, mutual understanding is a priority and achieved through the education relationship. Education exchanges and their effects create benefit by developing an understanding between the participating states.

In considering whether learning about each other improves understanding between Indonesia and the US, it is interesting to note that respondents who graduated from American universities, and who had lived in the US, showed a greater appreciation of Americans. The respondents who studied in the US for one year or less showed a greater appreciation of Americans, although they were cautious of losing their cultural identity. Similarly, American participants who have visited Indonesia show a greater appreciation of Indonesia's diverse cultures and its geopolitics. As one noted:

> I can't begin to describe all I've learned. . . . I think the bottom line is cross-cultural understanding, and we have those personal friendships that evolve and develop. As far as the faculty is concerned, I think that we learn a lot from one another. (*American respondent negotiating and administering MoUs (Respondent 16)*)

The respondent describes the benefits that accrue to each state. Studying abroad brings tremendous consolations and personal benefits. These benefits include personal friendships and understanding, and the professional advantages gained from learning through working collaboratively. Another respondent commented:

> I would say we would gain a better understanding of a very important country in the world, Indonesia, with a very large population and an increasingly important role in geopolitics, the Pacific. In addition, we would also gain by having some students come from Indonesia, to our university. They would then go back to Indonesia and be successful so that we would then have friends in companies or in government in Indonesia. We could then build connections for our local economy in Oregon. (*American vice-president for research and strategic partnership (Respondent 15)*)

For Respondent 15, friendship and relationships are exploited to best effect through international collaboration. Graduates returning from America become unofficial emissaries for the US, within Indonesia. The following respondent explained this:

> My kind of thinking is that we must overcome misunderstandings. I am fortunate to have lived in the United States for thirteen years. I know the real people besides the politics. . . . With exchange students there will be much better understanding between Western, American culture and Indonesian. (*Indonesian vice-president of US company (Respondent 9)*)

The comment is both powerful and persuasive, and the respondent is enthusiastic and optimistic about the understanding gained of America and Americans. Having been a recipient of education exchanges, the respondent champions the good of cultural understanding that education exchanges provide.

Whether learning about each other improves understanding between Indonesia and the US depends on a long-term commitment. It is unreasonable to expect that parties may understand each other based on only a short-term commitment. The US–Indonesia Comprehensive Partnership launched officially by President Obama and President Yudhoyono is based on long-term commitments, not a short-term partnership, which is often called an "opportunistic partnership," or partnership which is event-specific, and non-systematic.[31] Americans have the opportunity to study Indonesian culture, language, and arts, under Darmasiswa scholarships. Similarly, Indonesian youth have the opportunity for American Field Scholarship (AFS) exchanges for greater cultural understanding.

Most American and Indonesian respondents agreed that the education relationship was not about trying to bring political pressure on any of the parties. The following respondent stated:

> The Ford scholarships have been a really good model. USAID approached Ford when they heard Ford was cancelling and said they would fund it. Ford said they didn't want USAID to change it, make it political and bad. They negotiated and Ford is confident, at this point historically, that the scholarships will be the same kind as in the past, and they won't be politicised. That's one of the discussions that I was part of when I was in Jakarta. (*American respondent negotiating and administering MoUs (Respondent 16)*)

American negotiators are aware of the ramifications of political collaboration in the relationship, as any political pressure has the proclivity to cause a political furore and staunch opposition towards the US.[32] Likewise, any political conditions attached to the education relationship have the potential to incite hostility towards the US and thus impede the objectives of the Indonesia–US education relationship.

As indicated by most Indonesian and American respondents, learning from and about each other was preferred over any political connections. As one respondent commented:

> the dominant concern is to learn from each other; learn from other countries. There are numbers of interesting issues, such as agriculture, environment, opportunity for women, and so forth. This is essentially not a political relationship but a significant role we can play is to work with each other.

(*American respondent dealing with the US-Indonesia education exchange (Respondent 12)*)

This respondent indicated that any political relationship that serves the interests of the US is subjugated for the sake of collaboration. Working side by side benefits the understanding each state has for the other.

Of 16 Indonesian respondents, 12 claimed that the education relationship between Indonesia and the US must not have political agendas; nonetheless, the education relationship is a part of politics, which is unavoidable. Politically, Indonesia and the US have a love–hate relationship, as expressed by some scholars and government officials in the following ways:

> There was a period when Indonesia was very close to the US, and there was also a period when Indonesia told the US to go to hell with its aid. We tell the US to go away but come and help us![33]

> Some radicals can be annoying, they are not consistent. They hate Americans but they go to McDonald's and wear jeans, and listen to rock music. American education is still favoured by Indonesians. American pop culture is also favoured by most Indonesians. (*Indonesian government official (Respondent 5)*)

An ongoing vacillation is evident between pro-American and anti-American sentiments. The feelings towards the US among some Indonesians, nonetheless, were stated clearly at least by one respondent:

> They [fundamentalists] always say America is Satan. America is known by some as the United States of Arrogance. Especially when Americans occupy other countries, and are so aggressive to Pakistan, Afghanistan, Iraq and so on. But a lot of our lecturers and students would like to study in the US, England, and New Zealand. (*Former Indonesian rector who dealt with MoUs (Respondent 7)*)

Although, according to this respondent, the Islamic fundamentalists are those who have anti-American sentiments, many Indonesians regard Americans are arrogant. Yet, many still like to study in the US. Americans are aware of this love–hate relationship. A report published by Pew Research Centre, commented on the Indonesian opinion polls on the US:

Anti-Americanisation has not only deepened, but it has also widened. People see America as a real threat. They think we [America] are going to invade them.[34]

The negative and suspicious feelings towards the US among some Indonesians have the potential to weaken the bilateral relationship between the US and Indonesia. Building person-to-person relationships, which has been on the agenda in the Indonesia–US education relationship, is certainly an imperative. Most Indonesian respondents value the importance of building a relationship. As one respondent commented:

> I think we need to have this partnership in spite of the political tension. The political relationship is up and down and sometimes emotional. But I am sure through this education partnership, people can build a relationship people-to-people and tolerate and accept others' differences, and facilitate official diplomatic conflict solutions. (*Indonesian government official (Respondent 8)*)

Respondent 8 is clearly optimistic about the understanding gained from the relationship despite political tension attached to the Indonesian love–hate sentiments towards the US. Aspects of the relationship are described by Novotny as "the kind of a love and a hate from our side."[35] Novotny explains these aspects of the relationship:

> while the "love" aspect of the attitude means that Indonesia is seen as "part of the Western orbit," the "hate" aspect refers to the perception that the omnipresent influence of the West and particularly the United States' ability to interfere in Indonesia's internal affairs essentially constitute a threat to the country's national security.[36]

In referring to Indonesia being seen as "part of the Western orbit," Novotny describes this aspect as the "love" aspect of the relationship. One respondent noted:

> people think when they study in America they are in the centre of the world. My colleagues say, "What? Did you say you want to study in Australia? Why not study in the United States?" I answered "Why not? I got a scholarship to go to the best university in Australia". (*Indonesian director of the international office of a university in Indonesia (Respondent 10)*)

Australia is closely aligned with the US has had a high profile in Indonesia's education exchange, Australia also features significantly; Australia does not attract the same hostility the US has been prone to. For Indonesians, Australia is familiar, collegial, and a close neighbour, although for some, the US is preferred.

The following comment, however, illustrates the negative feelings towards foreigners (the West):

> We have been many times too trusting with foreigners. For instance, foreign scholars conducted research on tropical diseases like influenza but then when we want to know the outcomes of the research and the product they produce from the research, we must pay. Of course, that can make us angry. (*Indonesian research manager (Respondent 3)*)

Although Respondent 3 did not mention Americans, the comment that Indonesians have been too trusting, and Indonesians are angry with past events, would indicate there will be challenges in agreements because truly effective relationships are developed in a climate of trust and alliance. From Respondent 3's comment, it is clear that the dispute over research is not between education institutions. Yet, disputes over research in the past have influenced attitudes towards education collaboration.

Some Indonesian respondents claimed that the US, through USAID, has played an important role in enhancing the credibility of Indonesian research. As one respondent commented:

> If we are under the umbrella of USAID, our work is more credible. (*Indonesian research manager (Respondent 3)*)

Even though suspicion and opposition to the US have also been clearly evident in many cases, and close ties with the US ignited suspicion and opposition from many Indonesians, most Indonesian respondents perceived that the relationship in education with the US was beneficial.[37] Respondent 3, for instance, believes the relationship in education with USAID brings recognition and credibility to Indonesian education.

Even though the Indonesian government still maintains a relationship with the US (despite negative public sentiments towards the US), strengthening the relationship with civil society and its institutions is an important task.[38] Non-governmental organisations are influential in consolidating the perspectives on the US among Indonesians. Therefore, strengthening relationships with them has the potential to change negative images of the US. Nevertheless, other challenges to developing understanding between the US and Indonesia have arisen, which the following comment captures:

> not many people in Oregon know about Indonesia, and not many people know about Oregon so we have to work very hard to gain that awareness. (*Vice-president for research and strategic partnership* (*Respondent 15*))

Overcoming this obstacle of ignorance and hostility requires academic exchanges that include languages and cultural exchanges utilising both scholarships and fee paying funding. An issue, however, emerges, as the rich usually have the privilege of the exchanges. As the following comment illustrates:

> they [the scholarships] nearly always end up going to the wealthier, upper middle class student. The Indonesian government also funds fellowships, of course, to travel to the US. Who gets those fellowships? Well our experience has been that it is usually the sons and daughters of well-placed bureaucrats. What we call nepotism. So, that is interesting to look at. (*American respondent negotiating and administering MoUs* (*Respondent 16*))

The children of the rich get the privileges and advantages of an overseas degree, which puts them in good stead for a high position, and so the cycle is perpetuated. Only clearer guidelines directing the distribution of scholarship finances and close auditing will ensure equitable and fair education travel exchanges. Respondent 16 expresses valid frustration, as the scramble to attain high education qualifications corrupts the just distribution of resources made available through education aid.

However, the US has attempted to address the needs of Indonesia by establishing the largest English Language Fellow Program in Indonesia, and offering joint degrees, joint research projects, technical assistance, and scholarships.[39]

To summarise, Indonesian respondents were aware of political tensions and dynamics with the US. Nonetheless, all Indonesian respondents viewed that the relationship in education with the US was beneficial for Indonesia. It was an expectation therefore, of the Indonesian respondents, that there must not exist political agendas in education. Rather, the relationship is stressed for the purpose of enhancing understanding between Indonesia and the US. In order to build a stronger relationship, both Indonesia and the US have made long-term commitments through the US–Indonesia Comprehensive Partnership. Most respondents are clear that the education relationship must not have political agendas. Yet, the US–Indonesia Comprehensive Partnership is designed to serve the interests of each other's state. Thus, it is unavoidable that the Indonesia–US education relationship has the potential for political repercussions. It is important to note, however, that the relationship is not overtly trying to bring political pressure to bear on any of the parties involved in the education transactions.

Indonesia–Australia Education Relations

Indonesia–Australia relations, like Indonesia–US relations, have experienced many setbacks from Prime Minister Tony Abbott's refusal to confirm reports that the crews of asylum-seeker boats had been bribed to return to Indonesia, to Indonesia's unilateral action in cutting the live cattle quota. Recent setbacks relate to the executions of Australian drug smugglers Andrew Chan and Myuran Sukumaran. Following the executions, Australia withdrew its ambassador from Indonesia. Nonetheless, Julia Bishop states that the Australia–Indonesia relationship was "very strong and very good."[40] Marty Natalegawa, Indonesian foreign minister during Yudhoyono's presidency, expressed his hope that, "there is somewhere some kind of intensified communications. We cannot afford to let the relationship degenerate to a lower point."[41] The current Prime Minister Malcolm Turnbull has improved Australia's relationship with Indonesia.

In education, Australia has been one of the preferred destinations for study, with 63,000 Indonesians studying in Australia since 2002.[42] It is not surprising the head of the International Relations Department at the Australian National University, Matthew Davies, stated that Australia's relationship with Indonesia is "centrally important ... without Indonesia, all of Australia's key partner states are a long way away."[43] The Australian Minister for Education, the Hon Christopher Pyne, highlights the role of education in the relationship, particularly for strengthening intercultural and interfaith understanding.[44] As in the Indonesia–US relationship, the relationship in education is beneficial not only for Indonesia but also for Australia. The relationship does not bring overt political pressure to bear on any of the parties involved in the education transactions.

Concluding Remarks

Although the one-way transfer of knowledge from, and dependence on, foreign experts is evident, the Indonesian government has attempted to reduce dependence on foreign countries, whether that reliance was on knowledge or on finance.

Foreign financial assistance has been welcomed in Indonesia. Indonesia has, however, attempted to reduce dependence on foreign financial assistance in education by increasing its budget in education expenditure and by contributing financially to its education relationship with its developed state counterparts. Indonesia will continue, in the foreseeable future, to acquire education grants from a range of sources.

Indonesia is a unique case; the LDS is able to negotiate successfully, with its developed state counterpart, based on its interests. The significance of culture and cooperation shaping political objectives and the extent to which the relationship is used as a strategic culture by both parties provide valuable research domains.

Notes

1. USAID Indonesia, "SERASI-Education," http://www.indonesia.usaid.gov/en/usaid/activity/323/serasi_education
2. Unlike Australian higher education institutions, American institutions are perceived to be credible. See Anita Abbott, *Transnational education and educational sovereignty: The Indonesia–US education relations case study* (PhD thesis, The University of Waikato, 2014).
3. Department of Finance, "Focus Group Discussion: Researchers and Research Professors: Enhancing their Roles and Professionalism," http://www.fiskal.depkeu.go.id/2010/; *Republika*, "Minister of Research and Technology: Research in Indonesia is still in its Infancy," *Republika*, March 17, 2013.
4. BISNIS, "Indonesia Needs Millions of Young Entrepreneurs," Last modified February 15, 2017. http://kalimantan.bisnis.com/read/20161027/15/596443/indonesia-butuh-jutaan-wirausahawan-muda. Also see UPH, "Indonesia Needs Politicians Mastering Business," last modified February 20, 2017. http://www.uph.edu/id/component/wmnews/new/2797-indonesia-membutuhkan-politisi-yang-menguasai-bisnis.html
5. Muhammad Rakhmat, "Indonesia–UK Relations: Students Exchange Needed," last modified February 10, 2017. http://www.huffingtonpost.co.uk/muhammad-zulfikar-rakhmat/indonesiauk-relations-stu

6. For further information see http://curriculum.binus.ac.id/binus-international-education-program
7. See http://dikti.go.id/indonesia-belanda-tingkatkan-kerja-sama-pendidikan-tinggi-dan-sains/#66V1houcfKLMEk4z.99
8. David Jardine, "Indonesia: Universities' Poor World Ranking Probed," last modified February 10, 2017. http://www.universityworldnews.com/article
9. Boston Consulting Group predicts the number of Indonesia's middle and affluent consumer class will double by 2020, to roughly 141 million people. See. http://www.usindo.org/news/indonesias-rising-middle-class
10. MoUs set out the mutual benefits and agreements for initiating exchanges of teaching materials and literature, research collaboration, exchanges of scholars, and the conducting of joint workshops. For instance, see MoU of Ohio University, last modified December 10, 2012, http://www.oia.osu.edu/pdf/mou
11. See Presidential Decree, number 75 of 1999, concerning the employment of expatriates.
12. Franklin Weinstein (2007).
13. Franklin Weinstein, *Indonesia Foreign Policy and the Dilemma of Dependence: From Sukarno and Suharto* (Singapore: Equinox Publishing, 2007): 27.
14. During the Sukarno and Suharto eras, strong nationalism had been unconditional in any bargains with foreign powers. Any political attachment would terminate any negotiations.
15. Don Marut, "Can Indonesia do Without Foreign Aid?" *The Jakarta Post*, Thursday, December 1, 2011.
16. Indonesians tend to use indirect communication and hide their feelings. See Wahdi Yudhi, Marthin Nanere, and Apollo Nsubuga-Kyobe, "A Comparative Study of Negotiation Styles of Education Managers in Australia and Indonesia," *SEAMEO*, December 14, 2006.
17. Leon Tikly (2004); Gordon Crawford, *Foreign Aid and Political Reform: A Comparative Analysis of Democracy Assistance and Political Conditionality* (Basingstoke: Palgrave, 2001); Martin Carnoy, *Education as Cultural Imperialism* (New York: David McKay, 1975); Martin Carnoy and Diana Rhoten, "What Does Globalization Mean for Educational Change?: A Comparative Approach," *Comparative Education Review*, 46, (2002).
18. Crawford (2001); Carnoy (1975).
19. In the *Jakarta Globe*, "Indonesian Government Plans to Spend over US$ 34 billion on Education," *Jakarta Globe*, August 17, 2012.
20. Weinstein (2007).

21. The World Bank, "Internal debt Statistics 2013," last modified March 28, 2013, http://www.data.worldbank.org/sites/default/files. Also see Anti Debt Coalition, http://www.kau.or.id
22. USAID Indonesia, "United States Government Invests $19 Million in Indonesian Higher Education," last modified July 10, 2013 from http://www.indonesia.usaid.gov
23. *New Zealand Herald*, "New Zealand and Indonesia move past export dispute." Last modified February 18, 2017. http://www.nzherald.co.nz/business/news/article
24. Australian Department of Foreign Affairs and Trade, "Overview of Australia's Aid Program to Indonesia," last modified February 10, 2017. http://www.dfat.gov.au/geo/Indonesia/development
25. Some have speculated that the cut is related to the executions of Australian citizens. Some have said that the reduction is not retribution for Bali Nine executions. See *The Conversation*. "How will a 40% cut in Australian aid affect Indonesia?" Last modified February 20, 2017. http://theconversation.com/how-will-a-40-cut-in-australian-aid-affect-indonesia-41753
26. Ibid.
27. Daniel Novotny, *Indonesian Foreign Policy: A Quest for the Balance of Threat* (PhD thesis. The University of New South Wales, 2007).
28. Discussion of the political interests of the US and China in Indonesia is beyond the scope of this book.
29. Nor did the researcher probe questions surrounding political tensions and dynamic.
30. Melani Budianta, "Beyond the Stained Glass Window: Indonesian perceptions of the United States and the War on Terror." In *What They Think of Us: International Perceptions of the United States Since 9/11*. Ed. Farber D (NJ: Princeton University Press, 2007): 27–48.
31. Canto and Hannah (2001). The US–Indonesia Comprehensive Partnership is a long-term agreement with several aspects including defence and security, energy, trade and investment, climate change and environment, democracy and civil society, and education. See "US–Indonesia Joint Commission and Bilateral Meeting," Office of Spokesman, Department of State September 2010.
32. See Timo Kivimaki, *US–Indonesia Hegemonic Bargaining: Strength of Weakness* (Hants, England: Ashgate, 2003).
33. Speech by Dewi Fortuna Anwar. See Dewi Fortuna Anwar, "Indonesia's Perceptions of China and the US Security Roles in East Asia," *The Habibie Centre*, 2006.
34. Meg Bortin, "Polls Show US Isolation: In War's Wake, Hostility, and Mistrust," *The International Herald Tribune*, June 3, 2003.

35. In Daniel Novotny, *Indonesian Foreign Policy: A Quest for the Balance of Threats* (PhD thesis. The University of New South Wales, 2007).
36. Novotny (2007).
37. These aspects of suspicion and opposition to the US, and close ties with the US that ignited suspicion and opposition from many Indonesians, are beyond the scope of this article.
38. See Novotny (2007). It should be noted, however, some in the government held very negative views towards the US, e.g., Hamzah Haz (the former vice-president) and Amien Rais (leader of a political party).
39. US Department of State, "United States-Indonesia Education Cooperation," Bureau of Educational and Cultural Affairs, last modified August 10, 2012, http://www.exchanges.state.gov; The White House, "Fact Sheet: Higher Education Partnership with Indonesia," http://www.whitehouse.gov/sites/default/files/us-indonesia_higher_education_partnership; Alan Dessoff, "Building Partnerships: Indonesia and the United States," *Embassy of Indonesia*, http://www.embassyofindonesia.org/education.docpdf/building_partnerships_indonesia_us
40. David Wroe, "Australia-Indonesia Relations is in 'very good shape': Julia Bishop," *The Sydney Morning Herald*. Last modified February 2, 2017. http://www.smh.com.au/federal-politics/political-news/australiaindonesia-relationship-in-very-good-shape-julie-bishop-20151221-glsrus.html. Also see http://theconversation.com/australia-indonesia-relationship-is-back-to-normal-meaning-fragile-as-ever-45513
41. Ibid.
42. See http://ministers.education.gov.au/pyne/indonesia-and-australia-power-education-and-soft-diplomacy
43. CNN, Juliet Perry, Australia and Indonesia: A relationship too important to fail? http://edition.cnn.com/2017/01/05/asia/indonesia-australia-army/
44. Department of Education and Training, "Indonesia and Australia: Power of Education and Soft Diplomacy," Last modified January 30, 2017. http://internationaleducation.gov.au/News/Latest-News/Pages/article-Indonesia-and-AustraliaPowerofEducationSoft-Diplomacy.aspx

CHAPTER 5

Equality in the Indonesia–US Relations

While the balance of power between Indonesia and the US had not been one of the original ideas chosen for exploration in this book, the frequency with which the term *equality* occurred in the interviews suggests that this idea requires further consideration. The notion that the relationship with the US was equal was obviously of considerable importance to the Indonesian negotiators. Furthermore, their repeated reference to this term indicates their concern to position Indonesia in a particular way in these educational exchange agreements. In contrast, the term of equality does not appear in the interviews with Indonesian and New Zealand negotiators. When they were asked, however, they responded that equality was not an issue. Therefore, this chapter explores the concept of equality in terms of the way that equality is perceived in the relationship with Indonesia's American counterparts and how that reference to equality performs and, in relation to this, the extent to which educational sovereignty is retained by the Indonesian parties.

This chapter begins by reviewing the way the Indonesian negotiators emphasised equality in the relationship with the US. It discusses whether Indonesia is free in reality to negotiate as an equal party and whether it is in a position to pursue any exchange that it finds attractive. The chapter goes on to consider the question of whether foreign education provision weakens the educational sovereignty of Indonesia.

© The Author(s) 2017
A. Abbott, *Educational Sovereignty and Transnational Exchanges in Post-Secondary Indonesian Education*, DOI 10.1007/978-3-319-53985-0_5

Why Equality?

Equality in Indonesia's relationships with the US is referred to as shared contribution, benefits, responsibility, and commitment (as shown in the respondents' comments). In this context, equality is a descriptive concept. Equality is also a normative concept because it requires what Capaldi calls "special treatment."[1] This special treatment includes addressing inequality in order to maintain equality. In this section, the importance of Indonesia's need for equality in the relationship is explored because equality was obviously of considerable importance to the Indonesian negotiators.

The following comment illustrates how one respondent understood equality in the Indonesia–US education relationship. This respondent asserted:

> we are equals no matter who we are. ... That is why I will ask constantly for equal efforts from other countries also. ... If they are sending 10,000 compared with the population of Indonesia it should be the same effort from other countries to send their students to Indonesia, because it isn't fair. Let's say we have 17,000 students in Australia, while only a tiny number come to Indonesia. Only a few people know about Indonesia so the same effort applies to other countries, the US as well. I constantly ask the US government through the US embassy here to send their young students to come to Indonesia. (*Indonesian government official (Respondent 11)*)

Equality is perceived by this respondent as both a descriptive concept (people are equal) and a normative concept (equal efforts from other states are still required for realising equality in the relationship). The assertion of equal status, in this instance, was expressed as an expectation that the exchange of students should be mutual, and it led to calls to increase the number of American students studying in Indonesia. Believing that Indonesia was equal with other states, the respondent asked governments with which Indonesia had exchange agreements to send young students to Indonesia also.[2]

The idea of equality, and of being seen as an equal, was, therefore, of significant importance to the Indonesian respondents. Closely associated with this was a concern of not being taken advantage of:

We need to be equal. They must not exploit us because they think we are stupid and do not know anything! (*Indonesian research manager* (*Respondent 3*))

The assertion of equality in this sense, therefore, is an assertion of national and cultural pride, and a challenge to being positioned as backward or needy. That the two parties see each other as being fully equal in the education relationship was both a necessity and an expectation.

The assertion of equality was also linked to a concern with being "exploited," a possibility also expressed by another respondent:

We don't want to be exploited, to provide what they always want. We open the gate for the cooperation, we help them to find the data, [and] we help them to find a network among the government officials and Indonesian society. But they don't want to help [us], like when our scholars go to their country. So we don't want this kind of thing. (*Indonesian director of international office at an Indonesian university* (*Respondent 10*))

Here, the respondent saw the need to determine the essence of the educational experience of individuals when they study overseas. The respondent also reasons that Indonesia is taken advantage of if it continually subordinates its will to that of the US. Although equality, mutual respect, and mutual benefits are the guiding principles of the relationship, the output of the relationship is not always equally beneficial, as both states have different cultural norms.[3] This point is illustrated in the following comment:

We often have clash[es] of personality because of our different values. For instance, if we go to America, we have to do everything by ourselves whereas if they come here, we are so hospitable, making sure that everything would be ok for them. Here, if they go back to America, we will accompany them to the airport with our drivers but over there they won't care, go by yourself. (*Indonesian research manager* (*Respondent 3*))

Respondent 3's comment clearly stated that both Indonesia and the US have different cultural norms. As shown in Chap. 6, Indonesians value interdependence. Thus, the expectation to be independent, when a guest in someone else's country, is interpreted as the other [i.e., American] party being uncaring. The comments from Respondents 3 and 10 show that differences in attitude and cultural norms can result in a sense that some aspects of the relationship are indeed unequal.

Exercising autonomy, in terms of making independent decisions and entering beneficial agreements, was seen by some Indonesian respondents as the essence of equality. The idea of autonomy was discussed in Chap. 2, where each country was thought of as an autonomous state acting in accordance with its own interests. Further, the Indonesian Directorate of Higher Education defines equality in the relationship as being equally able to make decisions.[4] This is to say that equality is necessary for exercising autonomy. On this topic, the following respondent commented:

> We have the capacity to be equal. If we cannot agree with America and other Western countries, we can partner with Asian countries. (*Indonesian research manager (Respondent 3)*)

This strong assertion of equality shows the ability of Indonesian parties to accept or to refuse to cooperate with the US. This assertion, as noted in Chap. 6, informed the way the Indonesian parties entered into negotiations and was a way of maximising the benefits of the relationship.[5] The respondent expected to be respected as a coequal in the agreement. The following respondent's comment reflected the same concern:

> Some universities only want to bring some students from here. We don't want that. That's very much capitalism. I mean, if it is cooperation it should benefit both of us, not exploit. This is the thing, I think we can refuse. If they cooperate with us they don't want to provide us with professors but they want us to send students from Indonesia to study in their institutions. I think that is not fair. (*Indonesian director of international office at an Indonesian university (Respondent 10)*)

One of the defining features of educational sovereignty, as outlined in Chap. 2, is the need to challenge the arbitrary authority of power structures to determine the essence of individuals' educational experiences. The respondent (Respondent 10) saw the necessity not only of retaining control of the commercialisation of education within Indonesia but also of being able to refuse what would not be beneficial for Indonesia. For the respondent, individuals determine their own course of learning, and are not to be used only as a convenience and to bring pecuniary gains to education providers. Knowledge is accessible through experience rather than determined by the arbitrary pronouncements of a few powerful individuals manifested in international corporations or international education providers.

The discussion in Chap. 2 indicated that autonomy over national education is one of the defining features of educational sovereignty. Although exercising autonomy is clearly shown by the ability of the Indonesian government to regulate national education and to establish a character-based curriculum, Indonesian respondents dealing with curriculum emphasise the importance of the US's acknowledgement of Indonesian cultural norms. Such acknowledgement could be achieved only within the context of an equitable relationship. As discussed earlier, Indonesian respondents perceived American education to be superior. As expected, Indonesian respondents, particularly those who design education curriculum together with their American counterparts, claimed that equality involved having one's culture acknowledged. Hence, as the earlier discussion suggests, there is a link between equality and autonomy. Through equality, the Indonesian respondents believe that it is possible to retain autonomy. Further, it was clear that, for the success of the exchange agreements, the American parties had to acknowledge equality with their Indonesian counterparts.

Impact on Indonesia's Educational Sovereignty

The protection of the ability to make decisions independently and to refuse foreign involvement in education was a clear concern of the Indonesian respondents. Retaining the ability to refuse or accept foreign involvement in education and to make decisions independently are defining features of educational sovereignty. This connection implies that equality in the education relationship is fundamental to retaining educational sovereignty. Given the importance of these interconnected concerns, examination of questions around whether Indonesia's educational sovereignty is weakened by its involvement with American education providers forms the topic for this section. The intention here is to examine the actual extent to which assertions of equality are realised in the relationship, and thus the extent to which educational sovereignty is retained by the Indonesian parties.

As previously discussed in Chap. 2, critical education theorists stress that transnational education positions the LDSs as commercially and politically weaker than developed states and, consequently, vulnerable to exploitation. This vulnerability exists regardless of whether the objective is the commercialisation of education or the promotion of mutual understanding. As outlined in Chap. 4, educational links between the US and Indonesia that involve academic and research collaboration do tend to result in a one-way transfer of knowledge. Nguyen, Elliot, Terlouw, and Pilot have argued that through the transfer of knowledge, Western education influences both the cultures and educational systems of non-Western states.[6] In this context, Western education can be seen as having the potential to weaken or undermine the educational sovereignty of the LDS. It was emphasised in Chap. 4, however, that in the case of the Indonesia–US education relationship, the Indonesian respondents were enthusiastic about adopting American education and regarded it as being highly prestigious. The respondents were also clear in their positions in terms of what they were willing to accept and adopt, and what they would refuse. Thus, even though a one-way transfer of knowledge was evident, the relationship with the US did not necessarily mean Indonesia relinquished sovereignty in education.

The starting point for this examination of whether educational exchanges undermine the educational sovereignty of Indonesia is the work of authors such as Carnoy, Siqueira, Verger, and Bonal, who argue that educational requirements through the GATS have the potential to put the LDSs at risk by requiring compliance with international trade regulations. Such compliance leads, they suggest, to the loss of the authority to regulate internal education initiatives.[7] Green, for example, states:

> Liberalization of trade in education may weaken the government's commitment to an investment in public higher education, promote privatization, and put countries with weak quality assurance mechanisms at a disadvantage in their countries, by foreign providers.[8]

Three aspects of the liberalisation of trade in education, derived from Green's statement, are worth exploring: promotion of privatisation of education, weak quality assurance mechanisms, and commitment to investment in public higher education. With regard to the first aspect, privatisation involves the transfer of ownership and control of government or state assets, firms, and operations to the private investor.[9] A policy of privatisation has been encouraged in Indonesia, evident, for example, in the 2010 statement by Parikesit Suprapto, the Indonesian deputy minister for financial institutions.[10] Dissatisfaction with the performance of Indonesian public institutions was one motivation for the call for privatisation.[11]

Concerns, however, have been voiced over privatisation in the education sector. Winarno Surakhmad, former president of the Jakarta Teachers Training Institute, for instance, has argued that privatisation always culminates in higher costs; the rich will have access to education, whereas the poor will stay poor and will be unable to access higher education. He further argues that when privatisation of education is encouraged, foreign investors will own large parts of institutions.[12] In such a scenario, fees will rise, and education will become the privilege of those who can afford to pay for it.

It is important to note, however, although the credibility of foreign education—particularly American education—has attracted many Indonesian middle-class investors to foreign education,[13] the commercial presence mode of delivery is highly regulated. According to Presidential Regulation 77/2007, foreign education institutions are limited to 47% of shares in education institutions in Indonesia, and 80% of the educators must be Indonesian national.[14] In this context, foreign education institutions are recognised as Indonesian education institutions. It is necessary to note that privatisation of higher education at national level is facilitated due significantly to the government's recognition of private post-secondary education institutions through education law, and is encouraged by the government as a way of accommodating an overflow of high school graduates. The Indonesian government has tight restrictions on the operation of foreign education providers (commercial presence mode) in order to protect local education institutions from competition. In this context, the government of Indonesia still retains a high degree of regulation over the education sector, and, therefore, educational sovereignty.

The second aspect of liberalisation of trade in education is related to education quality assurance mechanisms. Frase and O'Sullivan in *The Future of Education under the WTO* argue that the quality of education should be questioned because there is little control over what is being taught by foreign education institutions.[15] As the commercial presence of foreign education providers is restricted, the issue of poor quality of education is not a consequence of the operation of American education providers. Besides, based on the interviews, the respondents clearly regarded American education as more prestigious and of a higher quality than Indonesian education. Collaborating with American education institutions was seen as having the potential to improve Indonesian education quality. Indonesian respondents also showed a willingness to collaborate only with universities that were higher ranked than Indonesian universities. In this context, once again, the respondents were clear on their positions in terms of what they were willing to accept.

The third aspect of liberalisation of trade in education is concerned with whether government expenditure in education is decreasing. Commercialisation of education typically, but not necessarily, entails user charges and it is often accompanied by corporatisation as well as deregulation, as seen in, for example, the removal of regulations sanctioning free education.[16] Understood in this way, the extent to which Indonesia's education sovereignty is weakened by the provision of American education programmes in Indonesia then can be evaluated based on the extent to which the government commits to an investment in public higher education. According to the World Bank, in 2007, Indonesia spent 17% of its total national expenditure on education. Although a small amount compared to its southeast Asian neighbours, public expenditure in education (elementary to tertiary education) had moved up from 11.4% of total national expenditure spent on education in 2001.[17] This spending illustrates Indonesia's commitment to investment in public education. The allocation of public expenditure to education has been mainly for primary education (75% of the total education budget). Fifteen percent of the total education budget has been allocated to secondary education. Only 10% of the total budget for education has been allocated to post-secondary education.[18]

Although government expenditure in education has increased, the government initiated autonomy in higher education. It means district tertiary education institutions are not only self-governing entities able to make independent decisions without central government, but also expected to be independent financially.[19] The autonomy policy is welcomed by Indonesian universities for its principle is to enable universities and district universities to make independent decisions without the control of central government.[20] Nonetheless, user pays policy as a way to be financially dependent has been a controversial issue because of the fear that post-secondary education is only for those who can afford to pay.[21] Here, user pays policy has been implemented not because educational requirements of the GATS have the potential to put Indonesia at risk by requiring compliance with international trade regulations. Rather, the concern surrounding user pays policy arises from the implementation of financial autonomy of Indonesian post-secondary education institutions.

Although the government expenditure in education has increased, not only has the financial autonomy of post-secondary education been initiated and supported, but also the active participation of non-state actors in the education sector is encouraged. The following respondent commented:

> Tier 2 is private-to-private as government does not have a significant role in higher education. Universities have their own autonomy. It is not enough we have only G to G [government to government]. (*Indonesian government official dealing with MoUs* (*Respondent 8*))

The relationship is not only between state actors but also between non-state actors, and state and non-state actors. At the public–private partnership (PPP) level, PPP institutions such as ExxonMobil, Intel, and ConocoPhillips have assisted financially in the establishment and improvement of education facilities.[22] At the university level, Indonesian and American higher education institutions have collaborated in both research and education exchanges. Increased contributions to the collaboration, as discussed in earlier chapters, are perceived by the Indonesian respondents to be necessary for maintaining equality in the relationship and, hence, to enable them to make independent decisions. Equality is thus an attribute of sovereignty because equality is necessary for retaining sovereignty.

The extent to which Indonesia's educational sovereignty is weakened by the provision of American education programmes in Indonesia can also be evaluated based on the extent to which the government has the capacity to implement regulations in the education sector and enforce national education law. The government of Indonesia has, over many years, regulated national education and enforced national education law. Indonesia's National Education Law of 2003 authorises transnational education in Indonesia's territory.[23] Foreign education in Indonesia, as noted earlier in the text, is highly regulated, particularly mode 3 (commercial presence), to protect local education institutions from competition with foreign providers. Foreign education services must also collaborate with an Indonesian provider, and together with its local partner, they must be registered as accredited education providers with the Ministry of National Education. In addition to prohibiting the commercial presence mode in Indonesia, under Presidential Regulation 111 of 2007 and Presidential Regulation 36 of 2010, academic directors and executives must be Indonesian citizens. Temporary entry for foreign experts engaged in education activities in Indonesia is also subject to approval by the Ministry of National Education. There is no evidence to suggest the government of Indonesia lacks the capacity to implement these regulations in the education sector.

As the interviews have illustrated, American education, particularly in management and technology, is highly regarded, and education exchanges and research collaboration provide supplementary support to Indonesian education. Improvements in facilities are also a priority for improving education quality. The issue then is not whether foreign education is preferred to national education or whether the two forms are in competition. Rather, transnational education, other than the commercial presence mode, is used to supplement national education. If foreign education is supplementary to national education, and is limited to the consumption abroad mode, then the provision of American education programmes in Indonesia does not put Indonesia at a disadvantage.

In summary, the extent to which Indonesia's educational sovereignty is undermined by the provision of American education programmes in Indonesia can be evaluated based on the extent to which the government commits to an investment in public higher education, and restricts transnational education to the mode that is beneficial for Indonesia. The government is able to commit to an investment in public higher education. The Indonesian government also has the capacity to regulate the modes of education delivery not only between state actors but also between non-state actors and between state and non-state actors. When the government is able to restrict transnational education modes by committing only to those modes which benefit Indonesia, the argument that foreign education weakens Indonesia's ability to regulate education within its borders is not supported. This finding signifies that American education does not diminish Indonesia's educational sovereignty.

A necessary starting point in assessing whether Indonesia's education sovereignty is undermined by foreign education providers has been established earlier in the text through an evaluation of the extent to which the Indonesian government commits to an investment in public higher education and restricts transnational education to the modes that are beneficial to Indonesia. The extent to which Indonesia agrees to and approves American education providers' operations is now examined. It is first worth making two brief points. The US is perceived by Indonesian respondents as having a good reputation in education and research, and with superior technology and management. Indonesia has offered scholarships and grants to Americans to learn Indonesian languages, arts, and culture; in return, the US has offered scholarships, grants, and technical assistance to Indonesia.[24] Both the US and Indonesian governments have a shared vision of increasing cooperation and ties that are critical to the bilateral relationship for addressing key regional and global challenges.[25] At the university level, there have been academic and research collaboration that benefitted Indonesia; American education institutions, by contrast, are able to recruit Indonesian students to study at their institutions. Mutual benefits can also be identified in PPPs. ExxonMobil and other international companies, for instance, are able to operate their businesses with wider social acceptance by promoting corporate responsibility, contributing financially to the establishment of public education facilities, improving education quality, and developing educated and competitive graduates.[26]

Secondly, as mentioned earlier in this chapter, respondents held the view that Indonesia entered into beneficial agreements. The typical comments included: "They do not dictate to us. We do not want that" (Indonesian government official dealing with curriculum (Respondent 1)); "Indonesia is not compelled" (Indonesian government official (Respondent 5)); "The government of America could not intervene with Indonesian national education because it is the authority of DIKTI" (Indonesian official working in a US governmental agency (Respondent 6)).

The following comments also illustrate that the Indonesian parties enter into agreements they find advantageous and are not coerced into accepting any agreement:

> We have a record for each university; whether we need to enhance, whether we should cooperate with this university or not. The policy at that time was that we should cooperate with universities that are better than us. If they are not better than us, then what's the point? We need to enhance our international standing so why should we cooperate with ones that are worse than us? This is in the consideration when we have an MoU. (*Indonesian director of international office at an Indonesian university (Respondent 10)*)

> The cooperation is beneficial ... mutually beneficial. I myself have gained benefits. Sandwich programmes, for instance, would not be established without cooperation and MoUs. Without MoUs it is not easy to get a letter of acceptance from a university in the US. So, with the partnership, we can go to the US much more easily. (*Indonesian chair of international cooperation of a university in Indonesia (Respondent 18)*)

Respondent 18 clearly claimed there were benefits from educational collaboration with the US. One of the benefits for Indonesian universities was clearly stated by Respondent 10, that collaboration should be with foreign universities that are well known and among the best ranked internationally, or with universities that have particular strengths that appeal to and fulfil Indonesia's needs.

The ability to retain educational sovereignty, however, requires negotiation and renegotiation for securing the exchange agreements, particularly in the areas which Indonesian parties perceive as unequal in the relationship, such as the better quality of American education. The following respondent shared her experience and perspective:

> usually we will try to negotiate. Because if it is a good university we cannot let them go. They said that if we do not want to cooperate with them, they will cooperate with Gadjah Mada University. We have to negotiate what we can give to them, and what we can get from them. I think in that case we would be ready to negotiate. If it is a good university we will try and negotiate, but if it's not the best university and it has no benefit for us, usually in that case we will not progress. (*Indonesian director of an international office* (*Respondent 10*))

The comment suggests that American providers are adept at shopping around for universities that will meet their needs, and that the threat to go to other universities weakens the bargaining position of potential Indonesian partners. The respondent vigorously pursued collaborations with US universities, and she would be prepared to make concessions that other Indonesian universities would not in order to secure an exchange agreement. It is clear here that American providers had a good deal of bargaining power in this situation. For the respondent, negotiation and renegotiation are often required when an agreement is not achieved; renegotiation often takes place, especially if the prospective university partner has world recognition.

In summary, this discussion establishes that Indonesian parties are at liberty to enter into agreements they find beneficial. The actual ability or capacity to implement regulations that retain Indonesian control over the education sector is shown from the relationship that is based on mutually agreed objectives and from the willingness of Indonesian parties to accept agreements. The comments of Indonesian respondents show that they are able to negotiate before signing off on MoUs that will be beneficial for Indonesia, and they are not coerced into accepting any agreements. Negotiations include manoeuvring towards securing foreign financial assistance in education, as is discussed in the following section.

AMERICAN FINANCIAL ASSISTANCE IN EDUCATION

The stronger financial position of the US was another aspect of the Indonesia–US education relationship that the Indonesian respondents highlighted as an area of inequality. This type of inequality, as Abrahamsen suggests, provides donor countries with the power to threaten to withdraw aid from the less-developed counterpart in the negotiation of agreements.[27] With regard to the Indonesian–US education exchanges, a question arising is whether the threat of withdrawing financial aid was a bargaining tool in the negotiation of exchange agreement.[28]

To examine whether the threat to withdraw aid by the US provides Americans bargaining power in the negotiation of agreements and thus weakens Indonesia's sovereignty, it is important to understand the history of the relationship between Indonesia and the US. To examine whether American financial assistance threatens the educational sovereignty of Indonesia requires, first, evidence of any obligatory and unwanted attachment of conditions to that assistance, and second, any limitations to the exercise of authority and autonomy over education within Indonesia's territorial boundaries.

To discuss whether American financial assistance threatens the educational sovereignty of Indonesia, one should understand the history of the relationship between Indonesia and the US in which the threat to withdraw aid by the US does not necessarily provide it with bargaining power in the negotiation of agreements. Indonesia has welcomed foreign aid since the 1950s, and the US was the main donor. It is necessary to note, even though Indonesia welcomed foreign aid, in the 1950s, Indonesia accepted more loan finance than grants because it did not want to align itself with the US (and the West).[29] Indonesian nationalism and its independent and active foreign policy have enabled Indonesia to adopt policies to secure national interests as well as be free from any burdens that may arise as a consequence of the alignment with the US.[30] Although the US leadership in international affairs was strong in the 1950s, despite the US threat to embargo Indonesia, Indonesia was able to gain economic assistance not only from the American aid but also from American compensation to Indonesia for the loss of export earnings caused by the US embargo.[31] In 1961, Indonesia, by balancing between the US and the Soviets, was able to gain both diplomatic support from the US in the Indonesia–Netherlands dispute over Western New Guinea, and military assistance from the Soviets. In negotiations with the US between 1961 and 1975, Indonesia was also assertive in its relations with the US and the West: Indonesia would neither commit itself to the Western block nor give the US a voice in any questions related to its domestic politics and foreign affairs.[32] Despite the US threat to ban military aid and training due to human rights abuses in East Timor, Indonesia was gradually able to gain military assistance from the US. From this brief discussion, it is clear that the threat to withdraw financial assistance does not necessarily provide the US with bargaining power in the negotiation of agreements with Indonesia. What is more, the education relationship is beyond politics; thus, there is no evidence that there is a threat to withdraw financial assistance based on political conditions attached to American aid. Moreover, any discrete threat or political conditions attached to American aid have the potential to provoke antagonism towards the US.[33] In this light, it is likely that political conditions attached to financial assistance in education would also create antagonism towards the US.

It is important to distinguish between foreign financial assistance received through multilateral relationships, through international financial institutions such as the World Bank and IMF, and through bilateral relationships, such as the Indonesia–US education bilateral relationship. Unlike assistance from the US, the World Bank and IMF provide loans, which have not reduced poverty but rather have increased debt. Indonesia is one of the top ten World Bank borrowers. In 2011, Indonesia's debt reached US$ 215.5 billion.[34] By borrowing money from the World Bank, Indonesia would have increased debt. As a result, the World Bank's policy implications for Indonesia have kindled resistance among Indonesians.[35] In contrast, USAID has not only assisted Indonesia with its governance strategy, but it has also contributed financially to Indonesian education.[36] In 2005, for example, the total USAID budget for Indonesia was $102.8 million, with more than 10% of the total budget being for policy reform and training.[37] The following respondent commented on the role of USAID in Indonesia:

> Our aim is at helping and building capacity of local education, increasing the quality of education, increasing the quality of education planning and management, and helping educators to improve their teaching skills. We started university partnership in research and teaching in 2009. We do it through student exchanges. The other programme is higher education leadership and management in 2011. We helped DIKTI with technical support and local financial management. (*Indonesian official dealing with financial management in a US governmental agency (Respondent 6)*)

The respondent's experience illustrates the significant role of USAID in improving the quality of Indonesian education. In the Aceh Polytechnic Programme project, USAID was involved in the process of hiring teachers and developing curriculum in accordance with Indonesian government regulations and industry needs in such areas as electronics engineering, information technology, and business accounting.[38]

The US places conditions on its assistance in education, based on the purpose of the US–Indonesia Comprehensive Partnership. It is a long-term commitment to elevating bilateral relations by enhancing cooperation and upgrading strategic consultations on key bilateral, regional, and global issues.[39] In the education sector, USAID's aims are to support initiatives, to expand access to quality basic education, to improve the quality and relevance of higher education, to embrace the US–Indonesia Comprehensive Partnership, and to recognise the leadership role Indonesia plays in its own development as well as development throughout the region.[40] Although democratisation and government reform and strategy are part of USAID's overall mission plan, USAID recognises the guiding principles of Indonesian authorities, both nationally and regionally. Hence, Indonesia retains authority and control over its education.

The extent to which foreign financial assistance may be seen as threatening Indonesia's educational sovereignty depends on the outcomes of negotiations. Indonesian education law comprises five sources: Pancasila, the 1945 constitution, customary law, laws enacted by the parliament, and presidential and ministerial regulations. The extent to which negotiations can effectively protect the educational sovereignty of Indonesia can be evaluated based on the adherence of transnational education transactions to these sources of Indonesian law.

Indonesian customary law or *adat* law governs civil behaviour and civil law. Every region in Indonesia has its own local wisdom based on *adat*. To protect Indonesia's educational sovereignty means protecting Indonesian customs (*adat*). Whether or not financial assistance in education will undermine Indonesia's educational sovereignty depends on whether transnational education transactions acknowledge Indonesian customary law. Based on laws enacted by the parliament, local governments have the responsibility and authority for all sectors of development and governance in their own regions except for international affairs, the judiciary, defence, monetary and fiscal policies, and other domains subject to central government authority.[41] Local government, therefore, is responsible for the observation and protection of local customary law. With regard to the Indonesia–US education relationship, USAID endeavours to work collaboratively and build the capacity of local institutions. USAID recognises the authority of Indonesia to control its national education and it cannot intervene in Indonesian national education, which is under the authority of DIKTI (*Direktorat Jenderal Perguruan Tinggi*). USAID also formulates and implements its policies in line with both the US mission strategy for Indonesia and education strategy set down in Washington, and with the Indonesian national education strategy. USAID also attempts to find ways to work closely with local institutions to build their capacity.[42]

Indonesian education law also includes *Tri Dharma Perguruan Tinggi* (Three pillars of higher education); these are education, research, and community service. Any research and education programme must be accompanied by character development objectives, which benefit society.[43] USAID and American education institutions have addressed Indonesia's industry needs in the fields of electronics engineering, information technology, and business accounting.

As indicated in the discussion, USAID works together with Indonesia's central and local governments in such a way as to demonstrate mutuality in commitment and responsibility in the relationship. Recognition of Indonesia's authority and the leadership role Indonesia plays in its own development, arguably, plays an important role in the acceptance of continuing cooperation with USAID.

American financial assistance has played an important role in Indonesia's development. Since gaining its independence, Indonesia has received financial assistance from foreign states, including the US. After independence, Indonesia had the enormous task of nation building. Nation building refers to activities or tasks in three broad categories: in the political (democratisation), economic (economic development), and social (unification of disparate ethnic groups) domains.[44] Economic development in Indonesia was supported by aid from former communist countries, from non-aligned states such as Yugoslavia and India (from 1959 to 1961), and from the US (from 1951). The US has been the nation's primary donor, contributing $7 million a year in technical assistance for 6 years, and providing $91.8 million in loans for various development projects.[45] Indonesia and the US first started working together in the 1950s when they signed their first economic and technical cooperation agreement. It aimed to address Indonesia's request of assistance to overcome food shortages, to solve critical health problems, and to rehabilitate the country's transportation facilities.[46] Between 1949 and 1961, Indonesia received $545 million from the US ($113.6 million of which was in the form of loans) and over $13 million was in Ford Foundation grants.[47] Tasks in reforming education in Indonesia after independence included increasing the rates of literacy, improving the quality of education, improving the quality of education facilities, and increasing the rate of participation in education. The World Bank played a significant role as it advanced loans for building education institutions and for improving the quality of education facilities. In 2005, the World Bank granted a loan of US$114,537,000 for the Relevance and Efficiency programme, a project in higher education.[48] The US, too, has played a significant role in Indonesian education through, for example, improvements to education facilities and teacher training.

Indonesia has experienced economic reconstruction since the late 1960s and following the financial crisis in 1997–1998. From the 1950s onwards, USAID, together with the Ford, Carnegie, and Rockefeller foundations, sponsored Indonesian students studying in the US.[49] When Indonesia experienced financial turmoil in the late 1960s, Indonesians who had graduated from American universities and who were cabinet ministers during the leadership of President Suharto, for example, Widjojo Nitisastro, Ali Wardhana, J.B. Sumarlin, and Emil Salim, successfully implemented economic policies for Indonesia's recovery. During the Suharto era, education focused on economic returns, and the government was able to both dominate and direct education institutions. Education attainment was regarded as one of the critical components in state and nation building and resilience, because it enabled people to improve their economic status, and hence address the issues of poverty and illiteracy. The role of education in economic development, both during and since the Suharto era, has been closely linked through government policy to the needs of the economy. Currently, Vice-President Boediono emphasises the role of education, from basic to post-secondary education levels, in Indonesia's development.[50] For Boediono, the development of the country depends on a strong Indonesian economy, and secure and stable government to ensure the needed achievement, with education playing a significant role by creating competent and skilled human capital.

American technical and financial assistance has played an important role in Indonesia's development. The following comment captures this point:

> USAID as an education agency also has a worldwide education strategy. Part of that is higher education, increasing the capability of the workforce in all the

countries we work in, in order to meet the development needs of the country. So it's broken down into USAID's focus on helping to increase the relevance and quality of higher education. USAID in Indonesia has programmes on that which is/are different to the scholarship programmes. That's because part of our higher education programme is increasing access for underserved communities to higher education opportunities. (*American respondent working in a US governmental agency (Respondent 17)*)

Through USAID, the US support for increasing the quality of education comes not only through improving education infrastructure, but also through training for educators and increasing access to higher education opportunities for the wider communities.[51] The following respondent commented on the role of USAID:

Support from the government of America for higher education is only for giving technical assistance for the DIKTI (Directorate General of Higher Education) for increasing management capacity and leadership. We are aimed at helping and building the capacity of local education, increasing the quality of education, increasing the quality of education planning and management, and helping educators to improve their teaching skills.... In 2011 we helped DIKTI with technical support, and local financial management. (*Indonesian official working in a US governmental agency (Respondent 6)*)

Respondent 6 observed that the support from the US is limited to giving technical assistance, enhancing cooperation at the higher education level, improving the quality of education, aiding educators to enhance their teaching skills, and building the capacity of local education establishments.[52]

Through SERASI (relief and development) project, USAID provides grants to support activities that expand access to quality education services in remote areas.[53] USAID has also sponsored cluster-based in-service training, training in education performance assessment, training in the use of information and communication technology, partnerships for enhanced engagement in research (PEER), and programmes to extend scholarships and training to achieve sustainable impacts (PRESTASI). This outreach prompted Teuku Rezasyah, University of Padjajaran's international relations specialist, to state that under the Obama administration, the US is generous.[54] USAID has also encouraged several companies, such as ExxonMobil, Intel, Anchora, and ConocoPhillips, to develop PPPs. USAID, together with Chevron, has supported Indonesia by providing scholarships for youth for vocational education courses that are perceived by Indonesian authorities as offering what is needed for the economy.[55] Courses included are automotive engineering, electronics, building and construction, electrical wiring, welding, and computer applications.

Indonesia's efforts, since independence, to produce a highly skilled population, and the role of the World Bank and international agencies, show the relevance of Carnoy's argument, outlined in Chap. 2, that as former colonies become independent from the European colonial powers, they have to catch up with European levels of development, and this progress is contingent upon producing a highly skilled workforce, for which appropriate financing is essential. Etzioni argues most of the elements of economic development (expeditious transportation of resources and goods, effective knowledge, secure supplies of power, a highly educated population, a high level of innovative capacity, supportive legal and financial institutions, and the accumulation of capital and capital goods) need to be present.[56] The LDSs are still catching up with Western levels of development, and not all the elements of economic development are present. As such, the LDSs still require foreign involvement in the form of importing foreign education in order to gain depth of knowledge and to create a highly educated population.

The extent to which American financial assistance furthers Indonesia's development will depend on the extent to which the outcome of negotiations with the US benefits Indonesia. As noted earlier, Indonesian respondents were not coerced into accepting financial assistance from the US, but, rather, entered into agreements they found beneficial. According to these respondents, there were no political stipulations made or implied in return for the assistance. To most Indonesian respondents, as noted earlier, the relationship with the US in education was beneficial for Indonesia as seen in the win-win climate of the negotiations in which Indonesian negotiators made independent decisions in the negotiations.

Working together in the relationship was perceived by the Indonesian respondents as a feature of an equal relationship. Both Indonesia and the US worked together towards the MDGs and the goal of US–Indonesia Comprehensive Partnership, and they regarded both these goals as advantageous.[57]

> The ultimate aim of the partnership is to improve understanding between two countries, and to increase human resources capital for achieving Millennium Development Goals. (*Indonesian official dealing with financial management in a US governmental agency* (*Respondent 6*))

Respondent 6 clearly indicated that the Indonesia–US education relationship is not only for improving understanding between Indonesia and the US, but also for increasing human capital for realising MDGs. In September 2006, Indonesia signed the Millennium Declaration at the United Nations Millennium Summit in New York. Education is the cornerstone for achieving the goals.[58] UNESCO outlines the importance of education in equipping people with the knowledge and skills they need to increase income and expand employment skills, and thus realise the first goal, which is to eradicate extreme poverty and hunger.[59] Anwar has argued that educational exchanges and foreign educational assistance are necessary for development, as they enable people to use educational attainment to improve their economic status, thereby helping to address the problems of poverty, illiteracy, and low education attainment that have trapped millions in Asia in a vicious cycle of misery and despair.[60] Education, according to UNDP, also plays important roles in realising other goals, such as reducing child mortality; eradicating HIV, malaria, and other diseases; and ensuring environmental sustainability. For UNESCO, these goals will be achieved by equipping students with the proper knowledge and skills. USAID has assisted Indonesia in training educators, another element which is necessary for achieving the aforementioned goals. As the following respondent stated:

> We change the way the teachers teach, the students learn, and change the learning environment to an environment conducive for learning, promoting participation in learning, strengthening leadership, and we help them to plan to achieve the overall goals. (*Indonesian official dealing with financial management in a US governmental agency (Respondent 6)*)

USAID has strengthened teaching and learning processes, which, in turn, has contributed to improved student learning.[61] For the respondent, teaching educators, changing the learning environment to one that is conducive to learning, promoting participation in learning, and strengthening leadership, all help Indonesia to achieve MDGs.

Although American financial assistance has played a role in Indonesia's development and education, most Indonesian respondents did not make any comments on the importance of American financial assistance in Indonesia's development and education. Rather, most Indonesian respondents, as noted in Chap. 4, carefully asserted that Indonesia is not financially dependent on the US. What is more, as also noted earlier in this chapter, Indonesian respondents wanted the dignity of being treated as equals, despite the significant financial contributions the US has made to Indonesian education. The US response of working together with Indonesia certainly aided Indonesians' acceptance and willingness to cooperate with the US.

American financial assistance can be, and has been, an instrument for Indonesia's development, if both American and Indonesian parties work together towards their shared goals. When both parties work together, any assertion that the American parties might be exploiting the Indonesian parties becomes irrelevant. An equal relationship is characterised by goal sharing between the parties involved in the relationship. Both the US and Indonesia have worked together as equal partners despite the financial resources contributed by the US being much greater than those of Indonesia. Importantly, the US recognises and respects Indonesia's regulations, and this recognition can be taken as a sign of respect for Indonesia's equal position in the relationship. What is more, education is beyond politics, and thus there is no political attachment to the assistance. For these reasons, American financial assistance has the potential to be an instrument for the development of Indonesia and its education.

Concluding Remarks

This chapter has discussed the importance of equality of Indonesia's relationships with developed states, particularly with the US. Interest in the topic of equality arose from the respondents themselves, especially the Indonesian respondents. Being equal enables the parties to make decisions independently, and also to refuse what would not be in Indonesia's own best interests. The ability to choose to refuse or freely accept foreign involvement in education and to make decisions independently are defining features of educational sovereignty. Equality in the relationship is regarded by the Indonesian parties dealing with curricula as important because Indonesian culture is acknowledged and accepted in the relationship and in the curriculum design and development. In the Indonesia–US education relationship, this equality has proved important in the maintenance of Indonesia's sovereignty in education.

The extent to which Indonesia's educational sovereignty is undermined by American education providers can be evaluated based on the extent to which the government commits to an investment in public higher education and restricts transnational education to the mode that is beneficial for Indonesia. The government is able to commit to an investment in public higher education. The Indonesian government also has the capacity to regulate the modes of education delivery not only between state actors but also between non-state actors and between state and non-state actors. When the government is able to restrict transnational education modes by committing only to those modes that benefit Indonesia, the argument that foreign education providers weaken Indonesia's ability to regulate education within its borders is not supported. For these reasons, the provision of American education programmes in Indonesia does not necessarily undermine Indonesian educational sovereignty.

Indonesian parties are at liberty to enter into agreements they find beneficial. The actual ability or capacity to implement regulations that retain Indonesian control over the education sector is shown from the relationship that is based on mutually agreed objectives, and is shown from the willingness of Indonesian parties to accept agreements. The comments of Indonesian respondents show that they are able to negotiate before signing off on MoUs that will be beneficial for Indonesia, and they are not coerced into accepting any agreements. The need to challenge the arbitrary authority of power structures to determine the essence of individuals' educational experience is also indicated by some Indonesian respondents.

USAID has played an important role in Indonesia's education through its financial contribution. Based on the purpose of the US–Indonesia Comprehensive Partnership—which is a long-term commitment to elevate Indonesia–US bilateral relations—the US places conditions on the educational assistance it offers Indonesia. USAID also recognises the leadership role Indonesia plays in its own development, and that Indonesia has authority over its education. There is no evidence that American financial assistance in education represents a threat to the educational sovereignty of Indonesia. Both the US and Indonesia have worked together as equal partners, despite the financial resources contributed by the US being much greater than those of Indonesia. Importantly, the US recognises and respects Indonesia's regulations.

Indonesian respondents sought to be treated equally, and although the US made significant financial contributions to Indonesian education, the US worked with Indonesia in realising Indonesia's development goals. Working together in the relationship is indeed perceived by the Indonesian respondents as a feature of an equal relationship.

Given the evidence presented here that the US and Indonesia work together as equal partners despite the financial resources contributed by the US being much greater than those of Indonesia, American financial assistance in education does not threaten the educational sovereignty of Indonesia. However, because US financial assistance can be, and has been, an instrument for Indonesia's development, and because education is beyond politics, there is no political attachment to the assistance. For these reasons, it is confirmed by the findings of this research that American financial assistance is an instrument for the development of Indonesia and for its education.

Notes

1. Nicholas Capaldi, "The Meaning of Equality." *Liberty and Equality*, ed. Tibor Machan (Stanford, CA: Hoover Press, Stanford University, 2002).
2. As discussed in earlier chapters, one of the objectives of the education relationship between Indonesia and the US is to enhance understanding between these two states. As a government official, the respondent has endeavoured to achieve the objective of improving understanding between Indonesia and the US.
3. Different cultural norms is only one factor that renders unequal output in the relationship. See The Indonesian Institute, "Indonesian-American Cooperation," last modified August 6, 2013, http://www.theindonesianinstitute.com
4. Directorate General of Higher Education, *RENSTRA (Strategic Planning) 2010–2014*.
5. Also see Timo Kivimaki, "Strength of Weakness: American-Indonesian Hegemonic Bargaining," *Journal of Peace Research*, 30, (1993): 391–408.
6. Phuong-Mai Nguyen, Julian Elliot, Cees Terlouw, and Albert Pilot, "Neo-colonialism in Education: Cooperative Learning in an Asian Context," *Comparative Education*, 45, (2009): 109–130.
7. Angela Siqueira, "The Regulation of Education through the WTO/GATS," *Journal for Critical Education Policy Studies*, 3, (2005) 1–16; Anthony Verger and Xavier Bonal, "Against GATS: The Sense of a Global Struggle," *Journal for Critical Education Policy Studies*, 4, (2006) 1–27; Martin Carnoy, *Education as Cultural Imperialism* (New York: David McKay, 1975); Andre Gunder Frank, "The Development of Underdeveloped," *Imperialism and Underdevelopment*, ed. Robert Rhodes (New York: Monthly Review Press, 1970).
8. Madeleine Green, "GATS Update," *International Higher Education*, 37, (2004): 3–5.
9. OECD, "Glossary of Statistical Terms," http://www.stats.oecd.org/glossary

10. Faisal Baskoro, "State firms to buy bonds in case of capital reversal," *The Jakarta Globe,* http://www.thejakartaglobe.com. Also see Rangga Fadilah, "SOEs' Net Profits Expected to Reach US$ 12.6 Billion this Year," http://www.embassyofindonesia.org/news
11. L. P. Jones, (ed), *Public Enterprise in Less Developed Countries* (New York: Cambridge University Press, 1987); R. P. Short, "The Role of Public Enterprises: An International Statistical Comparison," in *Public Enterprise in Mixed Economies: Some Macro-economic Aspects,* eds. Robert Floyd, Clive Gray, and R. P. Short (Washington, DC: International Monetary Fund, 1984); Nicolas Van De Walle, "Privatization in Developing Countries: A Review of the Issues," *World Development,* 17, (1989): 601–615.
12. See *Jakarta Globe,* "Education privatization bill encounters expert opposition." http://www.thejakartaglobe.com. It is important to note, however, although foreign investors such as ExxonMobil, Chevron, Intel, and Coca-Cola have contributed financially to education in Indonesia, they are not education institutions. Therefore, their activity in education is not competing with Indonesian post-secondary education institutions.
13. Centre for Middle Class Consumer Studies, "The Role of Middle Class in Indonesia and Its Differences from Those of Other Countries," http://consumer3000.net. Also see http://www.indonesia-digest.net/2420usrelations
14. Presidential Regulation 77/2007. See http://www.dephut.go.id/files/perpres-77
15. Peter Frase and Brendan O'Sullivan, "The Future of Education under the WTO," last modified December 2009, http://www.campusdemocracy.org
16. Corporatisation refers to the creation of an enterprise in place of an administered government department. See Simon Marginson *Markets in Education* (St. Leonards, NSW, Australia: Allen and Unwin, 1997).
17. The World Bank, "Investing in Indonesia's Education: Allocation, Equity, and Efficiency of Public Expenditures," http://www.sitesources.worldbank.org/INTINDONESIA/Resources/publication/280016-152,870,963,030/invest.Educationindo.pdf
18. Teguh Wicaksono, and Deni Friawan. "Recent Development in Higher Education in Indonesia: Issues and Challenges," *Financing Higher Education and Economic Development in East Asia,* eds. Shiro Armstrong and Bruce Chapman. Canberra: ANU E Press, 2011.
19. See Law of the Republic of Indonesia on Local Government, http://datahukum.pnri.go.id
20. Saiful Rizal, "7 state universities support autonomy," SH News, April 20, 2013.

21. Financial autonomy has been interpreted in various ways. For educators, financial autonomy can mean increased income because universities are free to make independent decisions with regard to salaries and tuition fees. For students, financial autonomy can mean the ability to reject increased tuition fees and choose between universities. For the Indonesian Ministry of Finance, financial autonomy means that the ministry is no longer responsible for financing Indonesian post-secondary education.
22. See USAID, "Education—USAID/Indonesia," http://www.indonesia.usaid.gov/en/programs/education; ExxonMobil, "ExxonMobil in Indonesia," http://www.exxonmobil.co.id
23. See "Indonesian Law of the National Education System," http://www.inherent-dikti.net. Also see Sofian Effendi, "Quality and Transparency: Indonesia's Approach to Cross-border Higher Education," http://www.sofian.staff.ugmac.id
24. USAID, "Fact Sheet: Higher Education Partnership with Indonesia," http://www.indonesia.usaid.gov; USAID, "Comprehensive Partnership," http://www.indonesia.usaid.gov; http://www.jakarta.usembassy.gov; US Department of State, "United States-Indonesia Education Cooperation," Bureau of Educational and Cultural Affairs, http://www.exchanges.state.gov; The White House, "Fact Sheet: Higher Education Partnership with Indonesia," http://www.whitehouse.gov/sites/default/files/usindonesia_higher_education
25. The Bureau of International Information Programs, "U.S.–Indonesia Joint Declaration on Comprehensive Partnership," http://www.america.gov. Sharing a vision of increasing cooperation and ties that are critical to the bilateral relationship for addressing key regional and global challenges signifies that the relationship is unavoidably related to political interests of both Indonesia and the US.
26. According to OECD, corporate responsibility is "the action taken by businesses to nurture and enhance mutual symbiotic relationships". See OECD, "Corporate Responsibility: Frequently Asked Questions," "Directorate for Financial and Enterprise Affairs," http://www.oecd.org/document
27. Rita Abrahamsen, "The Power of Partnerships in Global Governance," *Third World Quarterly*, 25, (2004): 1453–1467.
28. The US committed to invest $165 million over five years in the education programmes with Indonesia, through educational exchanges from 2010, which has assisted Indonesia in the improvement of Indonesian education quality and infrastructure. See Cameron Hume, "Number of Indonesian students in US doubled," *Jakarta Post*, Friday November 13, 2009; The US made a commitment to grant Indonesia $301 million for education, and environment and climate change development. See *Jakarta Post*, "US puts up $301 million for partnership with RI," http://thejakartapost.com; US

Embassy in Indonesia, "Ambassador Marciel's visit to eastern Indonesia," http://www.jakarta.usembassy.gov; USAID, "Fact Sheet: Higher Education Partnership with Indonesia," http://www.indonesia.usaid.gov
29. Donald Hindley, "Foreign Aid to Indonesia and Its Political Implications," *Pacific Affairs*, 36, (1963): 107–119.
30. See Timo Kivimaki (1993).
31. Ibid.
32. Ibid.
33. See Timo Kivimaki, "US-Indonesian Negotiations over the Conditions of Aid, 1951–1954, in *Power and Negotiation*, ed. I.W. Zartman (Ann Arbor, MI: The University of Michigan Press, 2002).
34. See The World Bank, "Internal Debt Statistics 2013," last modified March 28, 2013, http://www.data.worldbank.org/sites/default/files. Also see Anti Debt Coalition, http://www.kau.or.id
35. See KAU (Anti Debt Coalition), http://www.kau.or.id
36. USAID Indonesia, "Indonesia–Democracy and Governance Assessment," http://www.indonesia.usaid.gov
37. In Lena Kay, "Indonesian Public Perceptions of the US and their Implications for US Foreign Policy," *Issues and Insight*, 5, (2005): 3.
38. USAID and Chevron contributed US$12.3 million for these projects. See USAID Indonesia, "The Aceh Polytechnic Program-TAPP," http://www.indonesia.usaid.gov/en/usaid/activity
39. US Department of State, "United States-Indonesia Comprehensive Partnership," http://www.state.gov
40. USAID Indonesia, "Education—Preparing Indonesian students for learning, work, and community," http://www.indonesia.usaid.gov/en/programs/education
41. UNESCAP, "Country Report on Local Government Systems: Indonesia," http://www.unescap.org
42. See http://www.indonesia.usaid.gov
43. Mochtar Buchori and Abdul Malik, "The Evolution of Higher Education in Indonesia," *Asian Universities: Historical Perspectives and Contemporary Challenges*, eds. Phillip Albatch and Toru Umakoshi (Baltimore, MD: The John Hopkins University Press, 2004): 249–277.
44. Amitai Etzioni, "A Self-restrained Approach to Nation-building by Foreign Powers," *International Affairs*, 80, (2004): 1–17.
45. Hindley (1963): 107–119.
46. USAID, "History," http://www.usaid.govt/Indonesia/history
47. Ibid.
48. The World Bank, "Higher Education for Relevance and Efficiency," http://www.web.worldbank.org

49. Yashui Shin, "The Role of US-trained Economists in Economic Liberalization: The Cases of Chile and Indonesia," *Globalization and Transformation of Governance*, (2003): 71–94.
50. In *Kompas*, "Education as the Key to Development," August 27, 2012.
51. USAID, http://www.usaid.govt/Indonesia
52. Also see USAID Indonesia, http://Indonesia.usaid.gov
53. USAID, "About SERASI," last modified May 20, 2013, http://www.serasi-ird.org/index.php
54. In *Jakarta Post*, "US puts up $300 m for 'partnership' with RI," http://www.thejakarta.com/news/2010
55. http://www.usinfo.state.gov
56. Ibid., 27.
57. See USAID, "SERASI-Education," http://www.indonesia.usaid.gov/en
58. UNDP, "Millennium Development Goals," http://www.undp.or.id
59. See UNESCO website for further goals. UNESCO, "Millennium Development Programmes," http://www.unesco.org/new/en/education
60. See Chap. 2. Dewi Fortuna Anwar, "Human Security: An Intractable Problem in Asia," *Asian Security Order: Instrumental and Normative Features*, ed. Muthiah Alagappa (Stanford, CA: Stanford University Press, 2003).
61. Nisha Biswal, "New Teaching Methods and Resources Transform Indonesian Schools," *USAID*, http://blog.usaid.gov/2011

CHAPTER 6

Indonesian Identity and Cultural Values

INDONESIA'S IDENTITY AND CULTURAL VALUES

Indonesian culture has been formed by long interactions between the original indigenous culture (including tribal groups) and various foreign influences such as those from the Middle East, South Asia, and East Asia. These foreign cultures were strongly influenced by religions. The arrival of Buddhism in Indonesia began with the trading activity between Indonesia and India. The combination of Buddhism and original indigenous Indonesian beliefs can be found in *Bodha* belief among the *Sasak* ethnic group. The influence of Buddhism and Hinduism can also be found in Javanese literature and arts.

The arrival of Hinduism also happened because of the trading activity between Indonesia and India. In addition to being found in Javanese literature and culture, the influence of Hinduism is also seen in Balinese dances. Hinduism was combined with Animism, Buddhism, and Islam. The combination of Hinduism and Animism can be found in *Kaharingan* belief among the *Dayak* ethnic group.

Islam, however, has been the dominant religion in Indonesia for more than four centuries. One distinctive influence of Islam has been the adaptation of *musyawarah* (deliberation) and *mufakat* (consensus). Indonesian former foreign minister, Subiandro, stated that *mufakat* means searching

© The Author(s) 2017
A. Abbott, *Educational Sovereignty and Transnational Exchanges in Post-Secondary Indonesian Education*, DOI 10.1007/978-3-319-53985-0_6

for "amalgamation of the most acceptable views of each and every member, in which all parties have power over each other."[1] *Musyawarah* means,

> a leader should not act arbitrarily or impose his own will, but rather make gentle suggestions of the path a community should follow, being careful always to consult all other participants fully and to take their views and feelings before delivering his synthesis conclusion.[2]

In the negotiation process, *musyawarah* and *mufakat* take place, "not as between opponents but as between friends and brothers."[3] Cooperation is characterised by the conception and exercise of consensus. The terms *musyawarah* and *mufakat* are clearly stated in Pancasila: "people led or governed by wise policies arrived at through a process of consultation and consensus." Hinduism and Islam were syncretised and can be found in unorthodox Islamic belief, or the *Abangan*, among the Javanese ethnic groups.

The arrival of the first Europeans, the Portuguese, in the Indonesian archipelago marked the arrival of Christianity. Substantial Christian populations live in Indonesia, such as in North Sumatra, West Kalimantan, North Sulawesi, Tanah Toraja, Maluku, and West Papua. The influence of the Portuguese, nevertheless, was subsequently displaced following the arrival of the Dutch. The West (including the US) has strongly influenced Indonesian political systems, legal systems, science, and technology.

In summary, multiple foreign influences have helped to form Indonesian culture, particularly foreign cultures that were strongly influenced by religion. The process of these incoming religions interacting with indigenous values eventually developed a hybridised culture in which indigenous values survive. This hybrid form of culture is evident in Indonesian education practices.

The Influence of Cultural Values on Indonesian Education

Culture constitutes shared patterns of learned behaviours and interactions, to which individuals are exposed and bound by virtue of living within the culture. Putera and Brill have identified strong traditionalism, a deep sense of collectivism, hierarchy, communalism, and syncretistic attitudes as the basic features of Indonesian culture since the earliest period of Indonesian history.[4] Hinduism strengthened collectivist tendencies, in which "the basic unit of survival is a group."[5] In a collectivist culture, people tend to think of themselves as *we*—not only of their immediate family but also of their extended family.[6] When Indonesians study overseas, it is not surprising that adjusting to life in Western society is not easy for them. As this respondent said:

> Sometimes Indonesian exchange students get frustrated and one lecturer attempted suicide. She was sad because she was so lonely. (*Former Indonesian rector who negotiated MoUs (Respondent 7)*)

This comment illustrates how support from others is very important, particularly in offering a safeguard against life's stresses.[7] The respondent reflects on the consequences of loneliness when living abroad. Similarly, Giles and Goodwin, in their study, argue that in a collectivist society, the basic unit of survival is the group, and thus support from others is very important in this society.[8]

As noted in the earlier text, one distinctive influence of Islam has been the incorporation of *musyawarah* (deliberation) and *mufakat* (consensus) that are enshrined in Pancasila. In the educational setting, *musyawarah* and *mufakat* are taught in civic education. Indigenous cultural values are also evident in Indonesian education. The Javanese make up the largest ethnic group in Indonesian society, approximately 45% of the population, and many cultural aspects originating from the Javanese are typically found in education. The Javanese, for instance, hold to the principle of avoiding conflict. *Rukun* is a Javanese term meaning to avoid conflict through a willingness to compromise in order to achieve harmony in all relationships, including relationships among students and teachers. For the Javanese, to achieve harmony, one should have *ewuh pekewuh*, or uneasiness for controversy and conflict. *Ewuh pekewuh* discourages students from discussing any sensitive issues openly. The Javanese also have a principle of obedience or *manut lan miturut*. In the education setting, the principle of obedience is shown by refraining from direct eye contact when speaking with a teacher. Students should keep their heads down with their chin low to show obedience and respect.[9] The teacher is seen to be a moral authority, and students expect a teacher to know everything,[10] which discourages students from being independent learners and critical thinkers.

In summary, the Indonesian education system is culturally bound and has given guidance as to how people should live and act. Indonesia's collectivist culture originates from the influence of Hinduism (carrying out an obligation and duty through *gotong royong*), Islam (the tradition of *musyawarah* and *mufakat*), and the indigenous people groups (family and group oriented for individual security, dependence on teachers' knowledge, and avoiding conflict for achieving harmony). In Indonesian education, there are obligations as students and educators, duties (through *gotong royong*), tradition (*musyawarah and mufakat*), dependence on teachers' knowledge, avoiding conflict for achieving harmony, and obedience to authorities, such as educators.[11]

Where Indonesia interacts with foreign education, the question arises as to whether Indonesia's culturally bound education can be preserved. This question is addressed in the following section.

TRANSNATIONAL EDUCATION AND HOMOGENISATION PROCESSES

In seeking to answer the question of whether Indonesia retains control over its education curriculum, it is necessary to identify the control Indonesia has within each mode of transnational education. With regard to cross-border supply (mode 1) delivery, the movement of education programmes and materials takes only the forms of (a) programme articulation, (b) twinning, and (c) double degree (the double-degree programme is still in the process of negotiation). Programme articulations are inter-institutional arrangements between Indonesian and foreign education providers who agree to define jointly a study programme in terms of study credits and credit transfers. Twinning occurs when a foreign education provider collaborates with a provider in Indonesia to develop an articulated system that allows students to take course credits in one or both of the states. The arrangements for twinning programmes and awarding degrees usually comply with national regulations of the foreign education provider. In twinning, curricula are provided by foreign providers and are delivered by local institutions. Any programmes within Indonesia's territory are required to comply with Indonesian regulations. Because the twinning arrangements comply with American regulations, in the Indonesia–US education relationship, mode 1 is no longer limited to the provision of education services not requiring the physical movement of students. Double or joint degrees involve collaboration between the US and Indonesia to offer programmes for which students receive a qualification from each provider or a joint award from the collaborating partner. These arrangements usually comply with national regulations in both states. As the arrangements involve synchronising two different regulations, the double-degree programme, although desired by the Indonesians, is still in the process of negotiation (see Chap. 5).

In the consumption abroad mode (mode 2), such as Indonesian students studying overseas, the Indonesian government also does not have control because Indonesian students have to follow foreign education system.

In the commercial presence (mode 3) mode of delivery, the Indonesian government retains control over education as the presence of foreign education providers is restricted and closely regulated. Article 90 of the higher education law sets conditions for the presence of foreign education institutions in Indonesia: they have to be non-profit, or partner with Indonesian education institutions, and they must also be approved by the Ministry of Education.[12] This regulation has already had an impact on Indonesia's educational relationship with other institutions; for example, although expected to do so, Monash University could not establish a branch institution in Indonesia, and it established its branch in Malaysia instead.[13] However, through Australia's Asian Century White Paper, bilateral cooperation with Indonesia is expected to strengthen, and thus Monash University should be able to re-establish its branches in Indonesia.[14]

There have been controversies surrounding the presence of foreign education institutions in Indonesia. On the one hand, for those who oppose their presence, such as the Indonesian Deans' Forum, education is not a tradable product or commodity but has the moral value of maintaining and developing Indonesia's civilisation and culture.[15] Andreas Tambah, secretary-general of the National Commission for Education, argues that "foreign institutions will have more value than national universities. Students will choose foreign universities, and the national universities will be crushed."[16] On the other hand, for proponents, every government and private sector, including education, is impacted by globalisation.[17] According to Riady, it is important to build a "critical mass of citizens who understand the complexity of the world and can serve as bridges to other cultures and communities. ... A solid group of foreign educated citizens is essential to achieving this role."[18]

The Indonesian Deans' Forum, despite its rejection of the commercial presence of foreign education institutions in Indonesia, does not deny the important role of foreign education in improving the quality of education for Indonesian students.[19] There are a few good quality Indonesian higher education institutions such as the elite state universities and several private universities that operate in big cities. It has been reported in the *Jakarta Post* that only 60% of lecturers in bigger universities, institutes, and academies have master's degrees or higher, while the number of lecturers with master's degrees reaches only 40% in some other universities.[20]

It is necessary to note, however, that there is some inconsistency between Indonesian education laws regulating foreign education presence and the practice. Profit-making universities such as Limkokwing University for Creative Technology (Chinese education provider) and Gandhi Institute of Business and Technology (Indian education provider), for instance, have been operating in Indonesia, and Indonesia will open its borders to foreign universities from across ASEAN in the next few years.[21] In July 2013, Indonesia's Parliament endorsed a higher education bill allowing the entry of foreign universities.[22] According to Agus Hermanto, the Chairman of the House Commission, allowing foreign universities in Indonesia will encourage Indonesia's most brilliant students, who would otherwise prefer to study overseas, to stay in Indonesia.[23] Indonesia's tight regulations on entrance to Indonesian public universities, and the special entrance that is required by these universities, are also viewed as a valid reason for allowing foreign education institutions into Indonesia.[24] Mohammad Nuh, the Minister of Education and Culture, has made clear that foreign universities operating in Indonesia would operate under the government's control: they must be non-profit making, and must uphold the Constitution, Pancasila, and Indonesian religious values.[25]

As with modes 1 and 3, the Indonesian government retains sufficient control over the presence of natural persons (mode 4) mode of delivery. Mode 4 is subject to Indonesian labour and immigration laws and regulations; only directors, managers, and technical experts/advisors, unless mentioned otherwise, are allowed to stay for two years, which may be extended for a maximum of two times, subject to a two years' extension each time. Managers and technical experts (intra-corporate transfer) are allowed based on an economic needs test. The entry and temporary stay of business visitors is permitted for a period of 60 days and may be extended for a maximum of 120 days (see Chap. 3).

INDONESIA–US RELATIONS AND HOMOGENISATION PROCESS

As discussed in Chap. 2, the terms Westernisation, Americanisation, and homogenisation feature prominently in discussions surrounding transnational education. Tomlinson has used homogenisation and Westernisation synonymously.[26] Rizvi and Lingard have used the term Americanisation synonymously with homogenisation.[27] This book, as mentioned in Chap. 2, uses the terms homogenisation, Americanisation, and Westernisation interchangeably.

Since independence, Indonesia has adopted some aspects of American higher education, such as the credit hour system. After independence, the Dutch model of higher education was replaced by the Anglo-American higher education structure, because the former was regarded by the government as unsuitable—unstructured, resulting in low productivity, and lengthy periods of study.[28] In the 1950s, Indonesia built a relationship in education with the US. Through USAID and the Ford Foundation, university to university cooperation was initiated. In 1953, there was a shortage of textbooks for teacher training due to the lack of expertise of Indonesians in writing them.[29] USAID responded to this need by supplying textbooks and teaching aids for teacher training. An important corollary of the role of USAID and the Ford Foundation in facilitating university to university cooperation, and in supplying Indonesia with teaching aids and materials, was the influence of American scholarly literature in Indonesian higher education, and the adoption of the American credit hour system. In 1955, only six years after independence, the government of Indonesia started to adopt the American credit hour system. By 1974, the American credit hour system was fully institutionalised and, since 1989, all universities in Indonesia have used it. Nonetheless, restrictions in student subject choices and government regulations, which do not allow credit transfer among institutions and faculties, have weakened the effectiveness of the adoption of the credit hour system and other aspects of the American tertiary education system in Indonesia. For Regel, the adoption of foreign education in LDSs can be effective, if their higher education systems share similar organisational goals, such as high amounts of flexibility, curricula choice, and interfaculty and inter-institutional transfer.[30]

Some Indonesian respondents acknowledge that American academic patterns are sometimes imitated and modelled. Examples of such comments follow:

> It [American education system] is very clear, and very systematic. It is easy to follow. Perhaps Indonesian education is following American education, but it is very clear. They [Americans] have the credit system, which is the same as our credit system. Or we have the same credit system as they do. They have four years of study, which we can understand because we have the four years of study scheme over here. (*Indonesian dean of an Indonesian private education institution (Respondent 14)*)

I think American education is straightforward in terms of the structure, unlike education in Asia. (*Indonesian government official* (*Respondent 5*))

The system of American education is held in great esteem by most Indonesian respondents. At the post-secondary education level, clarity and systemisation are perceived as the benefits of the American academic model. For Respondent 5, the organisation of the teaching process and the American ways of structuring the organisation and delivery of higher education have much to offer Indonesia.

The following experience of one American respondent illustrates that Indonesian negotiators willingly adopt American academic patterns:

The administrators I met from the universities in Indonesia wanted to have more contact with American universities so they could learn how to structure their universities, how to set up research programmes, how to develop different kinds of degrees particularly in business and engineering. There was a lot of interest in learning how to have a programme accredited so it is officially acceptable in the world. So all of these things are what the United States can bring to Indonesia. (*Vice president for research and strategic partnership* (*Respondent 15*))

Respondent 15 indicated the willingness and interest of Indonesian university administrators in adapting the American ways of structuring education organisation. This raises the question: Does adopting these organisational approaches play a significant role in homogenisation processes? Although the organisation of teaching processes and the American ways of structuring the organisation and delivery of higher education are regarded as having improved Indonesia's capacity to deliver post-secondary education level courses, all international students in Indonesia are also required to learn *Bahasa* Indonesia as it is the language of instruction.[31] Throughout the sponsored education programmes of USAID, *Bahasa* Indonesia is used as the language of instruction. Whether this factor is sufficient to avoid homogenisation, remains open to question.

Siqueira, Verger, Bonal, and Pennycook have articulated their concerns about the possible threat to indigenous cultural values from the WTO GATS. The crux of their argument is that GATS regulations, which address Most Favoured Nations and National Treatment, forbid different treatment for national and foreign education providers, without regard to whether the foreign education providers develop courses that include the local language and cultural values.[32] In addition, many previously colonised state governments are still struggling to develop educational curricula suited to their cultures and histories, and thus transnationalism in education is seen as facilitating the demise of indigenous cultures.

The English language is nonetheless introduced in the Indonesian education curriculum. Folk tales and local stories are included in the teaching of English, as they are regarded as necessary both to preserve Indonesian cultural values and to prepare individuals for playing active roles in global competition.[33] English is also used as the language of instruction in professional development workshops involving foreign experts. The following respondent commented:

> Language is the barrier for the dual degree programme. We have English language programmes on our agenda but they have not developed. For dual degree programmes, when we want to send our students through USINTEC, they need to have English language skills and that's our weakness. The workshops are excellent; very practical, not only theoretical. Unfortunately, language is the barrier. Everything is interpreted. (*Indonesian chair of international cooperation* (*Respondent 18*))

The respondent clearly valued education collaboration with the US, and the comment illustrates that English language instruction is desirable in some circumstances, such as for professional development. The need for English, however, had been an impediment to such collaboration, particularly the dual-degree programmes that require students to have fluency in both *Bahasa* Indonesia and English. Although the government has emphasised the need to learn English in order to be able to get access to international communication networks,[34] the government of Indonesia has also developed a language-training centre, with a focus on training Indonesian educators and researchers in English. The government of America simultaneously established the largest English Language Fellow Program in Indonesia, which certainly helped to increase the number of Indonesians learning English.[35]

It is important to acknowledge, however, that Indonesian negotiators and those involved in the education exchange are cognisant of the loss of cultural values and identity. Foreign (particularly Western) influence through education is viewed by some respondents as a threat to Indonesian cultural values. The following respondent, in particular, commented that Indonesian cultural values have changed:

We are now too open and vulgar. These are not Indonesian cultural values but foreign values. Indonesians now are becoming self-centred, too open and vulgar. A long time ago we would not make any vulgar comments. (*Indonesian vice rector negotiating and administering MoUs (Respondent 2)*)

Like other Indonesian respondents, Respondent 2 is aware of the impact of foreign influences on Indonesian cultural values. One of the interesting points to emerge from the interview is the assuredness and confidence of Indonesians being able to preserve cultural values through education (see below). The efforts of the governments of developed states to increase the numbers of their students learning Indonesian language and culture, and their desire to grow in their understanding of Indonesian culture, all support the view that Indonesian culture is respected and pursued.

In summary, Indonesia has been willing to adopt American education, and the US has fulfilled a substantial number of the education needs of Indonesia. Immediately after Indonesia's independence, USAID responded to Indonesia's education need by supplying textbooks and teaching aids for teacher training. The US has also established the largest English Language Fellow Program in Indonesia, which addresses the needs of Indonesia by increasing the capacity of Indonesians to learn English. Accordingly, there would be some influence on Indonesian education, such as the influence of American scholarly literature in Indonesian higher education, and the establishment of Indonesia's system of higher education, based on some aspects of the US system. Yet, to argue that an education relationship with the US equates to the homogenisation of the curriculum in Indonesia (based on the aforementioned influences) is challenged in the Indonesian context. There is ample evidence to suggest that Indonesia retains control over its education curriculum and is not subject to homogenisation, as discussed next.

After years of colonialism, Indonesia gained its independence from the Netherlands in 1945, and a new constitution was implemented. The unification of a culturally diverse nation was crucial, and the Indonesian national language was considered essential in the unification process. The unification of cultural diversity, however, was not easy, as many Indonesians were illiterate in the Indonesian national language, *Bahasa* Indonesia. By 1980, however, 61.4% were literate,[36] and, according to the 1990 census, over 80% of Indonesians above the age of five were literate in the Indonesian national language.[37]

Despite its active participation in transnational education, Indonesia maintains Pancasila, the Constitution 1945 (UUD 1945), and religion as the foundation of its education and to prevent the loss of Indonesian identity and cultural values. Even though the Indonesian National Education Law of 2003 authorises transnational education within Indonesian territory, foreign education institutions must follow the Indonesian curriculum in Indonesia and not interfere with Indonesian national education because it is under the authority of the Directorate General of Higher Education. Despite the flow of education across borders, *Bahasa* Indonesia is the language of instruction, and religion is compulsory in the Indonesian education curriculum.[38] The following respondents also confirmed that religion is a compulsory subject.

> They [foreign students] need to follow our curriculum if they are in Indonesia, especially religion. Religion is the main and compulsory subject in our curriculum. (*Indonesian government official (Respondent 8)*)

> Religion is compulsory, yes. But we call it religious study. It is not religion as religion. (*An Indonesian dean dealing with MoUs, (Respondent 14)*)

Both comments show that religion is a compulsory subject in the Indonesian education curriculum. There are five official religions in Indonesia: Islam, Christianity, Catholicism, Hinduism, and Buddhism.[39] Students are required to study these religions. Religion is emphasised in the curriculum because, as noted earlier in this chapter, it is part of Indonesian cultural identity. In this context, the inclusion of religion as a compulsory subject is a way of maintaining control over the curriculum to sustain Indonesian culture.

Cooperation is conditioned by culturally informed perception. Indonesian culture has been formed by long interactions between the original indigenous culture and various foreign elements that were strongly influenced by religion. Individuals are exposed and bound by religions within the culture. Religion is part of Indonesian cultural identity. When the mode of transnational education involves Indonesia's territory, such as mode 3 (commercial presence) and mode 4 (the presence of natural persons), any collaboration and education transaction, therefore, includes religion as a compulsory subject.[40] The following respondent also stated:

students know Pancasila but if they have no religion, that is ridiculous. That's not competent. With the changes of curriculum, the subjects of national curriculum are religion, Pancasila, *bahasa* Indonesia, citizenship, math, statistics, and logical thinking. The subjects are [now] more comprehensive and competitive. (*Indonesian government official dealing with dealing with curriculum (Respondent 1)*)

The comment indicates that in addition to religion, Pancasila, citizenship, and Indonesian national language (*Bahasa* Indonesia) are also compulsory subjects. Religion, in particular, according to Indonesia's Chief of the Ministry of Religious Affairs in Riau province, Fairuz, plays an important role in sustaining a strong sense of national culture.[41] To be competitive at the international level, mathematics, statistics, and logical thinking are now also compulsory subjects, and there is a wider range of subjects than during the Suharto era. Pancasila and moral education are now separate subjects as are Pancasila and citizenship.

To argue that the transfer of American values, such as liberal democracy, leads to homogenisation of education is unsound, because the Indonesian government retains sufficient control over its national education within its territory to avoid such an outcome. Chapter 2 discussed how Siqueira, and Verger and Bonal were concerned with the GATS facilitating the process of the homogenisation of education, and contended there was the potential for a loss of local cultures.[42] They argued that the GATS' regulations regarding the Most Favoured Nation and National Treatment meant that there should not be differential treatment for national and foreign education providers, irrespective of whether or not foreign education providers develop courses that include local language and cultural values.[43] Tikly too has argued that in many previously colonised states, the governments are still struggling to develop education curricula suited to their cultures and histories.[44] In the case of the Indonesia–US education relationship, however, although English language is a complementary feature, the responses obtained in this research illustrate Indonesia's determination to regulate and control its education, as seen in its ability to regulate the inclusion of Indonesian language as the language of instruction, and to include Indonesian cultural values in the education curriculum. There are advantages to Indonesian education promoting both English and *Bahasa* Indonesia: learning English is essential if the students are to study in the US, and including *Bahasa* Indonesia as the language of instruction is essential in order to preserve cultural values and national identity.

As outlined in Chap. 2, the LDSs do not have control over the prevention of homogenisation. In the context of the Indonesia–US education relationship, Indonesia has the ability to preserve its cultural integrity and formulate regulatory policies inside its territory. Language and religion are compulsory in the education curriculum, and foreign students are required to learn and understand the Indonesian language. Although English is introduced in the curriculum as a way to prepare individuals for active roles in global competition, local stories are also included in the teaching of English language, as they are regarded as necessary in order to preserve Indonesian cultural values. There is insufficient evidence from the interviews with both Indonesian and American respondents to support the statement that the US deliberately transfers American values through the Indonesia–US education relationship. The adoption of American literature and an American credit hour system does not equate to the homogenisation of the curriculum because Indonesia retains sufficient control over its education curriculum through mode 3 and mode 4, as these modes take place in Indonesian territory. Additionally, Indonesian cultural values and identity are maintained in education curricula by making *Bahasa* Indonesia, religion, and Pancasila compulsory subjects. As education transactions are influenced by the values, ideas, customs, and traditions of Indonesia's education partners, whether Indonesia will be able to preserve its cultural autonomy through education, or instead share and combine those values, ideas, customs, and traditions, is discussed in the following section.

HYBRIDISATION OF CULTURE AND EDUCATION

The connection between transnationalism and hybridisation has been explained by Pieterse, who argues that transnationalism is one of the driving forces behind hybridisation.[45] Transnational transactions are characterised by the processes involving sharing values, customs, and traditions, through education as well as the forms of educational delivery, resulting in hybridisation or the combination of foreign and local cultural values in regard to education.

Drawing on the history of Indonesian culture that has been formed by long interactions between the original indigenous culture and various foreign cultural and religious influences, it could be argued that Indonesia has experienced forms of cultural hybridisation and the hybridisation of its education since before its independence. The arrival of Hinduism, Islam, and Buddhism has indeed shaped contemporary Indonesian culture. Islam became dominant, and since then Islamic values and cultural traits have been carried over into the Indonesian cultural context. The adoption of Hinduism, Islam, and Buddhism in Indonesian dances and arts is widespread. The original indigenous cultures are still preserved through the combination of animism and dynamism with Hinduism, Islam, and Buddhism. The hybridisation of religious values—Hinduism, Islam, and Buddhism—and indigenous values has been maintained in Indonesia by handing down local wisdom and values through local stories or folktales from generation to generation, particularly through formal education. Similarly, sets of religious values are also handed down from generation to generation, and through formal education.

Under its former coloniser (the Dutch), Western culture had an influence on both Indonesian education and culture. Between 1950 and 1952, one of the biggest Indonesian universities, the University of Indonesia, adopted the Dutch curriculum, textbooks, and Dutch language as the language of instruction.[46] Some aspects of Dutch culture were adopted, including Dutch cuisine: pinch cake *poffertjes* (pinch cake), *rijsttafel* (rice table), *bistik* (steak), and *kroket* (croquette). Many Dutch words have been assimilated into the Indonesian language. Nonetheless, Dutch is no longer used as an official language of government, ever since the Japanese prohibition during World War II. When the occupation of the Japanese was over, neither Dutch nor Japanese was taught as foreign languages. Indonesia introduced American English at elementary school in 1967.

After independence, the Indonesian government grappled to construct an autochthonous curriculum, drawn from its culture and history. Both Sukarno and Suharto successfully formulated an education curriculum based on Pancasila emphasising the importance of unifying Indonesia's diverse cultures. In the mid-1960s, several universities in Indonesia offered courses, in order to educate and train diplomats, in which American textbooks were extensively used.[47] Yet, while Indonesian national identity has been preserved through the education curriculum, American education and literature have influenced the Indonesian education curriculum at the postsecondary level.

Although Indonesia has adopted cultural ideas and practices from nations around the world, American culture has become the predominant foreign influence. The following comment illustrates the extent to which the creation of hybrid education programmes may be seen as having diminished Indonesia's educational sovereignty:

HYBRIDISATION OF CULTURE AND EDUCATION   149

We also need a change of culture. They [Americans] are disciplined and are on time. For Indonesians the slogan *alon-alon asal kelakon* (slow but sure) is not always relevant in modern times. That kind of cultural value can lead us to live in modern times. (*Indonesian vice rector negotiating and administering MoUs (Respondent 2)*)

The respondent clearly illustrates the willingness to adopt some aspects of American cultural values. Such values include what the respondent terms as "discipline" and "on time." Reconciliation of culture that is required in modern life is indicated by the respondent. As shown in previous chapters, most Indonesian respondents also claimed a willingness to adopt and reconcile cultures. Respondent 2 further stated:

In the cultural aspect, this is only my impression, we are not self-centred. We are not like we used to be. I guess that is because of foreign influence whether as a result of the penetration of popular culture or through education partnership. (*Indonesian vice rector negotiating and administering MoUs (Respondent 2)*)

Although the respondent indicated his preference for adopting some aspects of American culture, he was fearful of the implications of the strong degree of extranational influences (including American influence) through education transactions, as such an influence could potentially lead to the loss of highly valued and important Indonesian values and practices like social interdependence.

As foreign influence is viewed as a threat to Indonesian cultural values, it is to be expected that the Indonesian respondents would make clear about their determination to retain their own cultural values. The following comment illustrates this position:

We want internationalisation to enhance our identity, to make us stronger. We try to accept the good things but refuse the worst from outside. (*Indonesian director of the international office of a university in Indonesia (Respondent 10)*)

The respondent is clear that Indonesian parties should accept foreign involvement in education to the extent that Indonesia benefits but refuse foreign involvement that is not in the interests of Indonesia. Although the education relationship with the US is valued by Indonesian negotiators and government officials, the maintenance of cultural values remains a matter of some concern for Indonesian negotiators. Evidence underlying this assertion is clearly shown both in the government regulations on character-based curriculum, and by the statements of some Indonesian respondents. Some Indonesian respondents included statements such as "We have our own identity" (Indonesian government official dealing with curriculum (Respondent 1)); "We have our identity and that identity must not disappear" (Indonesian vice rector negotiating and administering MoUs (Respondent 2)); "We have regulated so that we will not imitate their values" (Indonesian government official (Respondent 8)); "Whatever the activities, they should not be in conflict with the values of Indonesian people" (Indonesian director of the international office of a university in Indonesia (Respondent 10)). Education transactions with the US, as indicated by most Indonesian respondents, are necessary for enhancing the quality and reputation of Indonesian higher education without losing national identity and cultural values. Booth clearly states, "Identity patterns are becoming more complex as people assert local loyalties but want to share in global values and lifestyles."[48] From these comments, not only do Indonesian respondents indicate the willingness to adapt to American culture and to reconcile both cultures, but they also clearly asserted that Indonesia had a self-identity that signified the sense of *who we are*. It is important to note, however, that for most Indonesian respondents, American education does not, in fact, impact Indonesian culture and values. As the following respondents stated:

> Foreign involvement in curriculum is not easily adapted in Indonesia. The government of America could not intervene with Indonesian national education because it is under the authority of the Director General of Higher Education. (*Indonesian official dealing with financial management in a US government agency* (Respondent 6))

> American education does not impinge on Indonesian culture and values. (*Indonesian government official* (Respondent 5))

Although foreign influence coming through interaction with American education could be viewed as a potential threat to Indonesia's own cultural values, Respondent 5 believes that Indonesia is protected from this threat because the Indonesian government has the ability to exercise its authority over national education. Consequently, these respondents claim the education relationship with the US does not impinge on Indonesian cultural values. Here, the notion of cultural domination does not apply in the case of the Indonesia–US education relationship.

It is during the negotiation of arrangements for MoUs that the implications of the education exchanges are considered, particularly the implications for maintaining cultural values. It is not surprising then that Indonesian negotiators have chosen to accept some aspects of American cultural values as desirable, indeed necessary, if they are to share fully in the benefits of the exchange. The willingness of the Indonesian negotiators to accept and adopt desirable aspects of American values, and the attempt to maintain Indonesian culture, illustrates the advantage of the hybridisation of cultures.

The following statement offers a good starting point for considering whether cultural values can be preserved through an education curriculum, while also gaining benefits from adopting American ideas or knowledge:

> American education does not impinge on Indonesian culture and values. They live here comfortably and enjoy living in Indonesia. They will understand and be tolerant with our culture, and vice versa. (*Indonesian government official (Respondent 5)*)

This observation of one Indonesian government official dealing with negotiations between Indonesia and the US notes three important things. First, American education is described as not impinging on Indonesian cultural values. Instead, the respondent is of the view that through the education relationship, Americans and Indonesians will understand and be tolerant to each other's cultures. As has been shown in Chaps. 4 and 5, Indonesia retains its authority over education within its territory. Second, through the Indonesia–US education relationship, there is the potential and promise of understanding and tolerance of each other's culture, as also indicated in the following comment:

> The other connection that I have is I play in a Javanese *gamelan* here in Portland. So part of my interest in going was to be able to hear *gamelan* in its native setting. (*An American vice president for research and strategic partnership (Respondent 15)*)

The interpenetration of both cultures, as Pieterse argues, is one of the defining features of cultural hybridisation.[49] The respondent's interest in *gamelan* (Javanese instrumental music) illustrates how educational exchange and collaboration enhance understanding, tolerance, and experience of each other's culture. The interpenetration of culture might be described as leading to cultural interdependence.[50] An example of cultural interdependence is best illustrated by the comment of the following respondent:

> Combination between two cultures is ok but we must not lose our identity. Those combinations include discipline, tolerance, being on time, accurate organisation, not self-centred. (*Indonesian vice rector negotiating and administering MoUs (Respondent 2)*)

The perspective of the vice rector illustrates the preference for cultural interdependence. Yet, there are concerns surrounding the negative effects of foreign cultural penetration, such as capitalism that renders individuals self-centred and competitive, thereby ruining Indonesian practices of collectivism and unity. The following respondent also commented:

> I hope American scholars and researchers could come here to educate in the area of early childhood; how to educate Javanese or how to educate Sundanese. But I think every region in Indonesia has its own wisdom. (*Indonesian vice rector negotiating and administering MoUs (Respondent 2)*)

This comment illustrates that although the respondent's preference for cultural interdependence is clear, and despite his admiration for American education, he is also concerned for the autonomy of the local culture. It is expected that although cultural interdependence is accepted, as the interviews illustrate, cultural values remain of significant importance in the education curriculum. Therefore, the government of Indonesia has attempted from time to time to preserve cultural values through the education curriculum.[51] This shows there is cooperation, conditioned by cultural ways of interaction for enhancing and improving understanding between the US and Indonesia. The cooperation involves interpenetration of culture, and cultural interdependence is expected to follow, according to the Indonesian respondents. In addressing the threat of foreign influences on Indonesian cultural values, the government is now actively promoting a character-based curriculum, aimed at strengthening Indonesian cultural values.[52] One respondent commented:

our government is now actively developing a character based curriculum. The aim is to strengthen our cultural values, character, and identity. Globalisation as an excuse is ok, but we are Indonesian and we have our own identity. Even though Indonesians are in America, they should not be afraid to say "Assalamualaikum" [peace be with you] in America because that's part of our culture, or, "Punten" [hello in Sundaneses]. We must be able to say that. (*Indonesian vice rector negotiating and administering MoUs (Respondent 2)*)

Nonetheless, it is a practically impossible task to develop regulations that prevent the inculcation of foreign values. For this reason, the preservation of cultural values will continue to be a challenge for Indonesia. Making religion a compulsory subject in the curriculum is important for preserving certain Indonesian religious values. Islam has the largest number of adherents of Indonesia's five official religions, and such Islamic values are often enshrined in the Indonesian culture. Guided by the character-based curriculum and the goal of national education to create individuals devoted to God, several education institutions in Indonesia have initiated the abolition of multiculturalism in education, and the obligation to read the Koran and pray in the education environment.[53]

The hybridisation of education results not only from an attempt to choose a set of values that is culturally relevant to include in the curriculum, but also from attempts to adopt new practices and learning experiences. Thus, the existing education curriculum combines with new practices and learning experiences. The benefits of new practices and learning experiences are best illustrated by the following responses:

> We learn only from books and mainly from American sources. With the partnership, our students can go directly to America and learn directly ... not solely from books or lecturers whose reading is based on American sources. That's amazing and has invaluable benefits. Many would agree that we use American sources for teaching and learning. If we can send students directly to America, they can learn directly from the authors and researchers, and so on. (*Indonesian vice rector negotiating and administering MoUs (Respondent 2)*)

The interviewee's comment clearly illustrates that American literature and American education structures give new learning experiences. The interviews also illustrate the willingness to adopt American education, because it is perceived as beneficial.

The adoption of American approaches to education is evident in the curriculum. In 2003, Indonesia shifted the focus of the curriculum from being a content-based curriculum to one which is competency based.[54] The changes have meant the subjects in the national curriculum are more comprehensive and competitive. Subjects include religion, Pancasila, *Bahasa* Indonesia, citizenship, mathematics, statistics, and logical thinking. The style of teaching has also shifted from teacher-centred to student-centred. The USINTEC (US–Indonesia Teacher Education Consortium) partnership provides opportunities for dual degrees and sandwich programmes (pursuing degrees in Indonesia with access to resources in the US), which enable Indonesian educators to improve their student-centred teaching quality.[55] In addition to USINTEC, USAID has also encouraged changes in teaching methods and in the ways students are encouraged to learn, and has sought to change the education environment, making it more conducive to learning by promoting greater participation in learning and strengthening leadership.[56] One respondent commented:

> The government of America focuses on teaching methods that should be student centred, language, science, and math. The national education of Indonesia has been set by the Ministry of Education and the Ministry of Culture, particularly the standard of content and process for achieving Indonesia's development goal for creating human capital who are devoted to God, knowledgeable and skilful in science, technology, art, and citizens who participate in development based on Pancasila and [the] Constitution 1945. (*Indonesian official dealing with financial management in a US government agency (Respondent 6)*)

This comment illustrates the role of the US in Indonesian curriculum development, by introducing student-centred teaching style. The adoption of American approaches to education is clearly evident in the curriculum: the shift from teacher-centred to student-centred education. It is necessary to note that the term *curriculum* is different for both American and Indonesian educators. Ayers and Tyler argue that Western educators generally define the term curriculum as the process and product of instruction occurring inside and outside the classroom.[57] On the other hand, Indonesian educators define the term curriculum as the written and standardised subjects for which the guidelines are provided by the national central office.[58] In this context, there are hybridisation processes at work in Indonesian education as a response to the Indonesia–US education relationship.

The struggle to maintain cultural values continues; however, McDonalds, jeans, and rock music are regarded as American cultural icons and are favoured by Indonesians. Since it is Indonesians adopting some aspects of American culture rather than Americans adopting some aspects of Indonesian cultures, there is some concern about the loss of Indonesian identity and cultural values. Booth argues that identity patterns are becoming complex, as people assert local loyalties but want to share in global values and lifestyles.[59] Such complexity in patterns of identity, coupled with the risk of cultural values fading away, has some bearing on education policy. As noted earlier, for instance, a character-based curriculum was developed in order to maintain national identity and cultural values through education.[60]

Transnational education, though one of the driving forces behind hybridisation, does not necessarily diminish Indonesia's educational sovereignty. The Indonesian authorities retain their ability to exercise influence over national education. In the case of Indonesia–US relations, an education relationship with the US should not impinge on Indonesian cultural values. Despite the penetration of foreign culture, and American culture through education transactions between Indonesia and the US, Indonesian identity and culture survive and are preserved through the national education curriculum. The idea of cultural imperialism in the relationship with the US, does not apply, as there is no indication of American cultural imposition, as most Indonesian respondents claimed a willingness to adopt some aspects of American culture. There is no indication of cultural dependence. In the case of the Indonesia–US relations, Indonesian respondents have clearly asserted that Indonesia has its own identity. Yet, whether hybridisation of education and culture diminishes educational sovereignty or not depends on the state. The state enacts regulations and is responsible for enforcing national education law, regulating education within its borders, prioritising development needs through education, and pursuing particular, chosen learning experiences from the West while maintaining national identity.

Concluding Remarks

This chapter has discussed identity and cultural values for Indonesia, and has explored the extent to which Indonesia is able to preserve its identity and cultural values. The Indonesian education system is culturally bound and derived giving guidance as to how people should live and act. Indonesian education is founded on obligations as both a student and an educator, duties (through *gotong royong*), tradition (*musyawarah and mufakat*), dependence on teachers' knowledge, avoiding conflict for achieving harmony, and obedience to the authorities, such as educators.[61] The adoption of Hinduism, Islam, and Buddhism in Indonesian dance and the arts is widespread. The original indigenous cultures are still preserved through the combination of animism and a dynamic relationship with Hinduism, Islam, and Buddhism.

Indonesia retains control over its education curriculum through mode 3 and mode 4, as these modes take place in Indonesia's territory. The government of Indonesia also retains control over cross-border supply delivery (mode 1). The twinning arrangements, however, require compliance with American education regulations. Because the twinning arrangements comply with foreign regulations, the twinning programme is limited to the physical movement of Indonesian students studying overseas. The Indonesian government does not have full control over the consumption abroad mode of delivery (mode 2), because Indonesian students have to follow foreign education system. A lack of control in this one situation does not mean, however, that Indonesian higher education curriculum is subject to homogenisation. Indonesia is able to preserve its cultural integrity and formulate regulatory policies inside its territory. Language and religion are compulsory in the education curriculum, and foreign students are required to learn and understand the Indonesian language. Although English is introduced in the curriculum as a way to prepare individuals for active roles in global competition, local stories are also included in the teaching of the English language, as they are regarded as necessary in order to preserve Indonesian cultural values. For these reasons, providing foreign education in Indonesia does not lead to the homogenisation or Americanisation in education through the transfer of Western and American cultures and values. Through the exercise of educational sovereignty, the Indonesian government retains sufficient control over its national education curriculum such that it is not subject to homogenisation.

Despite the penetration of foreign culture through education transactions, Indonesian identity and culture have survived and are preserved through the national education curriculum. Accordingly, the idea of cultural imperialism is not supported. In the case of the Indonesia–US relations, for instance, most Indonesian respondents claim they willingly adopt certain aspects of American culture because they consider it beneficial or advantageous to their own national interests to do so. Neither were there any indications of cultural dependence arising from the Indonesia–US education relationship, as Indonesian respondents have clearly asserted that Indonesia has its own identity. Whether or not hybridisation of education and culture diminishes educational sovereignty depends on the state which enacts regulations and is responsible for enforcing national education law, regulating education within its borders, prioritising development needs through education, and pursuing particular, yet chosen, learning experiences from the West, while maintaining national identity. For these reasons, the creation of hybrid education programmes does not diminish Indonesia's educational sovereignty. The creation of hybrid education programmes does not diminish the Indonesian government's ability to maintain its culture and values.

Transnational education cooperation is conditioned by culturally based perceptions and interactions. The maintenance of religion in the Indonesian education curriculum is necessary, and the cooperation is intended to enhance and improve international understanding. The cooperation involves interpenetration of culture, and cultural interdependence is expected to follow in the views of the Indonesian respondents.

Identity and language are constantly changing, and it is also the case for Indonesia. In this context, the notion that identity and culture are fixed, as implied by some critical educationalists, can be dismissed. An interesting point that these theorists are making is that, as this change takes place, it is, inevitably, the exchanges that need to be determined. Another interesting point they make is that culture and the capacity to remain in control of it is a central issue. In the case of Indonesia–US education relations, the loss of Indonesian culture is one of the highest concerns for Indonesian respondents, and thus the maintenance of culture is one of the highest priorities in the negotiations. However, in the case of Indonesia–New Zealand education relations, the Indonesian respondents do not have concerns for the loss of Indonesian culture. Nonetheless, the Indonesian respondents claimed that Indonesia has the ability to maintain Indonesian culture.

NOTES

1. In Amitav Acharya, "Culture, Security, and Multilateralism: The 'ASEAN way' and Regional Order," in *Culture and Security: Multilateralism Arms Control and Security Building*, eds. Keith Krause (NY: Frank Cass Publisher, 1999): 22.

2. Herbert Feith, *The Decline of Constitutional Democracy in Indonesia* (Ithaca, NY: Cornell University Press, 1962): 40.
3. Acharya (1999): 22.
4. Eka Darma Putera and E.J. Brill, *Pancasila and the Search for Identity and Modernity in Indonesian Society* (Leiden: The Netherlands, 1988).
5. Robin Goodwin and Sophie Giles, "Social Support Provision and Cultural Values in Indonesia and Britain," *Journal of Cross-cultural Psychology*, 34, (2003): 240–245.
6. H.C. Triandis, *Culture and Social Behaviour* (New York: McGraw, 1994); H.C. Triandis, R. Bontempo, H. Bettancourt, M. Bond, K. Leung, and A. Brenes, "The measurement of ethnic aspects of individualism and collectivism across cultures," *Australian Journal of Psychology*, 38, (1986): 257–267; Robin Goodwin and Sophie Giles (2003).
7. B. Muslim, Nia Nafisah, and Ika Damayanti, "Locality and Self-identity: Local Story Inclusion in Indonesian English Text Books," University of Indonesia, 2009. Also see Triandis et al. (1986); Goodwin and Giles (2003).
8. Robin Goodwin and Sophie Giles (2003).
9. Brett Noel, Ann Shoemake, and Claudia Hale, "Conflict Resolution in a Non-western Context: Conversations with Indonesian Scholars and Practitioners," *Conflict Resolution Quarterly*, 23, (2006): 427–446.
10. Fred Jandt, *Intercultural Communication: An Introduction* (London: Sage Publications, 2001).
11. Triandis (1994).
12. See http://www.bkpm.go.id
13. Bernard Lane, "Indonesia Outlooks Uncertain for Branch Campuses," *The Australian*, March 19, 2013. The reason the establishment of a Monash University branch in Indonesia was rejected is unknown.
14. See Australia in the Asian Century White Paper, http://www.dpmc.gov.au/sites/default/files/publications/annual_reports/2011-12/part-2/domestic-policy/aac.htm. Also see Bernard Lane, "Monash to Consider Setting up Campus in Indonesia," *The Australian*, February 20, 2003.
15. In Rudijanto, "Liberalization in education: A threat or a Necessity?" *The Jakarta Post*, Wednesday, January 26, 2005.
16. Professional International Education News, "Indonesia Opens up to Foreign Universities," last modified September 10, 2013, http://www.thepienews.com/news/Indonesia-opens-up-to-foreign-universities
17. Lane (2013).
18. John Riady, "Top Flight Foreign Educated Graduates can Help Indonesia Go Truly Global," *The Jakarta Globe*, January 15, 2010.
19. In Rudijanto (2005).
20. Ibid.

21. As reported by Dr Evi Fitriani, the Head of the International Relations Department, University of Indonesia. Also see James Smith, "Indonesian Universities Focus on Video Conferencing Opportunity," *Asia Pacific*, Thursday, August 29, 2013.
22. Lane (2013); Margaret Aritonang, "New Laws Open Doors to Foreign Universities," *Jakarta Post*, Saturday, July 14, 2013; Rudijanto (2005). This book, however, does not deal with the numbers of foreign education providers in Indonesia as the study is not quantitative.
23. In Aritonang (2013).
24. Ibid.
25. Ibid.
26. John Tomlinson, "Cultural Globalisation: Placing and Displacing the West," *European Journal of Development Research*, 8, (1996): 22–35.
27. Bob Lingard and Fazal Rizvi, "Globalisation and the Fear of Homogenisation in Education," *Change: Transformation in Education*, 1, (1998): 62–71.
28. Buchori and Malik (2004).
29. Francis Eugene Mooney, "Some Highlights of the Development of Secondary and Teacher Education in Indonesia," *Peabody Journal of Education*, 40, (1962): 137–141.
30. Ompron Regel, "The Academic Credit System in Higher Education: Effectiveness and Relevance in Higher Education," *Education and Employment Division*, July 1992.
31. Sri Soejatmiah, "Internationalisation of Indonesian Higher Education: A Study from the Periphery," *Asian Social Science Journal*, 5, (2009): 70–78.
32. Angela Siqueira, "The Regulation of Education through the WTO/GATS," *Journal for Critical Education Policy Studies*, 3, (2005): 1–16; Anthony Verger and Xavier Bonal, "Against GATS: The Sense of a Global Struggle," *Journal for Critical Education Policy Studies*, 4, (2006): 1–27.
33. Muslim et al. (2009).
34. Nikolaus Passasung, "Teaching English in an 'Acquisition Poor Environment': An Ethnographic Example of a Remote Indonesian EFL Classroom," (PhD Thesis, University of Sydney, 2003).
35. Embassy of the United States, "Language Fellow Program," last modified September 5, 2013, http://Jakarta.usembassy.gov/fellow.html (2013).
36. In Merle Ricklefs, "The Future of Indonesia," *History Today*, September 28, 2013. http://www.historytoday.com
37. Ibid.
38. Directorate General of Higher Education, "National Education Law 2003," http://www.inherent-dikti.net
39. Catholicism is not treated as a branch of Christianity.

40. As outlined in Indonesian national education law number 20/2003 chapter 18. See Indonesian Ministry of People's Welfare, http://www.menkokesra.go.id
41. In the District Ministry of Religious Affairs, "Currently Compulsory Religious Education is the Highest Priority," last modified August 20, 2013, http://riau.kemenag.go.id
42. Siqueira (2005): 1–16; Verger and Bonal (2006): 1–27.
43. Ibid.
44. Leon Tikly, "Education and the New Imperialism," *Comparative Education*, 40, (2004): 173–198.
45. Jan Nederveen Pieterse, *Globalization and Culture: Global Melange* (Lanham, Maryland: Rowman and Littlefield Publisher, 2009).
46. Bob Hadiwinata, "International Relations in Indonesia: Historical Legacy, Political Intrusion, and Commercialization," *International Relations of the Asia Pacific*, 9, (2009): 55–81.
47. Ibid.
48. Ken Booth in Ronald Lipschutz, "Reconstructing World Politics: The Emergence of Global Society," *Millennium*, 21, (1992): 396.
49. Jan Pieterse, "Globalization and Hybridisation," *International Sociology*, 9, (1994):161–184.
50. Ibid.
51. Research and Development Body, Ministry of Religion, "Character Based Curriculum," last modified July 29, 2013, http://www.balitbangdiklat.kemenag.go.id
52. Ibid.
53. Suara Pembaharuan, "Schools have Role in Abolishing Multiculturalism Values," last modified August 20, 2013. http://suarapembaharuan.com
54. Directorate General of Higher Education, "Guideline for Developing Competency Based Curriculum," 2008.
55. USINTEC, "Programs," last modified June 20, 2012, http://www.usintec.org/projects
56. USAID programmes, such as PRESTASI, from http://www.indonesia.usiad.gov/; US Department of State, "Background Note: Indonesia," http://www.state.gov
57. In Udin Saud and Marylyn Johnston, "Cross-Cultural Influences on Teacher Education Reform: Reflections on Implementing the Integrated Curriculum in Indonesia," *Journal of Education for Teaching*, 32, (2006): 3–20.
58. Ibid.
59. Ken Booth in Ronald Lipschutz (1992): 396.
60. Character-based curriculum is aimed at creating not only knowledgeable and skillful citizens but also citizens devoted to God. Character-based education

curriculum is based on national culture and identity. See Denny Setiawan, "Character Based Curriculum and its Implementation on Early Childhood Education," http://www.pustaka.ut.ac.id; Department of National Education, "General Policies of Curriculum Development," Department of National Education Research Development, Jakarta, 2000.
61. Triandis (1994).

CHAPTER 7

Normative and Non-normative Discourses in Indonesia–New Zealand Relationship in Education

A significant and provocative observation has arisen from this study: the respondents used the term *partnership* repeatedly. Similarly, relevant documents such as MoUs and media also use the term. This chapter discusses the normative and non-normative discourses of partnership by using the Indonesia–New Zealand relationship in education as a case study.

New Zealand has built free trade agreements with Indonesia, which includes agreements on educational programmes. The trade agreements include ASEAN–Australia–NZ FTA (AANZFTA) and the Regional Comprehensive Economic Partnership (RCEP). A total of 45% of Indonesian tertiary students studied in the university sector in 2014, with 38% enrolling in the Private Training Establishment (PTE) sector.[1]

As an emerging economy with a rising middle class, Indonesia is a promising partner that is beneficial for New Zealand's economy. It will be a missed opportunity for New Zealand if the country does not develop a sustained relationship with Indonesia. Important questions arise: "What factors are contributing to a sustained relationship in education?" "What factors impede a sustained relationship in education?" The understanding of non-normative and normative discourses of the partnership is essential in order to address these questions. Non-normative discourses relate to the definitions of the partnership in education. Normative discourses relate to the guiding principles of the partnership and what should comprise the partnership. With the understanding of non-normative and normative

© The Author(s) 2017
A. Abbott, *Educational Sovereignty and Transnational Exchanges in Post-Secondary Indonesian Education*, DOI 10.1007/978-3-319-53985-0_7

discourses, a framework is also proposed of whether transnational education negotiation will advance to collaboration.

This chapter firstly discusses Indonesia–New Zealand post-secondary education relations from 1945 to the present. Secondly, the definitions of partnership and normative and non-normative discourses of partnership are outlined based on literature. Finally, the experiences of negotiators in Indonesia–New Zealand education relations are analysed for the purpose of understanding non-normative and normative discourses in the relationship, and making recommendations for a sustained collaboration.

INDONESIA–NEW ZEALAND POST-SECONDARY EDUCATION RELATIONS

Indonesia–New Zealand Post-Secondary Education Relations from 1945 to 1970

The diplomatic relationship between New Zealand and Indonesia started in 1953 when New Zealand assisted Indonesia through the Colombo Plan. This included the establishment of a technical trade training institution, English language teaching, and short-term courses in dentistry. By 1960, a total of 99 Indonesians had been given scholarships to study in New Zealand, and 29 New Zealander expatriates had been sent to Indonesia.[2] In 1961, a Colombo Plan office was established in Jakarta. As part of the Colombo Plan, approximately 3500 Indonesian students came to New Zealand during the 1960s and 1970s.[3] New Zealand also opened its embassy in Indonesia in 1968.

Four main forms of relationship in education between New Zealand and Indonesia emerged from the 1950s to the 1970s. English-language teaching projects were the main form of technical assistance in Indonesia, while other forms of exchange included New Zealand experts working in Indonesia and Indonesian students training in New Zealand. Such technical assistance brought almost 900 trainees to Indonesia, particularly in engineering, agriculture, health, general education, and technical fields.[4] Yet another form of educational relationship was offshore study. For instance, Indonesian student Soedjati Djiwandono studied education, politics, and language at Otago University (New Zealand's oldest university).[5]

Indonesia–New Zealand Post-Secondary Education Relations from 1970 to 1997

During the Suharto New Order era, policies on development and modernisation were formulated in the endeavour to modernise Indonesia. Thus, the involvement of Indonesia on the international stage was emphasised during this era. As with many other Southeast Asian states, Suharto emphasised the importance of human resources as a key factor to improving Indonesia's economy. As such, the government actively sought international collaboration in the form of consultation and assistance, particularly in higher education, and sought such collaboration with New Zealand institutions.

The New Zealand government paid greater attention to Indonesia during the 1970s and 1980s, more than any other period during the Suharto era. Michael Green stated, "The potential of the relationship was more fully realized in the Suharto era. The two governments forged a rounded relationship comprising political links, development assistance, trade and economic ties, diplomatic coordination on regional problems, defence coordination and a range of people-to-people contacts."[6] In development assistance, New Zealand, like other donors, had laid emphasis on good governance for its assistance programmes to Indonesia.[7] During the New Order era, under Suharto's leadership in the early 1990s, the National Commission on Human Rights was established. To improve the Commission's research capabilities, New Zealand funded two senior Commission staff to study in New Zealand, and provided fellowships of two years each to seven Indonesians.[8]

Enthusiasm for Indonesia, however, waned in the New Zealand public mind following the Indonesian military's atrocities in East Timor. New Zealand had helped the Indonesian military with officer training from 1973. Maire Leadbeater, a human rights activist and critic of New Zealand's approach to assisting the Indonesian military, stated in the *New Zealand International Review*: "Most of the time, New Zealand's relations with Indonesia do not get onto the public radar. But in the 1990s, as news began to spread about atrocities in East Timor, the Foreign Affairs Ministry had to perfect a public relations strategy to account for the pro-Indonesia policy position."[9] The relationship in education between New Zealand and Indonesia, however, has continued since 1999.

Indonesia–New Zealand Post-Secondary Education Relations from 1999 to the Present

In 2002, the Prime Minister of New Zealand, Helen Clark, showed support for the relationship in a remark she made at a state dinner for Wahid's successor, President Susilo Bambang Yudhoyono, when he visited New Zealand in 2005. Clark stated:

> New Zealand is part of the Asia-Pacific and our closest neighbour in Asia is Indonesia. The dramatic political evolution means that there is much that it is positive to build on for the future, and we look forward to working with you and your government to strengthen our ties.[10]

New Zealand then began to improve its education ties with Indonesia by expanding cooperation in education. David Taylor, New Zealand ambassador to Indonesia and ASEAN, states that education is an area where New Zealand and Indonesia can work together very effectively.[11] Taylor also states that increased cooperation is reflected in the establishment of the bilateral Education Joint Working Group where both governments exchange best practices on education policy. Additionally, scholarships are offered for Indonesian students. In 2011, according to Taylor, 50 scholarships were offered to postgraduate studies, an increase from 15 in 2010. David Treacher, who was political counsellor at the New Zealand Embassy, states that New Zealand has made a commitment to offer up to NZ$6 million per year for the scholarship programme, which has led to the increased numbers of Indonesian students in New Zealand.

Opportunities in education relations also include joint research programmes and institutional links, teacher development training programmes, train-the-trainer programmes, cultural exchanges, onshore and offshore programmes, and government training programmes. According to Education New Zealand, there is also potential for collaboration in the areas of agriculture and food science, disaster risk management and planning, and geothermal energy and earth science.[12] Small grants in the four main areas—sustainable economic development, renewable energy, disaster risk management, and conflict prevention—are also included in the relationship.[13] There were 740 Indonesian students studying in New Zealand, and the year following, in 2014, that number increased to 865. New Zealand's stated objective is to increase the numbers of Indonesian students by 4000 in 2017.[14] Indonesia now has collaboration agreements with eight New Zealand universities for joint research, joint degrees, and pathways for Indonesian students to study in New Zealand.[15]

Both New Zealand and Indonesia consider the benefits of the collaboration. David Taylor, New Zealand's ambassador to Indonesia stated:

> The reasons for getting closer to Indonesia have never been more compelling. It's a trillion dollar economy now, and it will be a US$9 trillion economy by 2030, according to most estimates, which puts it in the top six economies in the world.... It's a no-brainer. It's so close to us geographically. There will be massive opportunities, and we have to work to get those opportunities. We have to build relationships and tend them well.[16]

It is clear that economic gain is one of the benefits of education collaboration for New Zealand. A 2011 World Bank report states that the number of Indonesians who spend between US$2 and US$20 a day had increased by 50 million in seven years.[17] Amris Hassan, chairman of Indonesia–New Zealand Friendship Council, states, "There are so many trade areas to be explored with the growing middle class. For New Zealand, it is a missed opportunity."[18]

EDUCATION PARTNERSHIP

Education relationship arrangements or collaborative activities are often referred to as education partnerships. This section presents normative and non-normative discourses of the transnational education partnership and thus offers an indicator of whether transnational education negotiations will advance to productive collaboration.[19]

Non-normative Discourse of Educational Partnership

Partnership is a collaborative activity and a concept that depicts reciprocal benefits between partners involved in the process.[20] The term *collaboration* then can be used synonymously with partnership, which is also used interchangeably with academic links.[21] The Africa Unit defines educational partnership, emphasising the elements of trust, transparency, and respect:

> A dynamic collaboration process between educational institutions that brings mutual though not necessarily symmetrical benefits to the parties engaged in the partnership. Partners share ownership of the projects. Their relationship is

based on respect, trust, transparency and reciprocity. They understand each other's cultural and working environment. Decisions are taken jointly after real negotiations take place between the partners. Each partner is open and clear about what they are bringing to the partnership and what their expectations are from it. Successful partnerships tend to change and evolve over time.[22]

Although the Africa Unit acknowledges reciprocal benefits as an element of a partnership, transparency is another important element of a partnership. Transparency means being open and clear about what the parties are bringing to the partnership and what their expectations are from it. Respect for and understanding of each other's cultural and working environments are also elements of a partnership.

Some authors, such as Bailey and Dolan, argue that to move beyond the vacuous rhetoric of partnership, it is necessary to examine what is entailed in a partnership. Morgan argues that partnership is process-oriented, and it must be viewed as a living system.[23] Thus, the definition of partnership requires further development. To conceptualise the term "partnership" in education, it is necessary to examine who appoints decision makers, who funds and evaluates the project or collaboration, and who owns the project.

Normative Discourse of Educational Partnership

Educational partnerships are often used as a mechanism for joint research opportunities between developed states and LDSs. As Kenneth King states, "Partnership is no longer a choice for Northern [developed states] researchers wanting to work in the developing world; it has become a condition of doing research in the South."[24] North–south partnerships enable teams of researchers to solve specific problems, such as climate change, poverty, or migration. In such partnerships, shared principles and objectives are essential in order to achieve a sustained collaboration. Abdou Diouf, former Senegalese president, states:

> The type of partnership we should promote cannot be founded on a vertical relationship based on authority, constraint, the imposition of an imbalance of power, substituted sovereignty and transposition of models, or paternalism and condescension. Instead, it should be founded on conditions such as authentic dialogue in a horizontal relationship in which the actors recognize each other as equals and participate in an exchange considered mutually useful and enriching by both parties.[25]

Diouf's statements suggest that the normative discourse of a partnership describes what a partnership should comprise: shared principles, interests, and objectives. These elements of shared principles, interests, and objectives are relevant for inclusion in educational partnerships. Examples of shared principles and objectives include developing regular channels for data and information sharing, exploring ways to enhance inter-agency cooperation, and recognising the importance of sharing best practices and experiences. Another example of shared interests and objectives in an education partnership is implemented in double-degree programmes leading to a certificate issued jointly by the participating higher education institutions. As double-degree programmes are developed together by several education institutions, they have shared objectives by developing curriculum and cooperation on admission and by producing learning outcomes recognised by all participating institutions.

Although partnership is a collaborative activity, the collaborative nature of a partnership is only one of the types of education partnership. Inter-institutional collaboration is an educational partnership that is supported by some kind of institutional commitment, based on a formal agreement between parties involved.[26] According to the Compassion Capital Fund National Resource Centre, there are several types of this partnership.[27] The first type is a collaborative type. This type comprises greater autonomy, with no permanent organisational commitment. The second type is an alliance type, which comprises shared decision-making power and being agreement-driven. The third type is an integration type, which involves changes to structure and control. The fourth type is a funding alliance type. This kind of partnership starts with separate organisations coming together in a recipient–donor relationship. The fifth type is a cost-sharing partnership. This type of partnership occurs when an organisation provides certain resources and the other organisation provides other different resources. Both parties share the benefits and costs. The type of partnership in education between New Zealand and Indonesia is explained later in this chapter.

Whether Indonesia–New Zealand relations in education will advance to collaboration or not, the experiences of negotiators are a good starting point, and these experiences will be analysed further in this chapter.

Partners can come together with shared objectives, but, in practice, things are not so simple.[28] An example is shown in Hannah's study. The British Council and the Brazilian Federal Agency signed an agreement to promote and facilitate academic collaboration between universities in Brazil and the UK. Hannah reports that from Brazilian perspectives, this agreement represented an opportunity to establish joint research and academic programmes that move beyond traditional forms of north–south collaboration. According to Hannah, however, constraints arising from historical and contemporary factors continue to pose barriers to genuine partnership.[29] A genuine partnership, as opposed to an instrumental partnership, is a type of partnership that provides a framework for identifying shared development objectives and for accommodating both "northern" accountability requirements and "southern" ownership.[30] The flow of students and experts, according to Canto and Hannah, is exclusively one-way. Canto and Hannah argue that the success of joint research projects can be genuinely of mutual interest in which both partners have a distinctive and complementary contribution to make. Without this, Canto and Hannah argue, there is a danger of degeneration into traditional forms of partnership where there is one-way transfer of knowledge and one-way movement of students and experts. Whether Indonesia–New Zealand collaboration is genuine or an instrumental partnership, is discussed further in this chapter.

INDONESIA–NEW ZEALAND EDUCATION COLLABORATION: A CLOSER LOOK AT NEGOTIATORS' EXPERIENCES

The partnership in education between Indonesia and New Zealand comprises greater autonomy and no permanent organisational commitment. Most Indonesian respondents indicate that the relationship with New Zealand in education is not bound and is not based on a long-term commitment. The following respondent, for instance, stated:

> We have a programme with Massey University in the electrical engineering department and physical science department where our lecturers study at Massey University. ... Although the MoU was signed for five years, it is not a binding agreement but we follow up every year. Massey also invited us for a visiting scholarship programme for one to two months. Massey, however, does not have enough funding so the programme can't continue. (*Head of International Relations and a negotiator at an Indonesian university* (*Respondent 21*))

Respondent 21 clearly stated that the MOU is not a binding agreement but has allowed the termination of agreed programmes, such as a visiting scholarship programme. At an early stage of the collaboration, most Indonesian respondents indicate that they do not see the reciprocal benefits and shared interests in the relationship. The reason for the absence of reciprocal benefits, pressing needs, and shared objectives is indicated by the following respondents:

> New Zealand doesn't seem to be very aggressive looking for opportunities to co-operate. Unfortunately, with the global image, Indonesians want to go to places like America, Australia, and in some cases Korea and Japan. ... With New Zealand, we just talked about our plan and the possibility of student exchanges or scholarship programmes. But we [both Indonesian and New Zealand parties] did not do anything. For us somehow there was no pressing need for it to happen. (*Head of International Relations and a negotiator at an Indonesian university (Respondent 22)*)

> The principle for the relationship should be based on mutual benefits but we do not see that. The relationship is not as strong as with other governments such as the US. New Zealand does not seem to be active. New Zealand does not have education fairs like those of Europe, Thailand, the US, India, and many other countries. New Zealand pays less attention and effort. Grants from the government of New Zealand are not as much as grants of other countries. New Zealand is also not a popular country like other countries. (*Head of International Relations and negotiator at an Indonesian university (Respondent 21)*)

Unlike other countries such as Singapore, Thailand, and the US, according to Respondents 21 and 22, New Zealand parties are not active in following up early discussions on the possibility to collaborate or conducting education fairs. For these respondents, the failure to actively follow up earlier discussions or conduct education fairs, the fact that grants from the New Zealand government are less than grants of other countries, and the possibility of collaboration with credible world universities, mean that many Indonesian students go to countries other than New Zealand.

> "The principle for the relationship should be mutual benefit. But we can't see this kind of principle in the relationship with New Zealand. No follow up. Very passive! We only talked." (*Head of International Relations and negotiator at an Indonesian university (Respondent 26)*)

> We have no relationship. We have had talks with University of Wellington but we don't have formal co-operation. We mainly have co-operation with American universities and Australian universities. (*Head of International Relations and negotiator at an Indonesian university (Respondent 29)*)

From the point of view of the Indonesian respondents, the passivity of the New Zealand parties and their failure to aggressively follow up with the initial discussion for collaboration mean there are no reciprocal benefits or shared objectives. It is important to note, however, that the respondents were representatives of higher education institutions rather than of government. Thus, the agreements are between Indonesian higher education institutions and New Zealand higher education institutions. Interestingly, most New Zealand respondents view the benefits as mutual. The following respondent, for instance, stated:

> The guiding principles are about cooperation and mutual benefits. So it's not just about gaining students or revenue. . . . we're very conscious that we need to be meeting the needs of the Indonesians. In particular, the Indonesian government. . . . It is a commercial model, so there are commercial realities. It's more about imparting academic, educational skills that can be applied in Indonesia. (*New Zealand negotiator for a New Zealand university* (*Respondent 22*))

When they were asked about what factors hinder or contribute to a successful collaboration, both Indonesian and New Zealand respondents had different perspectives.

> From our experience with those from America and Australia, they are very active in coming to Indonesia looking for opportunities for collaboration. Similarly, Korea and China, and even Malaysia are all very active. From an Indonesian perspective it is difficult to see New Zealand as a potential partner. We don't look at New Zealand as the most advanced technological country. (*Head of International Relations and negotiator at an Indonesian university* (*Respondent 22*))

> we would take great care to make sure cultural sensitivities are indeed allowed for. That is part of what cross-cultural education is about. New Zealand's future in large part is going to be dependent on relationships that we can build with our Asian neighbours and Indonesia is the largest of those with a population of some 265 million. So, it is very important that we build relationships with Indonesia and the fundamental of education is a wonderful foundation stone for those relationships. . . . I would only emphasise that the importance of personal relationships between the people on both sides and the need for a mutual understanding. Otherwise the contracts tend to be meaningless and very, very difficult to implement. (*New Zealand negotiator for a New Zealand university* (*Respondent 23*))

Clearly, the need for mutual understanding is required in the relationship. Most New Zealand respondents were not aware that the Indonesian respondents do not consider cultural differences to be an issue in the relationship. However, the passive response of the New Zealand parties was an issue for Indonesian respondents. The support of both Indonesian and New Zealand governments is considered by the Indonesian respondents to be an important factor that contributes to a successful collaboration. The following respondents said:

> Both government should discuss how to improve the relationship. The government of New Zealand should put Indonesia as one of the priority. The Indonesian government should support Indonesian universities by giving more funding or scholarship to New Zealand. University level is under the government, so we need financial support from the government. ... The government of New Zealand should be more active: more student exchanges, and more education fairs for informing us about New Zealand education. (*Head of International Relations and negotiator at an Indonesian university* (*Respondent 24*))

> Lack of money is the problem. We have no issue with national education law or cultural differences. We need support from our government and they [New Zealand institutions] can contribute by being active in promoting research and education collaboration. (*Head of International Relations and negotiator at an Indonesian university* (*Respondent 27*))

Lack of funding from both governments and lack of attention and effort from the New Zealand parties are considered by most Indonesian respondents to be the factors that impede a successful collaboration. The following respondents stated:

> New Zealand is not far. We are neighbours. But not many Indonesians prefer to study to New Zealand. In 2010, New Zealand only gave fifty scholarships but Australia gave more than one hundred scholarships. Giving scholarships is one of the ways to introduce New Zealand. ... Our government should support higher education both in financial aspect and guidance. (*Head of International Relations and negotiator at an Indonesian university* (*Respondent 21*))

> The biggest problem is money, not national education law or cultural differences or a language barrier. (*Head of International Relations and negotiator at an Indonesian university* (*Respondent 26*))

Cultural differences and Indonesian national education law are not the problem for a successful collaboration. From an Indonesian perspective it is difficult to see New Zealand as a potential partner. We don't look at New Zealand as the most advanced technological country. Talking about business studies, New Zealand is a relatively small country. It is much more advantageous to go to Europe, or Australia, or the United States. I think in the case of Victoria University they are one of the best in some studies, but they have to be active because New Zealand is a small country. (*Head of International Relations and negotiator at an Indonesian university (Respondent 22)*)

Clearly, from the Indonesian respondents' perspectives, funding from both governments and attention and efforts from the New Zealand parties are significant factors in achieving successful collaboration. More effort from New Zealand parties is especially required, as New Zealand is a small country that will need a bigger country's contribution, such as Indonesian students participating at New Zealand universities and benefitting New Zealand economically.

Although New Zealand Official Development Assistance (ODA) for Indonesia is New Zealand's largest Asian bilateral programme, the Indonesian respondents clearly do not view funding from the New Zealand government as being as significant as foreign aid in education from other states, such as the US.[31] Including the promotion of New Zealand aid in educational fairs, therefore, is essential in order to raise an awareness that New Zealand at least contributes to Indonesian education.

At the early stage of collaboration, identification of suitable partners, initiation of new collaborations, and preparation of joint research proposals that can be facilitated by the provision of small grants are essential elements that need to be taken into account for a successful collaboration. For most Indonesian respondents, collaborating with well-known universities is necessary. For Indonesian respondents (see Chap. 6), collaborating with universities with top international rankings is essential, as the Indonesian universities will learn more from the world's top-ranked universities. In the case of Indonesia–New Zealand education relations, some respondents also stated:

We like to partner with a university that has top international ranking, so we can learn from them. That is why they are selected, because they are number one in the world. Or, perhaps they have a very specific, high-quality programme. (*Head of International Relations and negotiator at an Indonesian university (Respondent 22)*)

Not all Indonesian universities use the world ranking university criteria in identifying suitable partners. But I think this is necessary. (*Head of International Relations and negotiator at an Indonesian university (Respondent 21)*)

Although New Zealand is Indonesia's neighbour, not paying attention to the concerns of Indonesian parties means that New Zealand will lose out in the competition with other provider countries such as Australia, India, the US, Singapore, China, and the UK.

Who plans the agreement, what are to be the outcomes of the partnership, what are the benefits and costs of the partnership, what kinds of assessment and evaluation are required, what is required to maintain the partnership, and what should be done if there are changes in the partnership? These questions are important to address in order to achieve a successful collaboration. In the case of New Zealand and Indonesia, however, these aspects cannot be evaluated fully as the collaborations are not actively developed.

TOWARDS A SUCCESSFUL INDONESIA–NEW ZEALAND EDUCATION COLLABORATION

Binder, in her work on Tunja's collaboration, outlines four important aspects to consider for insights into north–south partnership. Although her work does not deal with education, it informs some aspects that determine a successful collaboration in education and research. These aspects include encouraging local partners to develop a capacity for research leadership, reviewing progress early in the collaboration, focusing on the professors who will go on to teach future generations of researchers, and allowing a timeframe long enough for southern partners to develop a capacity for research leadership.[32] By taking these aspects into account, a framework emerges for accommodating the accountability of New Zealand and Indonesia.

In the case of Indonesia–New Zealand relations in education, although research collaboration and visiting professorship programmes were established, there were no follow-up or early reviews of progress in the collaboration. As a result, collaboration was unsustained. Understanding the collaboration partner and designing programme activities that also serve the interests of the partner are important for a successful collaboration to occur. Understanding the interests of New Zealand parties, understanding the needs of Indonesian parties such as the need for research collaboration, and understanding the concerns that the New Zealand parties are not active in the follow-up of the collaboration are necessary in order to achieve a successful partnership. The Overseas Development Institute (ODI) states that for research partnerships to work, the design of the programme activities needs to satisfy different partner-specific interests and objectives.[33] Research collaboration and visiting scholarship programmes are in the interests of the Indonesian parties. Developing these programmes, instead of only selling education courses to the Indonesian students, is therefore a good starting point in establishing collaborations with the Indonesian parties.

There is a conflict of interest that comes into play: the Indonesian parties prefer research collaboration and visiting scholarship programmes, whereas the New Zealand parties prefer selling education courses to the Indonesian students. Expanding the modes of delivery is necessary in the bilateral relation, as selling education courses to the Indonesian students, research collaboration, and visiting scholarship programmes are all beneficial for both governments and New Zealand education institutions. Through the New Zealand Aid programme, the Indonesian students are expected to return to Indonesia as soon as they complete their studies. This is beneficial for Indonesia. For Indonesia, brain drain is reduced, and for New Zealand, the burden of providing more jobs for graduates is reduced. However, offering courses to Indonesian students is beneficial for the New Zealand economy.

Understanding the collaboration partner and designing programme activities that also serve the interests of the partner are also contributing factors to establishing a genuine partnership rather than an instrumental partnership. As Canto and Hannah argue, a genuine partnership is a partnership that provides a framework for identifying shared development objectives and for accommodating both "northern" accountability requirements and "southern" ownership.[34] For the New Zealand parties to be sensitive to the needs and concerns of the Indonesian parties is a contributing factor in a sustained partnership. Likewise, understanding the interests of New Zealand parties is also a contributing factor in a sustained partnership.

Overall, a framework for accommodating the needs of both New Zealand and Indonesia includes follow-up and early reviews of progress in the collaboration, understanding and being transparent with each other's needs and concerns, designing programme activities that serve the interests of both parties, and developing programmes such as research collaboration and visiting scholarship and student exchange programmes, instead of solely selling education courses to the Indonesian students.

Concluding Remarks

As an emerging economy with the rise of the middle class, Indonesia is a promising partner that is beneficial for New Zealand's economy. In promoting education services, one of New Zealand's main challenges in Indonesia is raising awareness of New Zealand as a study destination for Indonesians. For New Zealand, it will be a missed opportunity if New Zealand does not develop a sustained relationship with Indonesia.

Although Indonesia and New Zealand have maintained their bilateral relationship in education since 1945, there have been several problems associated with the maintenance of the relationship. To identify the problems and to seek the solution, this chapter has offered a framework for analysis by exploring the normative and non-normative discourses of the partnership. In the case of Indonesia–New Zealand education relations, educational partnership is viewed by the Indonesian respondents as a mechanism for joint research opportunities. What the partnership should comprise, such as shared principles, interests, and objectives, however, still needs to be developed by both the Indonesian and New Zealand parties.

A framework for accommodating the needs of both New Zealand and Indonesia includes follow-ups and early reviews of progress in the collaboration, understanding and being transparent with each other's needs and concerns, designing programme activities that serve the interests of both parties, and developing programmes such as research collaboration and visiting scholar and student exchange programmes, instead of solely selling education courses to the Indonesian students.

Notes

1. Education New Zealand, "Fact sheet: Indonesia," last modified November 10, 2016, http://nziec.co.nz/wp-content/uploads/2015/08/Factsheet-Indonesia.pdf
2. Mike Green, "Governance Issues in Post-Soeharto Indonesia," Retrieved from http://www.asiaforum.org.nz/wpcontent/uploads/governance-issues-in-post-soehartindonesia.pdf. Paper was presented for Asia Forum, 12/02/2002.
3. Ibid.

4. Ibid.
5. Ibid.
6. Ibid. Also see Adam Schwarz, *A nation in waiting. Indonesia in the 1990s* (Sydney: Allen & Unwin, 1994). A detailed review of the New Zealand–Indonesia relationship in political links, and security and defence is largely beyond the scope of this book.
7. The Advisory Committee on External Aid and Development defined good governance as "the effective management of a country's resources in a manner that is participatory, transparent, and accountable." See Green (2002).
8. Ibid.
9. Maire Leadbeater, "New Zealand Aid Foster Impunity, Status Quo by Indonesian Security Forces," *New Zealand International Review*, 5, (35) September/October 2010.
10. Scoop, "PM Speech: State Dinner for Indonesian President," last modified August 30, 2016, http://www.schoop.co.nz/stories/PA0504/S00128.htm
11. In Jakarta Post, "New Zealand Highlights Education Relations with RI," last modified July 26, 2016, http://www.thejakartapost.com/news/2013/03/16/new-zealand-highlights-education-relations-with-ri.html
12. ENZ, "Market Opportunities," last modified September 5, 2016, http://www.enz.govt.nz/markets/indonesia/opportunities
13. The grants are administered through the $3 million Community Resilience and Economic Development Partnership with the University of Gadjah Mada.
14. ENZ, "Market Opportunities," last modified September 5, 2016, http://www.enz.govt.nz/markets/indonesia/opportunities
15. Ibid.
16. In The Listener, "Another Giant Awakes," last modified November 15, 2016, http://www.noted.co.nz/archive/listener-nz-2012/indonesia-another-giant-awakes
17. World Bank, "Indonesian Economic Quarterly," last modified August 20, 2016, http://documents.worldbank.org/curated/en/193681468044131489/pdf/601520revised010IEQ1Mar2011english.pdf
18. The Indonesia–New Zealand relationship has mainly involved trade in commodities, not services provision. In Frank Wilson, "Indonesia and its significance for New Zealand," *Asia New Zealand*, last modified August 30, 2016, http://www.asianz.org.nz/reports/wp-content/uploads/2015/08/21_Indonesia
19. Productive collaboration refers to achieving a sustainable collaboration and common objectives together.

20. Gerard Downes, "A Critical Analysis of North-South Educational Partnerships in Development Contexts," *Policy and Practice: A Development Education Review*, 16, (Spring 2013): 1–12, http://www.developmenteducationreview.com/issue16-editorial, last modified August 1, 2016.
21. J.M. Ishengoma, "Strengthening Higher Education Space in Africa through North-South Partnerships and links: Myths and Realities from Tanzania Public Universities," a paper presented at the Conference of Rectors, Vice-Chancellors, and Presidents (CORVIP) on Creating an African Higher Education Space, Stellenbosch, South Africa, May 30–June 3, 2011. It is important to note, however, the scope of partnership is wider than "academic links."
22. Nada Wanni, Sarah Hinz and Rebecca Day, "Good Practices in Educational Partnerships Guide," last modified November 25, 2016, http://www.gov.ul/government/uploads/system
23. G. Morgan, *Images of Organization* (2nd ed.). Thousand Oaks, California: Sage, 1998.
24. Kenneth King, "The New Politics of Partnership: Perils or Promise?" *NORRAG News*, December 2008, last modified August 2, 2016, http://www.norrag.org/fileadmin
25. Speech delivered by President Abdou Diouf at the ADEA Biennial Meeting, Dakar, Senegal, October 1997. See http://www.adeanet.org/adea
26. Michael Neil, *Research study on international collaboration between institutions of distance learning* (Milton Keynes, UK: Open University, 1981): 25, quoted in Louise Moran and Ian Mugridge, "Collaboration in distance education An introduction," in *Collaboration in Distance Education: International Case Studies,* ed. Louise Moran and Ian Mugridge, (London and New York: Routledge, 1993): 1.
27. Compassion Capital Fund National Resource Centre, "Partnerships: Frameworks for Working Together," last modified July 28, 2016, http://www.strenghteningnonprofits.org/resources
28. Alexandra Draxler, *New Partnerships for EFA: Building on Experience*, (Geneva: UNESCO International Institute for Educational Planning, and the World Economic Forum, 2008): 35. Last modified August 4, 2016, http://www.ungei.org/resources/files/Partnerships.pdf
29. Isabel Canto and Janet Hannah, "A Partnership of Equals? Academic Collaboration between the United Kingdom and Brazil," *Journal of Studies in International Education Spring*, 5, (2001): 26–41.
30. Hauck, V. and T. Land. 2000. "Beyond the Partnership Rhetoric: Reviewing Experiences and Policy Considerations for Implementing 'Genuine' Partnerships in North-South Cooperation," ECDPM Discussion Paper 20, last modified June 28, 2016, http://ecdpm.org/publications/beyond-partnership-rhetoric

31. In the higher education sector, a total of 428 Indonesians were studying in New Zealand as of July 31, 2000. A total of 351 students were full-fee-paying international students and 44 were on Ministry of Foreign Affairs and Trade scholarships. Thirty-three students came under the diplomatic/military and foreign research/postgraduate categories. See Parliament Library, "Indonesia's New Government: Stability at Last?" last modified November 20, 2016, http://www.parliament.nz/resource/mi.nz
32. Claudia Binder, "Research in Partnership with Developing Countries: Application of the Method of Material Flux Analysis in Tunja, Colombia," in *Future Cities: Dynamics and Sustainability*, 1, (2002): 227–240.
33. ODI, "North-South Research Partnerships: A guidance note on the partnering process," last modified May 28, 2016, http://www.odi.org/sites/odi.org.uk/files/odi-assets/publications-opinion-files/3508.pdf
34. Hauck, V. and T. Land. 2000. "Beyond the Partnership Rhetoric: Reviewing Experiences and Policy Considerations for Implementing 'Genuine' Partnerships in North-South Cooperation," ECDPM Discussion Paper 20, last modified June 28, 2016, http://ecdpm.org/publications/beyond-partnership-rhetoric

CHAPTER 8

Conclusion

The objective of this book was to examine questions about the ability of the Indonesian government to retain control over the content and delivery of education in an environment where Indonesia has a growing number of programmes offered through transnational education agreements with developed states.

The writing of the book was motivated by a concern to examine the arguments of critical education theorists who consider education to be a social and cultural process and who see foreign-controlled education as presenting a risk to a recipient nation's cultural integrity. Tikly, Pennycook, Nguyen, Elliot, Terlouw, and Pilot have all argued that cultural homogenisation tends to be the result of the educational relationships between the LDSs and developed states, and that these relationships disadvantage the former. For some of these writers, transnational education is seen as a means by which new forms of imperialism are perpetuated. Tikly, Carnoy, and Canto and Hannah contend that this new imperialism involves processes that reinforce knowledge-dependency, financial-dependency, and cultural-dependency. Together, these constitute a type of cultural imperialism and a continuation of the history of Western domination. Foreign forms of knowledge and expertise, and foreign education institutions, are considered to be the principal means of enforcing the new imperialism, reinforcing the dependence of LDSs on foreign knowledge, technology transfer, and foreign scientific skills.

8 CONCLUSION

The objective of this book is not to prove whether the perspectives of critical education theorists are wrong or right, but more comprehensively to provide the framework analysis, by including both state and non-state actors in the analysis, for explaining when educational sovereignty is and is not diminished by transnational education.

EVALUATING TRANSNATIONAL EDUCATION IN INDONESIA

Transnational education was defined as the mobility of education materials, students, and foreign education service providers across borders. Transnational education in Indonesia can be said to have its origins in the history of colonialism. While under the control of the Dutch, various professional colleges in which Dutch experts played significant roles were established.

Later, during the Suharto era, post-secondary education played a defining role in promoting Indonesia's economic development and stability. Education was regarded as an essential instrument for creating the human capital necessary for Indonesia's development. From that time onwards, education has been closely linked through government policy to the needs of the economy.

Knight's classification of different modes of delivery in transnational education (see Table 2.1) provides some defining clarity. Cross-border supply (mode 1) refers to the supply of education services in the consumer country; consumption abroad (mode 2) refers to the situations where students travel to the country of the education provider; commercial presence (mode 3) refers to education suppliers which establish institutions in the consuming country; and presence of natural persons (mode 4) refers to educators or scholars travelling to another country for the purpose of providing education services. Mode 1 takes a variety of forms: (a) programme articulations, (b) twinning, and (c) double or joint degrees. Twinning occurs when an overseas education provider collaborates with one in Indonesia to develop an articulated system that allows students to gain course credits in one or both of the states.

The arrangements for twinning programmes and awarding degrees usually comply with national regulations of foreign education provider. The definition of twinning is no longer indicated from Chap. 2, as it is no longer limited to the provision of education services that do not require the physical movement of students, because the twinning arrangements comply with foreign regulations. Any programmes within the Indonesian territory are required to comply with Indonesian regulations.

The commercial presence mode of delivery (mode 3) is highly regulated with foreign education institutions required to collaborate with Indonesian providers and ensure at least 80% of the educators are Indonesian nationals. They must be non–profit-making institutions or work in conjunction with a local partner, and they must be registered as accredited education providers with the Indonesian Ministry of National Education (see Chaps. 5 and 9).

The relationships with foreign education providers can be either competitive or collaborative. Indonesia has allowed foreign education providers to operate in Indonesia, subject to a number of stipulations, such as they must be non-profit education institutions. In this context, the relationship is collaborative, not competitive.

In Indonesia, the delivery of the programmes through the cross-border supply mode (mode 3) is often achieved through partnership arrangements, for example, the twinning programme between Jakarta International College and Western Michigan University. The aim of these forms of transnational education (twinning and the provision of double-degree programmes) is mainly to meet academic and cultural objectives. The delivery of the programmes through consumption abroad (mode 2) occurs not only through partnership arrangements but also through the independent initiative of Indonesian students who travel to the developed countries for study using self-funding. These forms of transnational education aim primarily at the achievement of academic and trade objectives. Commercial presence (mode 3), as noted earlier in the chapter, is highly regulated in Indonesia, with the delivery of programmes through the presence of natural persons (mode 4), and is typically achieved through partnership arrangements with foreign organisations and through academic and research collaboration conducted through partnership agreements.

Like the US, New Zealand has initiated a relationship in education with Indonesia. Unlike the US, New Zealand offers only limited delivery of the programmes, which includes consumption abroad through self-funding and scholarships from both governments. New Zealand's focus is more on trade, whereas the focus of the US is not only on trade but also on cultural objectives.

Overall, transnational education implies a platform for partnership through franchising and twinning arrangements, branch campuses, and corporate programmes, and the existence of a new type of relationship in which educational aid or assistance is part of that relationship.

Transnational Education and Indonesia's Educational Sovereignty

As set out in Chap. 2, this study defines educational sovereignty as the autonomy of the state to make independent decisions regarding national education policy, together with the authority of a state to control the movement of people, education materials, and institutions within and across national borders without intervention from external or foreign authorities, unless such intervention is sought. The question of whether transnational education diminishes the educational sovereignty of the LDS has been examined in this study through interviews with officials from Indonesia, New Zealand, and the US who negotiate and oversee transnational education, agreements, and the analysis of media reports, related publications, and journal articles.

Post-secondary education in Indonesia has its roots in a long history of colonisation. Given this history, there is a tendency towards suspicion of foreign involvement in education. Recent legislation, however, has opened access to Indonesia's education market for foreign providers, including New Zealand and American education institutions. Indonesia has had relationship in education with the US and New Zealand since independence. Education was one of the key components in the US–Indonesia Comprehensive Partnership negotiated in 2010. Education is regarded by both states as important for strengthening the bilateral relationship and promoting dialogue, advancing peace and tolerance, and facilitating mutual respect for each other's culture. The establishment of the Comprehensive Partnership has provided a framework for furthering the scope and provision in the bilateral agreement in education. In examining the dynamics of the Indonesia–US education relationship, this study sets out criteria for identifying educational sovereignty and threats to the loss of such sovereignty. Clearly, the capacity of the state to regulate national education and enforce national education law without interference from foreign authorities is critical here. Despite its active participation in transnational education, Indonesia maintains Pancasila, the Constitution 1945 (UUD 1945), and the inclusion of religion as the foundation of its education programmes, and these safeguards are instrumental in preventing the loss of Indonesian identity and cultural values. Even though the Indonesian National Education Law of 2003 authorises transnational education within Indonesian territory, foreign education institutions are required to follow the Indonesian curriculum, which is under the authority of Directorate General of Higher Education. Despite the flow of education across borders, *Bahasa Indonesia* is the language of instruction, and religion is compulsory in the Indonesian education curriculum. The freedom to control the mobility of education materials, programmes, and education institutions within the state's territory and across its borders is also an indicator of education sovereignty. Any programmes within Indonesia's territory are required to comply with Indonesian regulations. In the commercial presence mode of delivery (mode 3), the Indonesian government retains control over education, as the presence of foreign education providers is restricted and closely regulated. Article 90 of the higher education law sets conditions for foreign education institutions in Indonesia: they have to be non–profit-making organisations or partner with Indonesian education institutions, and they must also be approved by the Ministry of Education, although, as noted, there are exceptions to this last provision.

The financial aspects of education are a significant challenge for Indonesia, as Indonesia needs financial assistance. Thus, foreign financial assistance is certainly welcomed because research projects and education programmes require funding, particularly where there is a shortfall from fee-paying students. The government of Indonesia, however, has been selective with regard to receiving foreign financial assistance. In the 1950s, for example, Indonesia accepted more loan from the US, rather than grants, because it did not want to align itself with the US (and the West). During Megawati's presidency, the US' agenda on counter-terrorism ignited criticism from the Vice-President Hamzah Haz, who argued that the US had invited the terrorist attack launched by the Islamist terrorist group on September 11, 2001, and deserved such an attack.

The recognition of juridically independent territorial entities, which are equal and which can enter into voluntary contractual agreements, such as treaties and MoUs, is also a feature of educational sovereignty and has shown that most interactions between parties to the agreements differ in scope. Nevertheless, the principle of reciprocity remains: most agreements emphasise the ideal that exchanges and activities are to be mutually beneficial and there is to be mutual respect for each other's laws. This mutuality is highly significant in that the relationship involves a two-way effort in which Indonesia's educational sovereignty is retained.

Most of the agreements emphasise this mutual commitment. Agreements at the government level (G to G) are the most comprehensive and provide the guidelines for other parties at different levels (U-to-U or public–private providers). They cover not only the commitment of the state to facilitate favourable treatment for the mobility of education exchanges and cooperation with respect to visas, but also funding for the exchanges, the range of activities, executive agencies, obligations of both parties, recognition of each other's laws and sovereignty, governance, intellectual property, location of meetings, annual reports, annual budgets, settlement, commencement, amendments, and termination of the agreements.

At the government level, the principles of the relationship are outlined comprehensively in the agreement, which enshrines principles ensuring mutual benefits, carrying out activities that abide by Indonesian law, sovereignty and equality, mutual respect, mutual commitment, and transparency.

The ability to maintain local cultural values through education is also an indicator of educational sovereignty. In Chap. 2, homogenisation is defined both as a purposeful process of change to reflect foreign (Western) values, and the consequential transfer of those values as a result of contact with foreigners. Ensuring the preservation of indigenous cultures in Indonesia, the norms and practices that define the various peoples that make up the nation, and ensuring they are valued within the formal education system, represent a type of sovereignty that is closely guarded. The original indigenous cultures are still preserved through combining animism and dynamism with Hinduism, Islam, and Buddhism. The hybridisation of the religious values of Hinduism, Islam, and Buddhism, and indigenous values has been maintained in Indonesia by handing down wisdom and values through local stories or folktales, from generation to generation, particularly within formal education. Similarly, religious values are also handed down from generation to generation, and through formal education. Here, the concept of hybridisation, rather than homogenisation, is pertinent to the discussion of Indonesia's educational sovereignty.

Does Transnational Education Involving a Developed State and a LDS Diminish the Educational Sovereignty of the Latter?

The interviews indicated that the Indonesian negotiators of transnational education agreements highly valued the knowledge and technology provided by American education providers and that they had a strong interest in adopting them. As discussed in Chaps. 4 and 6, these respondents clearly indicated that they were not coerced, but rather were willing to learn and adopt new skills and knowledge in order to improve the quality of

Indonesian education, its graduates, educators, and researchers. There was no evidence to support a proposition that transnational education constitutes a new type of imperialism by perpetuating knowledge dependency through heavy reliance on foreign experts. One important factor here was the way the Indonesian government endeavoured to be less dependent on foreign experts. These attempts include regulations that require academic directors and executives to be Indonesian citizens, unless the education providers are wholly owned by foreigners. This has been a very effective measure for protecting local institutions and ensuring expatriates do not dominate local academic staffing.

Although Indonesia receives financial assistance from its developed state counterparts, the findings suggest that the relationship is characterised by recognition and respect, and as a partnership between equals. Through USAID, for instance, Indonesia has received grants for the purpose of nation building. USAID was found to work closely with local institutions to build their capacity, while recognising the authority and determination of Indonesia to control those institutions.

Education remains under the authority of the Directorate General of Higher Education. Not only does USAID recognise the leadership role Indonesia plays in its own development, but it also formulates and implements its policies according to both the US mission strategy to Indonesia and the Indonesian national education strategy. Indonesia has endeavoured to reduce dependence on foreign financial assistance, including American financial assistance, by increasing its budget in education expenditure and contributing financially to its education relationship with the US. Indonesia has various relationship choices for education aid and is not dependent on the US as its principal donor. Indonesia will continue in the foreseeable future to require education grants from a range of sources.

One prominent argument of critical education theorists is that recipient countries become dependent on the knowledge and financial aid of the provider countries. Although dependence on foreign expertise and the one-way transfer of knowledge are evident, the Indonesian government has repeatedly encouraged self-reliance, rather than dependence on foreign countries for knowledge or aid. The Indonesian government through national education laws has been active in limiting its dependence on foreign countries, whether that reliance was on knowledge, education professionals, or on finance. Accordingly, the relationships with developed state counterparts do not conform to a new type of imperialism. The argument, therefore, that transnational education contributes to the development of a new imperialism by perpetuating knowledge and financial dependency through the transfer of foreign knowledge and aid in education is not supported in the case of Indonesia.

In summary, gaining new skills and knowledge was regarded by the Indonesian respondents to be one of the benefits of the relationship, as new skills and knowledge improve the quality of Indonesian education, its graduates, educators, and researchers. The implication for Indonesia's educational sovereignty was examined through a framework specifically constructed for analysing the extent of educational sovereignty. The Indonesian respondents were aware of the risks of the relationship, such as being dependent on knowledge and financial assistance from developed states. Thus, the Indonesian government has been active in limiting its dependence on foreign countries, whether that reliance was on knowledge, education professionals, or finance, through national education laws. In this context, the government of Indonesia has control over national education laws.

Does Transnational Education Advance Learning About Other States and Has the Potential to Improve Relationships and Promote International Understanding?

The relationships between Indonesia and its developed state counterparts have not always been without obstacles. Yet, Indonesia, with developed states such as the US, has endeavoured to build a stronger relationship by making long-term commitments through the US–Indonesia Comprehensive Partnership. The Americans have the opportunity to study Indonesian culture, language, and arts, under Darmasiswa scholarships, while Indonesian youth are offered the opportunity of American Field Scholarship (AFS) exchanges for gaining greater cultural understanding. Indonesia's relationships with developed states such as the US and Australia are politically related, their educational arrangements being replete with political potential from the outset. In the case of the Indonesian–US relationship, for instance, Indonesia seeks to advance its development interests and the US seeks to advance its interests in the region. Both are concerned about the rise of China politically and economically, and also with the stability of the region. Consequently, Indonesia and the US have some economic and political agendas that are similar. It is unavoidable that the Indonesia–US relationship is politically motivated towards serving each other's interests. For example, from Indonesia's perspective, the US has been a counterbalance in the South China Sea (located to the North of Indonesia) dispute and the US market has contributed to the profitability of Indonesia's rubber and allied products. Additionally, the education relationship with the US can be seen to serve the interests of Indonesia, given that prestigious US technology, science, and engineering play an important role in *ketahanan negara*, or state resilience. Education relationships with other states, such as Australia and New Zealand, also serve to address the needs of Indonesia's graduates and experts in business, through the courses that Australia and New Zealand have offered. The relationship enhances and improves academic and research collaboration between Indonesia and its developed state counterparts.

The respondents who studied in the US for one year or less showed a greater appreciation of America, while continuing to be cautious about losing their cultural identity. Similarly, American participants who had visited Indonesia showed a greater appreciation of Indonesia's diverse cultures and its geopolitics. The evidence from this study is that transnational education does advance learning about other states and does have the potential to improve relationships and promote international understanding.

Does Foreign Financial Assistance in Education Threaten the Educational Sovereignty of Indonesia?

There were two main aspects in determining whether foreign financial assistance has been a threat to the educational sovereignty of Indonesia. The first is related to the question of whether there was any evidence that there had been, and whether there are conditions attached to foreign financial assistance, which could be seen as a threat to Indonesia's sovereignty. The second aspect is related to the question of what limitations there were on the exercise of authority and autonomy over education by developed states within Indonesian territorial boundaries.

To examine whether there was any evidence that there had been conditions attached to American financial assistance, which could be seen as a threat to Indonesian education sovereignty, it is necessary to understand first how much US aid was given to Indonesia. Although during the George W. Bush administration, US assistance targeted terrorism, arguably benefitting the US, most US assistance to Indonesia targeted such areas as health and military training. The assistance in these areas addressed needs identified by the Indonesian government, with one of the major US aid initiatives being the six-year, $157 million education programme that began in 2004.

There was no evidence that American financial assistance in education was considered a threat. USAID has played an important role in Indonesia's education through its financial contribution. The US does place conditions on its assistance in education, based on the purpose and aims of the US–Indonesia Comprehensive Partnership, which is a long-term commitment to foster Indonesia–US bilateral relations. There was no evidence of any attachment of conditions for the assistance. USAID endeavours to work collaboratively and build the capacity of local institutions, while recognising the authority of Indonesia to control its national education, and thus does not seek to intervene in Indonesian's national education, which is under the authority of DIKTI. USAID, therefore, formulates and implements its policies in line with both the US mission strategy to Indonesia and the education strategy set down in Washington, and with the Indonesian national education strategy. USAID also recognises the leadership role Indonesia plays in its own development and respects the position that Indonesia has authority over its education.

To avoid aid dependency, not only has Indonesia allocated finance for development projects, but also has improved cooperation with other states such as Korea, Japan, and China. For Indonesia, foreign financial assistance complements the national budget. It means, without foreign financial assistance, Indonesia's development projects will still continue within its national budget. Since 2003, the government of Indonesia had also passed a number of regulations that are aimed to prevent dependency on foreign states. These regulations include Law of Finance number 17/2003, Law of National Treasury number 1/2004, and the National Development Plan number 25/2004. These regulations limit the quota of foreign financial assistance to Indonesia and prevent foreign states dictating with regard to Indonesia's development policies.

The US, Australia, and New Zealand have taken advantage of the economic opportunities of Indonesia's growing middle class; thus, any disputes arising will not necessarily weaken the relationships. Indonesia has taken a clear stance that it does not depend on foreign financial assistance.

Does the Indonesian Government Retain Sufficient Control Over Its National Education Curriculum?

Despite its active participation in transnational education, Indonesia maintains Pancasila, the Constitution 1945 (UUD 1945), and religion as the foundation of its education and as a means to prevent the loss of Indonesian identity and cultural values. Even though the Indonesian National Education Law of 2003 authorises transnational education within Indonesian territory, foreign education institutions need to follow the Indonesian curriculum in Indonesia, and may not interfere with Indonesian national education because it is under the authority of Directorate General of Higher Education. Despite the flow of education across borders, *Bahasa* Indonesia is the language of instruction, and religion is compulsory in the Indonesian education curriculum (see Chap. 6).

Culture is the central issue in the discussion surrounding transnational education. From the interviews, the comments of Indonesian respondents clearly show that they were willing to adopt the American education system and some American cultural values, such as the need to be punctual. The respondents were aware of the risks in all their exchanges with the Americans, such as losing the ability to maintain control in education curriculum, and they felt they were certainly in control. The Indonesian government also has established and developed a character-based curriculum for maintaining cultural values through education. In this context, although Indonesians have adopted the American education system and some useful aspects of American cultural values, the Indonesian government is still committed to retaining and disseminating Indonesian cultural values through education. Despite the penetration of American culture through education transactions between Indonesia and the US, Indonesian identity and culture have survived and are preserved through the national education curriculum. Indonesian respondents confirmed that Indonesia retains control over its national educational curriculum and that education generally is not subject to homogenisation. By using and safeguarding its authority over education within its territorial borders, Indonesia has made agreements with other sovereign states, such as the US. Thus, Indonesia is able to preserve its cultural autonomy and formulate regulatory policies inside its territory. Indonesian authority is evident in the way foreign students are required to learn and understand the Indonesian language. *Bahasa* Indonesia and religion are compulsory in the education curriculum, and although English is introduced in the curriculum as a way to prepare individuals to be ready to play active roles in global competition, local stories are also included as part of the English language curriculum, thereby ensuring knowledge and preservation of Indonesian cultural values. For these reasons, the Indonesian government retains sufficient control over its national education curriculum so that it is not subject to homogenisation.

DOES THE CREATION OF HYBRID EDUCATION PROGRAMMES DIMINISH INDONESIA'S EDUCATIONAL SOVEREIGNTY?

As noted in Chap. 6, the hybridisation of the religious values of Hinduism, Islam, and Buddhism with indigenous values has been maintained in Indonesia by handing down local wisdom and values through local folktales, from generation to generation, and through formal education. At post-secondary education level, religious study is compulsory.

Under its former coloniser (the Dutch), Western culture had an influence on both Indonesian education and culture. Some aspects of Dutch culture were adopted, including Dutch cuisine and language. Nonetheless, since Indonesia introduced American English at elementary school in 1967, American education and literature have influenced the Indonesian education curriculum at the post-secondary level (see Chaps. 3 and 6).

For most Indonesian respondents, American higher education is highly prestigious. Education transactions with the US, as indicated by most Indonesian respondents, are necessary for enhancing the quality and reputation of Indonesian higher education. Most Indonesian respondents also expressed a willingness to adopt American cultural values. Yet, the issue of the inclusion of cultural values for most Indonesian respondents remains crucial; the preservation of Indonesia's cultural identity is the foremost concern for Indonesian respondents. This concern reflects the validity of the critical educationalists arguments. Accordingly, as it is mainly Indonesian respondents who prefer to adopt American cultural values and education, it is to be expected that the maintenance of cultural values is a matter of some concern for Indonesian negotiators. Therefore, the government of Indonesia has attempted from time to time to preserve cultural values through the education curriculum. In addressing the threat of foreign influences on Indonesian cultural values, the government is now actively promoting a character-based curriculum, aimed at strengthening Indonesian cultural values.

Unlike in the case of Indonesia–US education relations, where the loss of Indonesian culture is one of the highest concerns for Indonesian respondents, in the case of Indonesia–New Zealand education relations, the Indonesian respondents do not have concerns for the loss of Indonesian culture.

From the data gathered for this study, there is no indication of American cultural imposition, with most Indonesian respondents claiming they willingly adopt certain aspects of American culture because they consider it beneficial or advantageous to their own national interests. Accordingly, the idea of cultural imperialism is not supported. Neither were there any indications of cultural dependence arising from the Indonesia–US education relationship, as Indonesian respondents have clearly asserted that Indonesia has its own identity. For these reasons, the creation of hybrid education programmes does not necessarily diminish Indonesia's educational sovereignty.

Towards a Successful Education Partnership

There is a significant and pertinent aspect arising from this study. The American and New Zealand respondents used the term partnership repeatedly. Indeed, education relationship arrangements or collaborative activities are often referred to as education partnerships. It is argued that reciprocal benefits, respect for, and understanding of, each other's cultural and working environments are elements of a partnership.

The case of the Indonesia–New Zealand relationship in education shows that the Indonesian negotiators did not see mutual benefits in the relationship with New Zealand. It can be argued that the absence of any notion of reciprocal benefits is because the transnational education mode of delivery between New Zealand and Indonesia is the consumption abroad mode, whereas the interests of Indonesian parties include research collaboration and visiting scholarship programmes.

As an emerging economy with the rise of the middle class, Indonesia offers a promising partnership that is beneficial for New Zealand's economy. For New Zealand, it will be a missed opportunity if New Zealand does not develop a sustained relationship with Indonesia.

In the case of Indonesia–New Zealand relations in education, educational partnership is viewed by the Indonesian respondents as a mechanism for joint research opportunities. What the partnership should comprise, such as shared principles, interests, and objectives, however, still needs to be developed by both the Indonesian and New Zealand parties.

A framework for accommodating the needs of both New Zealand and Indonesia should include follow-ups and early reviews of progress in the collaboration; understanding and being transparent with each other's needs and concerns; designing programme activities that serve the interests of both parties; and developing programmes such as research collaboration and visiting scholar and student exchange programmes, instead of solely selling education courses to the Indonesian students.

Final Remarks

This book has endeavoured to clarify the defining features of educational sovereignty. Thus, it is hoped that this book will make both theoretical and empirical contributions to the study of transnational education. At the theoretical level, this book offers a framework analysis for assessing whether educational sovereignty has diminished and, if so, the extent to which this loss has occurred. Empirically, this study has provided an understanding of the complexity of the relationship between the LDSs and developed states.

The empirical limitations of the evidence of the study should be acknowledged. Using the case study approach has distinctive disadvantages as its findings are less generalisable because it is context-specific. Nonetheless, it is important to take into account that the interviews conducted in this study bring insights that simply cannot be gained by other methods. It is important to note that it is essential to treat cases of Indonesia–New Zealand and Indonesia–US education relations not for the purpose of generalisation, but rather for the ways in which they illustrate processes in the negotiations, perceptions, and objections, and also provide insight into how the communication between participants functions.

It is necessary to note that this book uses only Indonesia as a subject for the study of educational sovereignty. Using other southeast Asian countries, such as Malaysia, for the study of educational sovereignty is a valuable future research avenue.

BIBLIOGRAPHY

Abdulgani-Knapp, Retnowati. 2007. *The Life and Legacy of Indonesia's Second President*. Singapore: Marshall Cavendish International.
Abrahamsen, Rita. 2004. The Power of Partnerships in Global Governance. *Third World Quarterly* 25: 1453–1467.
Acharya, Amitav. 1999. Southeast Asia's Democratic Moment. *Asian Survey* 39 (3): 418–432.
Ackerly, Brooke, and Jacqui True. 2010. *Doing Feminist Research in Political and Social Science*. New York: Palgrave Macmillan.
Adlung, Rudolf. 2006. Public Services and the GATS. *Journal of International Economic Law* 9 (2): 1–29.
Agnew, John. 2005. Sovereign Regimes: Territoriality and State Authority in Contemporary Politics. *Annals of the Association of American Geographers* 95: 437–461.
Albatch, Philip. 1981. The University as Centre and Periphery. *Teachers College Record* 4: 601–621.
———. 2004a. Higher Education Crosses Borders: Can the United States Remain the Top Destination for Foreign Students? *Change* 36: 18–25.
———. 2004b. Globalisation and the University: Myths and Realities in an Unequal World. *Tertiary Education and Management* 10: 3–25.
Albatch, Philip, and G.P. Kelly. 1978. *Education and Colonialism*. New York: Longman.

Albatch, Philip, and Viswanathan Selvaratnam. 1989. *From Dependence to Autonomy: The Development of Asian Universities*. Dordrecht: Kluwer Academic.
American Indonesian Chamber of Commerce. *Culture and Business Trip*. Last modified 10 May 2013. http://www.aiccusa.org/culturaltips
Anis, Chowdhury, and Imam Sugema. 2005. How Significant and Effective Has Foreign Aid to Indonesia Been? *ASEAN Economic Bulletin* 22: 186–216.
Antara News Agency. *Demonstration of Thousands of Students Against BHMN-BHP Status*. http://www.antara.co.id/arc
Anwar, Dewi. 2003. Human Security: An Intractable Problem in Asia. In *Asian Security Order: Instrumental and Normative Features*, ed. Muthiah Alagappa. Stanford: Stanford University Press.
———. 2006. *Indonesia's Perceptions of China and the U.S. Security Roles in East Asia*. Jakarta: The Habibie Centre.
APLU. Recommendations on US-Indonesia Enhanced Cooperation in Higher Education Under the Planned Comprehensive Partnership. *Report of the US Higher Education Leaders Mission to Indonesia*. Last modified 10 July 2011. http://www.aplu.org/netcommunity/document
Aritonang, Margaret. New Laws Open Doors to Foreign Universities. *Jakarta Post*, 14 July 2013.
Arrifahmi, Dian. Industry Minister: Indonesia Is Not Ready for Newly Signed ASEAN-China FTA. *The Jakarta Globe*. http://www.thejakartaglobe
ASEAN. *Indonesia: Schedule of Specific Commitment*. Last modified 20 November 2012. http://www.aseansec.org
Asia Times. *US-Indonesia in a Tentative Embrace*. Last modified 10 June 2014. http://www.atimes.com
Aust, Anthony. 1986. The Theory and Practice of Informal International Instruments. *The International and Comparative Law Quarterly* 35: 787–812.
———. 2010. *Handbook in International Law*. 2nd ed. Cambridge: Cambridge University Press.
Baldwin, David. 1998. Exchange Theory and International Relations. *International Negotiations* 3: 139–149.
Ballard. 1995. Some Issues in Teaching International Students. In *Reaching More Students*, ed. L. Conrad and L. Phillips. Queensland: Griffith Institute for Higher Education.
Baptista, May. 2013, January 20. *Students Conduct Research and Study at the US Embassy's Information Resource Center in Jakarta, Indonesia*. http://www.america.govt
Baskoro, Faisal. 2012, November 20. State Firms to Buy Bonds in Case of Capital Reversal. *The Jakarta Globe*. http://www.thejakartaglobe.com
Bauer, Peter. 1969. Dissent on Development. *Scottish Journal of Political Economy* 16: 75–94.
BBC. *Obama Hails Indonesia as Example for World*, 13 May 2013.

Bert, Wayne. 1993. Chinese Policy and US Interests in Southeast Asia. *Asian Survey* 33: 317–322.
Binder, Claudia. 2002. Research in Partnership with Developing Countries: Application of the Method of Material Flux Analysis in Tunja, Colombia. *Future Cities: Dynamics and Sustainability* 1: 227–240.
Biswal, Nisha. New Teaching Methods and Resources Transform Indonesian Schools. *USAID*. http://blog.usaid.gov/2011
Bodin, Jean. 1967. *The Six Books of a Commonwealth* (ed. and trans: Michael Tooley). Oxford: Blackwell.
Bortin, Meg. Polls Show U.S. Isolation: In War's Wake, Hostility, and Mistrust. *The New York Times*, 5 June 2003.
Bray, M. 1993. Education and the Vestiges of Colonialism: Self-determination, Neocolonialism and Dependency in the South Pacific. *Comparative Education* 29: 333–348.
Brinkerhoff, Jennifer. 2002. Choosing the Right Partners for the Right Reasons. In *Partnership for International Development: Rhetoric or Results?* Boulder: Lynne Rienner.
Brock Utne, Brigit. 2000. *Education for All: The Recolonialization of the African Mind*. New York: Falmer Press.
Brodjonegoro, Satryo. n.d. *Higher Education Reforms in Indonesia*. Last modified 28 August 2012. http://www.worldreform.com
Buchori, Mochtari, and Abdul Malik. 2004. The Evolution of Higher Education in Indonesia. In *Asian Universities: Historical Perspectives and Contemporary Challenges*, ed. Philip Altbach and Toru Umakoshi. Baltimore: The John Hopkins University Press.
Budianta, Melani. 2007. Beyond the Stained-Glass Window: Indonesian perceptions of the United States and the War on Terror. In *What They Think of Us: International Perceptions of the United States Since 9/11*, ed. D. Farber, 27–48. Princeton: Princeton University Press.
Burbules, Nicholas, and Carlos Torres. 2000. *Globalization and Education: Critical Perspectives*. New York: Routledge.
Cai, Deborah, et al. 2000. Culture in the Context of Intercultural Negotiation: Individualism-Collectivism and Paths to Integrative Agreements. *Human Communication Research* 26: 591–617.
Canto, Isabel, and Janet Hannah. 2001. A Partnership of Equals? Academic Collaboration Between the United Kingdom and Brazil. *Journal of Studies in International Education* 5: 26–41.
Capaldi, Nicholas. 2002. The Meaning of Equality. In *Liberty and Equality*, ed. Tibor Machan. Stanford: Hoover Press.
Carnegie Endowment. *Where the War on Terror Is Succeeding*. Last modified 30 November 2012. http://www.carnegieendowment.org

Carnoy, Martin. 1975. *Education as Cultural Imperialism*. New York: David McKay.
Carnoy, Martin, and Diana Rhoten. 2002. What Does Globalization Mean for Educational Change? A Comparative Approach. *Comparative Education Review* 46: 1–10.
China Daily. *Obama Warms Indonesia Ties: Volcano May Cut Trip*, 13 May 2013. http://chronicle.com/article
Cialdini, R.B. 1993. *Influence: Science and Practice*. New York: Harper Collins.
Collins, Christopher. 2007. A General Agreement on Higher Education: GATS, Globalization, and Imperialism. *Research in Comparative and International Education* 2: 1–14.
Compa and Jeffrey Vogt. *Labor Rights in the Generalized System of Preferences: A 20-Year Review*. http://www.digitalcommons.ilr.cornell.edu
Conversi, Daniele. 2007. Homogenisation, Nationalism and War: Should We Still Read Ernest Gellner? *Nations and Nationalism* 13: 371–394.
Cox, Robert. 1981. Social Forces, States, and World Orders: Beyond International Relations Theory. *Millennium: Journal of International Studies* 10 (2): 126–155.
Cookson, Peter. 2002. The Hybridisation of Higher Education in Canada: Cross National Perspectives. *The International Review of Research in Open Distance Learning* 2 (2): 1–4.
Crawford, Gordon. 2001. *Foreign Aid and Political Reform: A Comparative Analysis of Democracy Assistance and Political Conditionality*. Basingstoke: Palgrave.
———. 2003. Partnership or Power? Deconstructing the 'Partnership for Governance Reform' in Indonesia. *Third World Quarterly* 24: 139–159.
Cribb, Robert, and Audrey Kahin. 2004. *Historical Dictionary of Indonesia*. Lanham: Scarecrow Press.
Dahana, A. 2006. *Indonesia's Perceptions of China and the U.S. Security Roles in East Asia*. Jakarta: The Habibie Centre.
Daniel, John. Building Capacity in Open and Distance Learning. *OECD/UNESCO Australia Forum on Trade in Education Services*, 12 October 2004, Sydney.
Denzin, Norman, and Yvonna Lincoln. 2003. *Strategies of Qualitative Inquiry*. Thousand Oaks: Sage.
Department of National Education. *Strategic Plan of the Department of National Education 2005–2009*. Last modified 10 October 2013. http://www.planipolis.iip
Department of State. Plan of Action to Implement the Indonesia-US Comprehensive Partnership. *Bureau of East Asian and Pacific Affairs*, 17 September 2010.
———. US-Indonesia Joint Commission and Bilateral Meeting. Office of Spokesman, September 2010.
DeRosa, Dean. 2004. US Free Trade Agreements with ASEAN. In *Free Trade Agreements: US Strategies and Priorities*, ed. Jeffrey Schott. Washington, DC: Institute for International Economics.

Dessoff, Alan. Building Partnerships: Indonesia and the United States. *Embassy of Indonesia*. http://www.embassyofindonesia.org/education.docpdf/building

Dharmawan, Frederik, and Eric Koo Peng Kuan. Adopting International Curricula for the Indonesian Context. *Jakarta Post*, Sunday, 9 November 2008.

DIKTI. *Long Term Framework for Developing Higher Education 1996–2005*. Last modified 9 June 2012. http://www.dikti.org/kpptjp.html

———. *Scholarship Programme Guidelines*. Last modified 30 May 2013. http://www.dikti.net

Directorate General of Higher Education. *RENSTRA (Strategic Planning) 2010–2014*. Last modified 23 June 2017. http://www.dikti.org

———. *Competition Based Curriculum Development*. Last modified 30 June 2013. http://www.akademik.dikti.go.id

Directorate General of Islamic Education. *Foreign Students Are Reluctant to Do Research in Indonesia*. Last modified 20 March 2013. http://pendis.kemenag.go.id

Donnans, Hastings, and Thomas Wilson. 1999. *Borders: Frontiers of Identity, Nation, and State*. Oxford: Berg.

Drysdale, Robert. 1975. Education as a Cultural Imperialism: Book Review. *School of Review* 84: 147–151.

Easterlin, Richard. 1981. Why Isn't the Whole World Developed? *The Journal of Economic History* 41: 1–19.

Economy, Elizabeth. 2005. China's Rise in Southeast Asia: Implications for the United States. *Journal of Contemporary China* 14: 405–425.

Education New Zealand. *Fact Sheet: Indonesia*. Last modified 10 November 2016. http://www. http://nziec.co.nz/wp-content/uploads/2015/08/Factsheet-Indonesia.pdf

Effendi, Sofian. *Quality and Transparency: Indonesia's Approach to Cross-Border Higher Education*. http://www.sofian.staff.ugm.ac.id

Egege, Sandra, and Salah Kutieleh. 2004. Critical Thinking: Teaching Foreign Notions to Foreign Students. *International Education Journal* 4: 75–85.

Elbe, Stefan. 2010. Haggling over Viruses: The Downside Risks of Securitizing Infectious Disease. *Health Policy and Planning* 25: 476–485.

Embassy of the Republic of Indonesia. *Indonesian Scholarship*. Last modified 10 January 2013. http://embassyofindonesia.org

———. *Bilateral Relations*. Last modified 15 August 2014. http://www.embassyofindonesia.org

Embassy of the United States. *Language Fellow Program*. Last modified 5 September 2013. http://Jakarta.usembassy.gov/fellow.html

Eng, P.V., and D. Southeast. 2004. *Asia: A Historical Encyclopaedia from Angkor Wat to East Timor*. Santa Barbara: ABC-CLIO.

Etzioni, Amitai. 2004. A Self-Restrained Approach to Nation-Building by Foreign Powers. *International Affairs* 80: 1–17.

ExxonMobil. *ExxonMobil in Indonesia*. Last modified 20 March 2013. http://www.exxonmobil.co.id

Fadilah, Rangga. *SOEs' Net Profits Expected to Reach US$ 12.6 Billion This Year*. Last Modified 20 April 2012. http://www.embassyofindonesia.org/news

Fahmi, Mohammad. *Indonesian Higher Education: The Chronicle, Recent Development, and the New Legal Entity Universities*. http://www.lp3e.fe.unpad.ac.id

Fasimpaur, Karen. *Massive and Open MOOCs*. Last modified 8 August 2014. http://www.files.eric.ed.gov/fulltext/EJ1015163.pdf

Fetsch, Frank P., and Alice Landau. 2000. Symmetry and Asymmetry in International Negotiations. *International Negotiation* 5: 21–42.

Firestone, William. 1987. The Rhetoric of Quantitative and Qualitative Research. *Educational Researcher* 16: 16–21.

Fischer, Karin. Obama Begins Rebuilding Academic Ties to Indonesia. *The Chronicle of Higher Education*. Last modified May 2012. http://www.chronicle.com/article

———. 2010. A New Start for U.S. and Indonesian Higher Education. *The Chronicle of Higher Education*. http://www.chronicle.com/article/a-new-start-for-us

Fox, Christina. 2007. The Questions of Identity from a Comparative Education Perspective. In *Comparative Education: The Dialectic of the Global and the Local*, ed. Robert Arnove and Carlos Torres, 134–138. Maryland: Rowman and Littlefield Publishers.

Frank, Andre. 1984. The Development of Underdevelopment. In *The Political Economy of Development and Underdevelopment*, 3rd ed. New York: Random House.

Frase, Frase and Brendan O'Sullivan. *The Future of Education Under the WTO*. Last modified December 2009. http://www.campusdemocracy

Gargano, Terra. 2009. (Re)conceptualizing International Student Mobility: The Potential of Transnational Social Fields. *Journal of Studies in International Education* 13: 331–346.

GATRA. *Numbers of Indonesian Students Drop*. Last modified 17 July 2012. http://www.gatra.com/article.php/id

Global Alliance for TNE. *Certification Manual*. Last modified 28 July 2012. http://www.edugate.org

Gonzales, Alfonso, and Jim Norwine, eds. 1998. *The New Third World*. Boulder: West View Press.

Goodwin, Robin, and Sophie Giles. 2003. Social Support Provision and Cultural Values in Indonesia and Britain. *Journal of Cross-Cultural Psychology* 34: 240–245.

Granado, F.J., Wolfgang Fengler, Andy Ragatz, and Elif Yavuz. Investing Indonesia's Education: Allocation, Equity, and Efficiency of Public Expenditure. *The World Bank Policy Research Working Paper*, August 2007.

Green, Madeleine. 2004. GATS Update. *International Higher Education* 37: 3–5.

Green, Mike. *Governance Issues in Post-Soeharto Indonesia*. Retrieved from http://www.asiaforum.org.nz./wpcontent/uploads/governance-issues-in-post-soehartindonesia.pdf. Paper was presented for Asia Forum, 12 February 2002.

Gürüz, Kemal. 2008. *Higher Education Student Mobility in the Global Knowledge Economy*. New York: State University of New York University Press.

Hadiniwata, Bob. 2009. International Relations in Indonesia: Historical Legacy, Political Intrusion, and Commercialization. *International Relations of the Asia-Pacific* 9: 55–81.

Hadiz, Vedi, and Daniel Dhakidae. 2005. *Social Science and Power in Indonesia*. Singapore: Equinox.

Hara, Abubakar. *Promoting Women Security as Human Security: Indonesian Women Attempt to Find Their Place in the Newly Indonesia Democracy*. http://www.humansecurityconf.polsci.chula.ac.th/Documents/.../Abubakar.doc

Harden, Nathan. The End of University as We Know It. *The American Interests*, 11 December 2012.

Hardihardaja. 1996. Private Higher Education in Indonesia: Current Developments and Existing Problems. In *Private Higher Education in Asia and the Pacific*, ed. Ongsothorn Tong-In and Yibling Wang. Bangkok: UNESCO, PROAP and SEAMO RIHED.

Harian Andalas. *Aceh Government Was Asked to Tighten Rules on Permits for Foreign Education*. http://www.harianandalas.com

Harian Global Post. *Perguruan Tinggi Asing Dibatasi Dalam Penerimaan Mahasiswa*. Last modified 28 January 2013. http://www.harian-global

Hart, L.A. 2012. *Concept of Law*. Oxford: Oxford University Press.

Heath, Joseph. 2004. Liberalization, Modernization, Westernization. *Philosophy and Social Criticism* 30: 665–690.

Hein, Gordon. 1988. *Suharto's Foreign Policy*. Ann Arbor: UMI Dissertation Information Service.

Held, David. 2002. Law of States, Law of Peoples: Three Models of Sovereignty. *Legal Theory* 8: 1–44.

Henkin, Louis. 1979. *How Nations Behave*. 2nd ed. New York: Columbia University Press.

Herbert, Werlin, and Harry Eckstein. 1990. Political Culture and Political Change. *The American Political Science Review* 84: 249–253.

Higgott, Richard. 1998. The Asian Economic Crisis: A Study in the Politics of Resentment. *New Political Economy* 3: 333–356.

Hindley, Donald. 1963. Foreign Aid to Indonesia and Its Political Implications. *Pacific Affairs* 36: 107–119.

———. 1967. Political Power and the October 1965 Coup in Indonesia. *The Journal of Asian Studies* 26: 237–249.

Hinsley, Francis Harry. 1986. *Sovereignty*. 2nd ed. Cambridge: Cambridge University Press.

Huang, Futao. 2007. Internationalization of Higher Education in the Developing and Emerging Countries: A Focus on Transnational Higher Education in Asia. *Journal of Studies in International Education* 11: 421–432.

Idrus, Nirwan. 2003. Transforming Quality for Development. *Quality in Higher Education* 9: 141–150.

Indonesian Department of Finance. *Focus Group Discussion: Researchers and Research Professors: Enhancing Their Roles and Professionalism.* http://www.fiskal.depkeu.go.id/2010/m

———. *Anggaran Pendidikan 2010–2015.* Last modified 20 January 2013. http://www.depkeu.go.id

Indonesian Institute of Arts. *Foreign Students Are Reluctant to Do Research in Indonesia.* Last modified 30 September 2012. http://www.isi-denpasar.ac.id/berita/mahasisa-asing-mulai-enggan-meneliti-di-indonesia

Indonesian Investment Coordinating Board. *Facts of Indonesia: Natural Resources.* Last modified 4 May 2013. http://www.bpkm.go.id

Indonesian Ministry of Defence. *Pendidikan karakter di Amerika Serikat.* https://balitbangdiklat.kemenag.go.id/download/read/984-1-pendidikan-karakter-di-USApdf

Indonesian Ministry of National Education. *Character Based Education.* Last modified 10 January 2013. http://www.perpustakaan.kemendiknas

———. *Republic of Indonesia and the United States Cooperation in Research.* Last modified 12 January 2013. http://www.kemendiknasgo.id

———. *Strategic Planning'.* Last modified 20 May 2013. http://www.kemendiknas.go.id

Indonesian Ministry of National Education and Culture. *Cooperation in education and accreditation.* Last modified 15 January 2013. https://www.kemdikbud.go.id/main

Indonesian Ministry of Research and Technology. *About Indonesian Higher Education.* http://risbang.ristekdikti.go.id/regulasi/uu-12-2012.pdf

Institute of International Education. About: The US- Indonesia Partnership Program. http://www.iie.org/research

Irwin, Rachel. 2010. Indonesia, H5N1, and Global Health Diplomacy. *Global Health Governance* 3: 1–21.

Jakarta Globe. Indonesian Government Plans to Spend over US$ 34 Billion on Education. *Jakarta Globe*, 17 August 2012.

———. *Education Privatization Bill Encounters Expert Opposition.* http://www.thejakartaglobe.com

Jakarta Post. US Most Popular Foreign Study Destination. *Jakarta Post*, 26 February 1997.

———. Number of Indonesian Students in US Doubled. *Jakarta Post*, 13 November 2009.

———. 9/11 Attack Brings US, RI Closer. *Jakarta Post*, 9 September 2011.

———. *Aussie, US, UK, and Singapore Top Choices for Overseas Study*. http://www.thejakartapost.com/news/2010/08/10/aussie-us-uk-and-singapore-top-choices-overseas-study.html

———. NAMRU-2: For Who? *Jakarta Post*, 10 November 2012.

———. *People-to-People Relations, Key in Education Partnership*. Last modified 25 January 2013. http://www.thejakartapost.com/news

———. *US Puts Up $301 Million for Partnership with RI*. http://thejakartapost.com

Jandt, Fred. 2001. *Intercultural Communication: An Introduction*. London: Sage.

Jing, Gu Jian. 2009. Transnational Education: Current Developments and Policy Implications. *Front Education China* 4: 624–649.

Jones, Roger. 1995. Why Do Quality Research? *British Medical Journal* 311: 2.

Jones, L.P., ed. 1997. *Public Enterprise in Less Developed Countries*. New York.

Kay, Lena. 2005. Indonesian Public Perceptions of the US and Their Implications for US Foreign Policy. *Issues and Insight* 5: 3–64.

Kilby, Christopher. 1999. Aid and Sovereignty. *Social Theory and Practice* 25: 79–92.

King, Kenneth. The New Politics of Partnership: Perils or Promise? *NORRAG News*, December 2008, Last modified 2 August 2016. http://www.norrag.org/fileadmin

Kivimaki, Timo. 1993. Strength of Weakness: American-Indonesian Hegemonic Bargaining. *Journal of Peace Research* 30: 391–408.

———. 2003. *US-Indonesia Hegemonic Bargaining: Strength of Weakness*. Aldershot: Ashgate.

Kleden, Ignas. 1986. Alternative Social Science as an Indonesian Problematique. *New Asian Visions* 3: 6–22.

Knight, Jane. 1997. Internationalization of Higher Education: A Conceptual Framework. In *Internationalization of Higher Education in Asia Pacific Countries*, ed. Jane Knight and Hans De Wit. Amsterdam: European Association for International Education.

———. 2004. Internationalization Remodelled: Definition, Approaches, and Rationales. *Journal of Studies in International Education* 8: 5–31.

———. 2006a. Cross-Border Education: An Analytical Framework for Program and Provider Mobility. *Higher Education* 21: 345–395.

———. 2006b. Higher Education Crossing Borders: A Guide to the Implications of the General Agreements on Trade in Services (GATS) for Cross-Border Education. *A Report Prepared for the Commonwealth of Learning and UNESCO*.

———. 2010. Higher Education Crossing Borders: Programmes and Providers on the Move. In *Higher Education in a Global Society*, ed. D. Bruce Johnston, Madeleine D'Ambrosia, and Paul Yakoboski. Northampton: Edward Elgar Publishing.

Kompas. American Students' Enthusiasm in Learning Indonesian Language. *Kompas*, 17 July 2012.

———. Education as the Key to Development. *Kompas*, 27 August 2012.

———. Let's Study in the US. *Kompas*. Last modified 18 July 2012.

Krasner, Stephen. 2001a. Sovereignty. *Foreign Policy* 122: 20–28.

———. 2001b. Abiding Sovereignty. *International Political Science Review* 22: 229–251.

Kroef, Justus. 1955. Higher Education in Indonesia. *The Journal of Higher Education* 26: 366–377.

Lane, Bernard. Monash to Consider Setting Up Campus in Indonesia. *The Australian*, 20 February 2003.

———. Indonesia Outlooks Uncertain for Branch Campuses. *The Australian*, 19 March 2013.

Larson, Deborah. 1998. Exchange and Reciprocity in International Negotiations. *International Negotiation* 3: 121–138.

Leifer, Michael. 1983. *Indonesia's Foreign Policy*. London: Allen and Unwin.

Lingard, Bob, and Fazal Rizvi. 1998. Globalisation and the Fear of Homogenisation in Education. *Change: Transformation in Education* 1: 62–71.

LIPI. *LIPI Sees the Quality of Indonesian Education Is Still Low*. http://lipi.go.id/berita/single/LIPI-nilai-Kualitaspendidikan-di-Indonesia-masih-rendah

Lipschutz, Ronald. 1992. Reconstructing World Politics: The Emergence of Global Society. *Millennium* 21: 389–420.

Loughlin, Martin. 2003. Ten Tenets of Sovereignty. In *Sovereignty in Transition*, ed. Neil Walker. Portland: Hart.

Lum, Thomas, et al. China's 'Soft Power' in Southeast Asia. *CRS Report for Congress*. 4 January 2008. https://fas.org/sgp/crs/row/RL34310.pdf

Lum, Thomas. U.S. Foreign Aid to East and South Asia: Selected Recipients. *CRS Report for Congress*. Last modified 5 October 2013. http://www.fpc.state.gov/documents

Marginson, Simon. 1997. *Markets in Education*. St. Leonards: Allen and Unwin.

Marginson, Simon, and Grant McBurnie. 2004. Cross-Border Post-Secondary Education in the Asia Pacific Region. In *Internationalisation and Trade in Higher Education: Opportunities and Challenges*. Paris: OECD.

Maroy, Christian. 2009. Converges and Hybridization of Educational Policies Around Post-Bureaucratic Models of Regulation. *Compare: A Journal of Comparative and International Education* 39: 71–84.

Marut, Don. Can Indonesia Do Without Foreign Aid? *The Jakarta Post*, Thursday 1 December 2011.

Maulia, Erwida. *MIT Tops Rankings for the First Time, Indonesia Universities' Positions Drop.* http://www.thejakartaglobe.com
Maulina, Erwida. Government to Retain Universities' Autonomy. *The Jakarta Post,* 13 April 2010.
Maxwell, Sarah, et al. 2003. The Wrath of the Fairness-Primed Negotiator When the Reciprocity Norm Is Violated. *Journal of Business Research* 56: 399–409.
McBurnie, Grant, and Christopher Ziguras. 2001. The Regulation of Transnational Higher Education in Southeast Asia: Case Studies of Hong Kong, Malaysia and Australia. *Higher Education* 42: 85–105.
———. 2007. *Transnational Education: Issues and Trends in Offshore Higher Education.* New York: Routledge.
McClure, Maureen. 2007. Sustainable University Partnerships: National Education Reform Challenges in Decentralizing Indonesia. *International Studies in Education* 8: 5–6.
Metronews. *Foreign Students Reluctant to Do Research in Indonesia.* Last modified 10 January 2013. http://www.metronews.com
Meyer, Michael. 2008. Using Documents. *Qualitative Research in Business and Management* 151–160.
Ministry of Foreign Affairs of the Republic of Indonesia. *Bilateral Cooperation: United States.* http://www.deplu.go.id
Ministry of Religion. *Character Based Curriculum.* Last modified 29 July 2013. http://www.balitbangdiklat.kemenag.go.id
Ministry of Research Technology and Higher Education Republic of Indonesia. *Law of the Republic of Indonesia No. 20 of 2003 on the National Education System.* http://www.inherent-dikti.net
Moll, Luis. The Concept of Educational Sovereignty. *The Ethnography Forum,* The University of Pennsylvania, 1 March 2002.
Moll, Luis, and Elizabeth Arnot-Hopffer. 2005. Socio-cultural Competence in Teacher Education. *Journal of Teacher Education* 56: 242–247.
Mooney, Francis. 1962. Some Highlights of the Development of Secondary and Teacher Education in Indonesia. *Peabody Journal of Education* 40: 137–141.
Morris, Paul. 1996. Asia's Four Little Tigers: A Comparison of the Role of Education in Their Development. *Comparative Education* 32: 95–109.
Morrow, Raymond, and Carlos Torres. 2007. The State, Social Movements, and Educational Reforms. In *Comparative Education: The Dialectic of the Global and the Local,* ed. Robert Arnove and Carlos Torres. Maryland: Rowman and Littlefield Publishers.
Munck, Ronaldo. 2004. Dependency and Imperialism in Latin America: New Horizons. In *The Political Economy of Imperialism: Critical Appraisals,* ed. Ronald Chilcote. Lanham: Rowman and Littlefield.
Murphy, Ann. Strategic Posture Review: Indonesia. *World Politics Review,* 20 September 2011.

———. 2010. US Rapprochement with Indonesia: From Problem State to Partner. *Contemporary Southeast Asia: A Journal of International and Strategic Affairs* 32: 362–287.

Muslim, B., Nia Nafisah, and Ika Damayanti. 2009. *Locality and Self-Identity: Local Story Inclusion in Indonesian English Text Books.* University of Indonesia.

Naidoo, Rajani. 2007. Higher Education as a Global Commodity: The Perils and Promises for Developing Countries. *The Observatory on Borderless Higher Education* 14 (2): 1–19.

National Bureau of Asian Research. 2010, November. Politics, Public Opinion, and the U.S.-Indonesia Comprehensive Partnership. *Special Report* Number 25.

Nguyen, Phuong-Mai, et al. 2009. Neo-colonialism in Education: Cooperative Learning in an Asian Context. *Comparative Education* 45 (1): 109–130.

Noel, Brett, Ann Shoemake, and Claudia Hale. 2006. Conflict Resolution in a Non-western Context: Conversations with Indonesian Scholars and Practitioners. *Conflict Resolution Quarterly* 23: 427–446.

Novotny, Daniel. 2007. *Indonesian Foreign Policy: A Quest for the Balance of Threats.* Dissertation, University of New South Wales.

Nuffic Neso Student Survey. *Annual Report June 2009.* Last modified 10 July 2010. http://www.nuffic.nl

Nye, Joseph. *Soft Power and Higher Education.* Last modified 20 July 2011. http://www.et.educause.edu/ir/library/pdf

OECD. *Corporate Responsibility: Frequently Asked Questions.* Directorate for Financial and Enterprise Affairs. http://www.oecd.org

———. *Glossary of Statistical Terms.* http://www.stats.oecd.org/

———. 2004, August. Internationalisation of Higher Education. *Observer, Policy Brief* 1–8.

Oliver, Paul, and Victor Jupp. 2006. Purposive Sampling. In *The Sage Dictionary of Social Research Methods.* London: Sage.

Orlikowski, Wanda, and Jack Baroudi. 1991. Studying Information Technology Organisations: Research Quality in Qualitative Approaches and Assumptions. *Information System Research* 2: 1–28.

Orlinkowski, Wanda, and Jack Baraoudi. 2002. Studying Information Technology in Organizations: Research Approaches and Assumptions. In *Qualitative Research in Information Systems: A Reader*, ed. Michael Myers and David Avison. London: Sage.

Oxford Dictionary. http://www.oxforddictionaries.com

Paasi, Anssi. 1998. Boundaries as Social Processes: Territoriality in the World of Flow. *Geopolitics* 3: 69–88.

Pardoen, S. 1998. Assessment of Private Investment in Private Higher Education in Indonesia: The Case of Four Private Universities. In *Centre for Societal Development Studies*. Jakarta: Atma Jaya Catholic University.

Parliament Library. *Indonesia's New Government: Stability at Last?* Last modified 20 November 2016. http://www.parliament.nz/resource/mi.nz

Passasung, Nikolaus. 2003. *Teaching English in an 'Acquisition Poor Environment'. An Ethnographic Example of a Remote Indonesian EFL Classroom*. Dissertation, University of Sydney. http://sydney.edu.au/library/theses/finding.html
Pennycook, Alastair. 1994. *The Cultural Politics of English as an International Language*. Harlow: Longman.
Pereira, Ana. 2005. The Liberalization of Education Under the WTO Services Agreement (GATS): A Threat to Public Education Policy. *Journal of International Economy* 2 (3): 1–40.
Pieterse, Jan. 1994. Globalisation as Hybridisation. *International Sociology* 9 (2): 161–184.
———. 2009. *Globalization and Culture: Global Melange*. Lanham: Rowman and Littlefield.
Pike, Graham. 2000. Global Education and National Identity: In Pursuit of Meaning. *Theory in Practice* 39: 64–73.
Purwadi, A. 2001. Impact of Economic Crisis on Higher Education in Indonesia. In *Impact of the Economic Crisis on Higher Education in East Asia*. Paris: IIEP/UNESCO.
Putera, Eka, and E.J. Brill. 1988. Pancasila and the Search for Identity and Modernity in Indonesian Society. *Journal of Southeast Asian Studies* 21 (2): 19–66.
Raychadaudhuri, Ajitava, and Prabir De. 2003. Barriers to Trade in Higher Education Services: Empirical Evidence from Asia Pacific Countries. *Asia Pacific Trade and Investment Review* 3: 67–88.
Regel, Ompron. 1992. The Academic Credit System in Higher Education: Effectiveness and Relevance in Higher Education. In *Education and Employment Division*. Washington, DC: The World Bank.
Report to the US Higher Education Leaders Mission to Indonesia. 2009. Recommendation on US-Indonesia Enhanced Cooperation in Higher Education Under 'the Planned Comprehensive Partnership'.
Republika. Minister of Research and Technology: Research in Indonesia Is Still in Its Infancy. *Republika*, 17 March 2013.
Riady, John. Top Flight Foreign Educated Graduates Can Help Indonesia Go Truly Global. *The Jakarta Globe*, 15 January 2010.
Ricklefs, Merle. 2001. *A History of Modern Indonesia Since c.1200*. Stanford: Stanford University Press.
———. The Future of Indonesia. *History Today*, 28 September 2013. http://www.historytoday.com
Riker, David, and Brandon Turner. Manufacturing and Services: Economics Brief. *US Department of Commerce*. Last modified 12 September 2012. http://www.trade.gov/mas
Rizvi, Fazal. 2000. International Education and the Production of Globalization Imagination. In *Globalization and Education: Critical Perspectives*, ed. N.C. Burbles and C.A. Torres. London: Routledge.

Robertson, Susan, et al. 2002. GATS and the Education Service Industry: The Politics of Scale and Global Territorialization. *Comparative Education Review* 46: 472–495.
Robertson, Raymond, et al. 2009. Globalization and Working Conditions: Evidence from Indonesia. In *Globalization, Wages, and the Quality of Jobs: Five Country Studies*, ed. Raymond Robertson et al. Washington, DC: The World Bank.
Robinson, William. 2007. Beyond the Theory of Imperialism. *Societies Without Borders* 2: 5–26.
Rowe, William, and Vivian Schelling. 1991. *Memory and Modernity: Popular Culture in Latin America*. London: Verso.
Rudijanto. Liberalization in Education: A Threat or a Necessity? *The Jakarta Post*, Wednesday, 26 January 2005.
Saito, Masaru. 1975. Introduction of Foreign Technology in the Industrialization Processes: Japanese Experience Since the Meiji Restoration. *Journal of Developing Economies* 13: 1–19.
Sajarwo, Gandang. Indonesia: The US Enhance Cooperation in Education. *Kompas*, 20 April 2012.
Said, Edward. 1993. *Culture and Imperialism*. New York: Vintage Books.
Samoff, Joel. 1999. International Influence. In *Comparative Education: The Dialectic of the Global and Local*, ed. Robert Arnove and Carlos Torres. Lanham: Rowman and Littlefield.
Sanou, Sini. 2004. Critical Transnational Education. *Western Humanities Review* 60: 141–153.
Santos, Boaventura. 2006. The University in the 21st Century: Toward a Democratic and Emancipatory University Reform. In *The University, States, and Market: The Political Economy of Globalization in the Americas*, ed. Robert Rhoads and Carlos Torres. Stanford: Stanford University Press.
Saud, Udin, and Marylyn Johnston. 2006. Cross-Cultural Influences on Teacher Education Reform: Reflections on Implementing the Integrated Curriculum in Indonesia. *Journal of Education for Teaching* 32: 3–20.
Sauve, Pierre. 2002. *Trade, Education and the GATS: What's In, What's Out, What's All the Fuss About?* Prepared for the OECD/US Forum on Trade in Services, Washington, DC.
Schatzman, Leonard, and Anslem Strauss. 1973. *Field Research: Strategies for a Natural Sociology*. Englewood Cliffs: Prentice Hall.
Schwartz, S.H. 1990. Individualism-Collectivism: Critique and Proposed Refinements. *Journal of Cross-Cultural Physiology* 21: 139–157.
Schwarz, Adam. 1994. *A Nation in Waiting. Indonesia in the 1990s*. Sydney: Allen & Unwin.
Schwindt, Erika. 2003. The Development of a Model for International Education with Specific Reference to the Role of Host Country Nationals. *Journal of Research in International Education* 2: 67–81.

Scoop. *PM Speech: State Dinner for Indonesian President.* Last modified 30 August 2016. http://www.scoop.co.nz/ stories/PA0504/S00128.htm

Segall, Marshall. 1999. *Human Behaviour in Global Perspective: An Introduction to Cross-Cultural Psychology.* 2nd ed. Boston: Allyn and Bacon.

Setiawan, Denny. *Character Based Curriculum and Its Implementation on Early Childhood Education.* http://www.pustaka.ut.ac.id

Shale, Douglas. 2002. The Hybridisation of Higher Education in Canada. *The International Review of Research in Open Distance Learning* 2: 1–5.

Short, R.P. 1984. The Role of Public Enterprises: An International Statistical Comparison. In *Public Enterprise in Mixed Economies: Some Macro-Economic Aspects*, ed. Robert Floyd, Clive Gray, and R.P. Short. Washington, DC: International Monetary Fund.

Sihaloho, Markus, and April Aswadi. *Health Ministry to Reopen NAMRU.* Last modified 30 November 2012. http://www.thejakartaglobe.com/news

Siqueira, Angela. 2005. The Regulation of Education Through the WTO/GATS. *Journal for Critical Education Policy Studies* 3 (1): 1–16.

Smith, Anthony. 2003. Reluctant Partner: Indonesia. *Asian Affairs* 30: 142–150.

———. 2005. A Glass Half Full: Indonesia-US Relations in the Age of Terror. *Contemporary Southeast Asia Journal of International and Strategic Affairs* 25: 449–472.

Smith, James. Indonesian Universities Focus on Video Conferencing Opportunity. *Asia Pacific*, Thursday, 29 August 2013.

Soejatmiah, Sri. 2009. Internationalisation of Indonesian Higher Education: A Study from the Periphery. *Asian Social Science Journal* 5: 70–78.

Soesastro, Hadi. Towards a US-Indonesia FTA. *Economics Working Paper Series.* Last modified August 2014. http://www.csis.or.id/papers/wpe08

Sofaer, Shoshanna. 1999. Qualitative Methods: What Are They and Why Use Them? *Health Service Research* 34: 1101–1118.

Spilimbergo, Antonio. 2009. Democracy and Foreign Education. *The American Economic Review* 99: 528–543.

Stake, Robert. 1995. *The Art of Case Study Research.* Thousand Oaks: Sage. Stanford University Press, 2001.

Statistics Canada. *Definition of Post-Secondary Education.* http://www.statcan.gc.ca

Strauss, Anselm, and Juliet Corbin. 1998. *Basics of Qualitative Research: Techniques and Problems for Developing Grounded Theory.* Thousand Oaks: Sage.

Stromquist, Nelly, and Karen Monkman, eds. 2014. Defining Globalization and Assessing Its Implications for Knowledge and Education, Revisited. In *Globalization and Education*, 1–19. Lanham: Rowman and Littlefield Education.

Suara Pembaharuan. *Schools Have Role in Abolishing Multiculturalism Values.* Last modified 20 August 2013. http://suarapembaharuan.com

Sukma, Rizal. 1997. Indonesia's *Bebas Aktif* Foreign Policy and the 'Security Agreement' with Australia. *Australian Journal of International Affairs* 51: 231–241.
Sukmadinata, Nana. 1997. *Curriculum Development: Theory and Practice.* Bandung: PT Remaja Rosdakarya.
Sundhaussen, Ulf. 1981. Regime Crisis in Indonesia: Facts, Fiction, Predictions. *Asian Survey* 21: 815–837.
Syarief, A.H. 1993. *Curriculum Development.* Pasuruan: Buana Indah.
Tagliacozzo, Erica, and Tineke Hellwig. 2009. *The Indonesia Reader: History, Culture, Politics.* Durham: Duke University Press.
Tangkilisan, William. *Why a Comprehensive Partnership with the US Is Crucial for Indonesia.* Last modified 20 October 2011. http://www.thejakartaglobe.com
Teichler, Ulrich. 2003. Mutual Recognition and Credit Transfer in Europe: Experiences and Problems. *Journal of Studies in International Education* 7: 312–341.
Tempo. *58 Public Universities Are Still Non-tax Revenue.* http://www.tempo.co/news
———. *Students of Indonesian Education University in Bandung Reject the Draft of BHP Legislation.* http://www.tempointeractive.com/hg/nusa/Jawamadura
The House of Representatives, Indonesia. *UUD 1945.* Last modified 18 January 2013. http://www.dpr.go.id/id/uu-dan-ruu
The Indonesian Institute. *Indonesian-American Cooperation.* Last modified 6 August 2013. http://www.theindonesianinstitute.com
Thomas, Robert. 1973. *A Chronicle of Indonesian Higher Education.* Singapore: Chopmen.
Thompson, Hayden, and M.C. Williams. 1995. The Crossing Frontiers. *International Schools Journal* 15: 13–20.
Thompson, Jeff, and Mary Hayden. 1995. International Schools and International Education: A Relationship Reviewed. *Oxford Review of Education* 21: 327–345.
Thomson, Janice. 1995. State Sovereignty in International Relations: Bridging the Gap Between Theory and Empirical Research. *International Studies Quarterly* 39: 213–233.
Tickner, Arlene. 2003. Seeing IR Differently: Notes from the Third World. *Millennium Journal of International Studies* 32: 295–324.
Tikly, Leon. 1999. Postcolonialism and Comparative Education. *International Review of Education* 45 (5): 603–621.
———. 2004. Education and the New Imperialism. *Comparative Education* 40 (2): 173–198.
Tilak, Jandhyala. 1988. Foreign Aid for Education. *International Review of Education* 34: 313–335.
———. 2002. Knowledge Society, Education and Aid. *Compare* 32 (3): 1–15.

Toby Harnden. Barack Hussein Obama: US 'One of the Largest Muslim Countries in the World'. *Telegraph*. Last modified 14 May 2001. http://www.telegraph.co.uk/news

Tomlinson, John. 1996. Cultural Globalisation: Placing and Displacing the West. *European Journal of Development Research* 8: 22–35.

Torres, Carlos. 2002. Globalization, Education, and Citizenship: Solidarity Versus Markets? *American Educational Research Journal* 39 (2): 363–378.

Triandis, H.C. 1994. *Culture and Social Behaviour*. New York: McGraw.

Triandis, H.C., R. Bontempo, H. Betancourt, M. Bond, K. Leung, A. Brenes, J. Georgas, C.H. Hui, G. Marin, B. Setiadi, J.B.P. Sinha, J. Verma, J. Spangenberg, H. Touzard, and G. de Montmollin. 1986. The Measurement of Etic Aspects of Individualism and Collectivism Across Cultures. *Australian Journal of Psychology* 38: 257–267.

Tujan, Antonio, Audrey Gaughran, and Howard Mollett. 2004. Development and the Global War on Terror. *Race and Class* 46: 53–74.

UGM. *Indonesian Government Regulation number 30/1990*. http://luk.staff.ugm.ac.id/atur/PP30-1990PendidikanTinggi.pdf

UNESCAP. *Country Report on Local Government Systems: Indonesia*. http://www.unescap.org

UNESCO. 2001. *Council of Europe's Code of Good Practice in the Provision of Transnational Education*. http://unesco.org/upload/Indonesia

———. 2005. *OECD Indicators*. Paris: Organisation for Economic Cooperation and Development.

———. *Millennium Development Programmes*. http://www.unesco.org/new/en/education

———. *Trends in Global Higher Education*. Last modified 30 July 2012. http://www.unesdoc.unesco.org

United Nations. 2006. *Treaty Handbook*. New York: Treaty Section of the Office of Legal Affairs.

US Embassy in Indonesia. *Ambassador Marciel's Visit to Eastern Indonesia*. http://www.jakarta.usembassy.gov

USAID. *Education – USAID/Indonesia*. http://www.indonesia.usaid.gov/en/programs/education

———. *Comprehensive Partnership*. http://www.indonesia.usaid.gov

———. *Fact Sheet: Higher Education Partnership with Indonesia*. http://www.indonesia.usaid.gov

———. *Syiah Kuala: Aceh Teacher Training Support*. http://www.indonesia.usaid.gov/en/Usaid/activity/218/syiah_kuala_aceh_teacher_training_support

USAID Indonesia. *Education – Preparing Indonesian Students for Learning, Work, and Community*. http://www.indonesia.usaid.gov/en/programs/education

———. *Indonesia–Democracy and Governance Assessment*. http://www.indonesia.usaid.gov

———. *SERASI-Education.* http://www.indonesia.usaid.gov/en/usaid/activity/323/serasi_education

———. *The Aceh Polytechnic Program – TAPP.* http://www.indonesia.usaid.gov/en/usaid/activity/233/The_Aceh_polytechnic_program_TAPP

———. *United States Government Invests $19 Million in Indonesian Higher Education.* Last modified 10 July 2001. http://www.indonesia.usaid.gov

US Department of Education. *Secretary Duncan's Remarks at the US-Indonesia Higher Education Summit.* Last modified 10 January 2013. http://www.ed.gov/news/speeches/secretary-duncans-remarks-us-indonesia-higher-education

US Department of State. *Background Note: Indonesia.* Last modified 20 February 2013. http://www.state.gov

———. *Developing a Comprehensive Partnership with Indonesia.* Last modified 18 February 2009. http://www.state.gov/secretary

———. *Guidance on Non-binding Documents.* Last modified 8 January 2013. http://www.state.gov/s/l/treaty/guidance

———. *Indonesia: Country Specific Information.* Last modified 12 May 2013. http://www.travel.state.gov

———. *United States-Indonesia Comprehensive Partnership.* Last modified 15 May 2013. http://www.state.gov

———. *United States-Indonesia Education Cooperation. Bureau of Educational and Cultural Affairs.* Last modified 10 August 2012. http://www.exchanges.state.gov

———. *United States-Indonesia Education Cooperation. Bureau of Educational and Cultural Affairs.* http://www.exchanges.state.gov

US Trade Information Center. *Political and Economic Environment.* Last modified 12 May 2013. http://export.gov/Indonesia/

USINDO. The 2009 US-Indonesia Comprehensive Partnership: Engaging the Non-government Sector, 16–17 April 2009. http://www.usindo.org/resources/the-2009-u-s-indonesia-comprehensive-partnership-engaging-the-nongovernment-sector/

———. *The Origin of the Indonesian Nation: The Indonesian Revolution of 1945–1949.* Last modified 30 June 2012. http://www.usindo.org/resources

———. *US-Indonesia Summer Studies Programme.* http://www.usindo.org

USINDO Brief. *US-Indonesia Relations: The Next Phase.* Last modified 20 January 2013. http://www.usindo.org

USINTEC. *Programs.* Last modified 20 June 2012. http://www.usintec.org/projects

Van Heek, Marieke. Holland Attracting Few Indonesian Students. *The Jakarta Post,* 2 June 1998.

Van der Kroef, Justus. 1970. Indonesian Communism Since the 1965 Coup. *Pacific Affairs* 43: 34–60.

Van De Walle, Nicolas. 1989. Privatization in Developing Countries: A Review of the Issues. *World Development* 17: 601–615.
Vaughn, Bruce. 2013. *Indonesia: Domestic Politics, Strategic Dynamics, and U.S. Interests.* Washington, DC: Congressional Research Service.
Verger, Anthony, and Xavier Bonal. 2006. Against GATS: The Sense of a Global Struggle. *Journal for Critical Education Policy Studies* 4 (1): 1–27.
Vincent-Lancrin, Stephan. *Cross-Border Higher Education for Development.* Last modified 10 June 2013. http://www.oecd.org/education/research
Voice of America. US Boosts Higher Education Exchanges with Indonesia, 5 April 2011. https://www.voanews.com/a/us-boosts-higher-education-exchanges-with-indonesia-119321869/137595.html
Waelchli, Heinz, and Shah Dhavan. 1994. Crisis Negotiations Between Unequals: Lessons from a Classic Dialogue. *Negotiation Journal* 10: 129–145.
Walker, Melanie, and Pat Thomson, eds. 2010. *The Routledge Doctoral Supervisor's Companion: Supporting Effective Research in Education and Social Sciences.* New York: Routledge.
Waters, Malcolm. 1995. *Globalisation.* New York: Routledge.
Weinstein, Franklin. 2007. *Indonesia Foreign Policy and the Dilemma of Dependence: From Sukarno and Suharto.* Singapore: Equinox.
Welch, A.R. 2007. Blurred Vision? Public and Private Higher Education in Indonesia. *Higher Education* 54: 665–687.
White House. *Fact Sheet: Higher Education Partnership with Indonesia.* Last modified 10 February 2013. http://www.whitehouse.gov/sites/.defaultfiles/us-indonesia_higher_education_partnership
Wicaksono, Teguh, and Deni Friawan. 2011. Recent Development in Higher Education in Indonesia: Issues and Challenges. In *Financing Higher Education and Economic Development in East Asia*, ed. Shiro Armstrong and Bruce Chapman. Canberra: ANU Press.
Wilhelm, Ian. Building on Presidential Bonds: US and Indonesia Seek Ways to Increase Academic Partnerships. *The Chronicle of Higher Education*, 31 October 2011.
Winter, Richard. 1987. *Action Research and the Nature of Social Inquiry: Professional Innovation and Educational Work.* Aldershot: Gower.
Wise, William. Indonesia's War on Terror. *USINDO*, August 2005. Last modified 20 July 2014. http://www.terror.wcke.org
Wolfensohn, James. *A Partnership for Development and Peace.* Last modified 10 August 2012. http://www.worldenergysource.com
World Bank. *Indonesia Managing Higher Education for Relevancy and Efficiency*, 12 April 2011.
———. *Internal Debt Statistics 2013.* Last modified 28 March 2013. http://www.data.worldbank.org/sites/default/files

———. *Investing in Indonesia's Education: Allocation, Equity, and Efficiency of Public Expenditures.* http://www.sitesources.worldbank.org/INTINDONESIA/Resources/publication/280016-1152870963030/InvestEducationindo.pdf

———. *Pages from World Bank History: The Pearson Commission.* Last modified 20 August 2012. http://www.web.worldbank.org

WTO. 2011. *Education Services – WTO.* http://www.wto.org/

———. *Education Services – WTO. Council for Trade in Services.* Last modified 23 December 1998. http://www.wto.org

Yanow, Dvora, et al. 2008. Case Study Research in Political Science. In *Encyclopedia of Case Study Research*, ed. Albert Mills, Gabrielle Durepos, and Elden Wiebe. London: Sage.

Yin, Robert. 1994. *Case Study Research: Design and Methods.* 2nd ed. London: Sage.

Yudhi, Wahdi, et al. A Comparative Study of Negotiation Styles of Education Managers in Australia and Indonesia. *SEAMEO,* 14 December 2006.

Zajda, Joseph. 1998. Globalising Education: Designing a Renewed Agenda for Teacher Education. *Education and Society* 16: 87–98.

Zartman, I.W. 2008. *Negotiation and Conflict Management: Essays on Theory and Practice.* London: Routledge.

Zartman, Ira William, and Guy Faure. 2005. The Dynamic of Escalation and Negotiation. In *Escalation and Negotiation in International Conflicts*, ed. Ira William Zartman and Guy Faure. New York: Cambridge University Press.

INDEX

A
Abangan, 136
Abbott, Anita, 103n2
ABC-CLIO, 199
abolish, 64
abolition, 153
Abrahamsen, Rita, 15, 31, 32, 47n35, 53n123, 53n124, 119, 133n27
academy, 2, 3, 5, 13, 14, 20, 21, 38, 39, 41, 57, 64, 72, 73, 75, 76n7, 81, 85, 88–95, 101, 112, 115, 117, 139, 141, 142, 167, 172, 183, 187, 189
accommodation, 58
accountability, accountable, 15, 31, 63, 78n37, 170, 175, 176, 178n7
accreditation, 59, 63, 64, 73, 77n16, 115, 142, 183
Acharya, Amitav, 157n1, 158n3
achievement, 183
activity, 2, 5, 9, 27, 31, 37, 42, 63, 115, 122, 124, 130n12, 135, 150, 167, 169, 175–7, 185, 186, 193, 194
actors, 4, 15–18, 20, 31, 37, 42, 43, 48n45, 49n61, 115, 116, 128, 168, 182

adaptation, 19, 29, 35, 135, 150
ADEA Biennial Meeting, 179n25
Adlung, Rudolf, 45n15, 45n16
administration, 14, 35, 124, 189
admission, 169
advisors, 62, 140
Advisory Committee on External Aid and Development, 78n37, 178n7
affiliation, 10, 39
affluent, 39, 40, 104n9
Afghanistan, 98
Africa, 54n136, 179n21
agency, 4, 13, 15, 18, 19, 24, 32, 46n24, 117, 123, 125, 186
agenda, 95, 98, 99, 101, 102, 143, 185, 188
Agnew, John, 55n154
agriculture, 2, 68, 69, 97, 164, 166
airport, 109
Alagappa, Muthiah, 6n1, 51n96, 133n60
Albatch, Philip, 2, 6n1, 15, 18, 19, 21, 48n54, 48n55, 49n64, 49n66, 49n67, 50n72, 50n76, 50n84,

Note: Page numbers followed by "n" refers to notes.

50n85, 53n113, 53n114, 53n126, 132n43
Alexander, Bryan, 10
alignment, 119
All Asia Aviation Academy (AAA Academy), 70–1
alliance, 18, 43, 100, 169
allocation, 114
amalgamation, 136
ambassador, 69, 70, 102, 166, 167
American Field Scholarship (AFS), 97, 188
Americanization, 21, 24, 29, 140, 141
Amin, Samir, 52n104
Amris, Hassan, 70, 167
Amsterdam, 51n94
analysis, 3, 4, 9–55, 177, 182, 184, 194
Anchora, 124
Angkor Wat, 199
Anglo-Chinese, 74
animism, 135, 148, 156, 186
antagonism, 120
anti-American, 98
Anwar, Dewi Fortuna, 6n1, 26, 51n96, 105n33, 126, 133n60
APBN, 77n20
appointments, 168
archipelago, 136
Aristotle, 48n46
Aritonang, Margaret, 159n22, 159n23
Armstrong, Shiro, 76n2, 76n6, 130n18
Arnot-Hopffer, Elizabeth, 54n144
Arnove, Robert, 48n51, 50n80
article, 4, 17, 106n37, 184
articulation, 10, 11, 39, 138, 182
ASEAN. *See* Association of Southeast Asian Nations (ASEAN)
ASEAN-Australia-NZ FTA (AANZFTA), 163
ASEAN Framework Agreement on Services (AFAS), 60

Asia, 14, 21, 26, 32, 33, 54n136, 58, 69, 126, 142, 166
Assalamualaikum (Peace be with you), 153
assessment, 2, 3, 17, 19, 37, 43, 92, 124, 175
assets, 112
assistance, 3, 5, 13–15, 20, 23, 26, 27, 31, 33, 36, 39, 46n24, 46n27, 66–8, 81, 91–4, 101, 103, 116, 118–29, 164, 165, 174, 183, 185, 187–90
Association of Southeast Asian Nations (ASEAN), 69, 70, 92, 140, 166
Atma Jaya Catholic University, 206
atrocities, 68, 69, 165
attainment, 26, 123, 126
attitude, 3, 24, 26, 99, 100, 110, 136
Australia, 14, 71, 85, 87, 93–4, 99, 100, 102, 108, 171–5, 188–90
authentic, 168
Authoritarian, 35
automotive, 59, 60, 125
autonomy, 19, 20, 37–8, 43, 61, 63, 64, 74, 75, 110, 111, 114, 115, 119, 131n21, 147, 152, 169, 170, 184, 189, 191
avenues, 6, 194
Ayers, 154

B

Badan Akreditasi Nasional Perguruan Tinggi (BAN-PT), Accreditation Board of National Higher Education, 63
Badan Hukum Milik Negara or State Legal Entity (BHMN), 61, 63, 64, 75
Badan Hukum Pendidikan or Education Legal Body (BHP), 63, 64, 75
Balinese, 135

INDEX   217

Ballard, 54n143
Baltimore, 6n1, 132n43
Bandung Institute of Technology (ITB), 58, 88
Bangkok, 76n5
Baptista, May, 78n25
barrier(s), 14, 16, 38, 40, 44, 143, 170, 173
Baskoro, Faisal, 130n10
Bauer, Peter, 26, 51n98, 52n101
Bebas Aktif, 209
behaviour, 30, 121, 136
Belgium, 90
Berkeley (University of California-Berkeley), 83
Bert, Wayne, 196
Bettancourt, 158n6
BHMN. *See* Badan Hukum Milik Negara or State Legal Entity (BHMN)
BHP. *See* Badan Hukum Pendidikan or Education Legal Body (BHP)
bilateral, 5, 34, 37, 66, 67, 69, 72, 88, 99, 116, 120, 121, 128, 131n25, 139, 166, 174, 176, 177, 184, 190
Binder, Claudia, 175, 180n33
biodiversity, 67
Biswal, Nisha, 133n61
blueprint, 74
Bodha, 135
Bodin, Jean, 47–8n43, 48n46
Boediono, Vice-Pres, 66, 77n21, 123
Bogor Institute of Agriculture, 4, 58
bombardments, 90
Bonal, Xavier, 3, 7n10, 18, 22, 35, 36, 48n50, 50n75, 50n83, 54n140, 112, 129n7, 142, 146, 159n32, 160n42
Bontempo, 158n6
Booth, Ken, 150, 155, 160n48, 160n59

border(s), 1, 3, 9, 11–13, 16, 21, 27, 30, 31, 34, 35, 39, 42, 43, 59, 60, 70, 71, 75, 87, 116, 128, 138, 140, 145, 155–7, 182–5, 191
borderless, 3, 30
Bortin, Meg, 105n34
Boston, Massachusetts, USA, 32, 53n122, 74, 104n9
Boulder, Colorado, USA, 47n33, 54n136
boundary, 25
Bourdieu, Pierre, 22
brainer, 70, 167
Brazil, 75, 169
Brenes, A., 158n6
Brett, Noel, 158n9
Brill, E.J., 136, 158n4
Brinkerhoff, Jennifer, 47n33
Brock-Utne, Brigit, 23, 31, 51n86
Brodjonegoro, Satryo, 76n6, 77n11
Buana Indah, 210
Buchori, Mochtar, 6n1, 63, 76n1, 77n12, 132n43, 159n28
Buddhism, 135, 145, 147, 148, 156, 186, 192
budgetary, 65, 91–4, 103, 114, 120, 186, 187, 190
Budianta, Melani, 95, 105n30
Burbules, Nicholas, 19, 34, 52n113, 53n114, 53n133, 54n144
Bush, Pres. George, 66, 78n27, 189

C

cabinet, 123
Cai, Deborah, 197
campus, 10–12, 15–17, 27, 40, 42, 43, 87, 183
Canada, 14, 71
Canto, Isabel, 47n35, 105n31, 170, 176, 179n29, 181

Capaldi, Nicholas, 108, 129n1
capita, 54n136
capitalism, 110, 152
Carnegie Endowment, 197
Carnoy, Martin, 18, 19, 22, 23, 31, 32, 35, 36, 49n58, 49n62, 50n76, 50n78, 50n85, 50n86, 51n87, 53n113, 53n125, 53n126, 54n141, 54n144, 91, 104n17, 104n18, 112, 125, 129n7, 181
Catholicism, 145, 159n39
census, 144
certificate, 169
chancellor, 16
Chapman, Bruce, 76n2, 76n6, 130n18
chapter, 1–55, 57–79, 81–133, 135–61, 163–94
charities, 58
chess, 59
Chevron, 124, 130n12, 132n38
Chilcote, Ronald, 49n57, 50n85
Chile, 133n49
China, 75, 93, 94, 105n28, 105n33, 172, 175, 188, 190
Chowdhury, Anis, 196
Christianity, 136, 145, 159n39
Cialdini, R.B., 198
citizen, 2, 17, 32, 33, 64, 89, 91, 105n25, 115, 139, 154, 160n60, 187
citizenship, 59, 146, 154
civic, 137
civilization, 30, 139
Clark, Helen (Prime Minister), 69, 166
classification, 182
classroom, 83, 154
climate, 6n4, 14, 100, 105n31, 125, 131n28, 168
Coca-Cola, 130n12
coequal, 110
collaboration, 2, 6, 11, 16, 58, 68, 70, 72, 73, 82–6, 90, 96–8, 100, 104n10, 112, 115–18, 143, 145, 152, 164–77, 178n19, 189, 193, 194
collectivism, 136, 152
Collins, Christopher, 23, 50n81
Colombia, 180n33
Colombo Plan, 14, 67, 164
colonialism, 1, 13, 50n77, 52n104, 144, 182
colony, 125
combination, 24, 25, 29, 135, 147, 148, 152, 156
commercialization, 14, 15, 17, 22, 34, 36, 43, 63, 64, 110, 112, 114
communalism, 136
communication, 2, 30, 102, 104n16, 124, 143
communism, 14
compensation, 119
competence, 154
competition, 61, 64, 65, 77n18, 113, 115, 143, 156, 175, 192
competitiveness, 36, 65, 89
complementary, 18, 146, 170
completion, 13, 24, 176
complexity, 3, 20, 43, 139, 155, 194
compliance, 112, 114, 156
component, 82, 123, 184
compulsory, 12, 145–7, 153, 156, 185, 191, 192
conceptual, 18, 30, 48n45, 168
concessions, 118
Conference of Rectors, Vice-chancellors and Presidents (CORVIP), 179n21
confidence, 144
confidentiality, 16
conform, 3, 21, 27, 187
conforming, 21
confusion, 74, 75
conjunction, 59, 73, 183
connection, 66, 85, 96, 97, 111, 147, 151

Conoco, 15, 115, 124
Conrad, L., 54n143
consciousness, 36
consensus, 135–7
consequence, 3, 21, 30, 35, 65, 76n7, 92, 113, 119, 137
consideration, 26, 28, 107, 117
consolations, 96
constitute, 37, 91, 94, 99, 136, 181
constitution, 16, 64, 65, 121, 144
constraint, 168, 170
construction, 125
consultancy, 39
consultant, 90
consultation, 66, 68, 121, 136, 165
consumer, 30, 104n9, 182
consumption, 9, 10, 12, 13, 38, 40, 59, 71, 75, 86, 87, 116, 139, 156, 182, 183, 193
context, 3, 19, 25–7, 29, 33, 43, 83, 108, 111–13, 144, 145, 147, 148, 154, 157, 183, 188, 191
contribution, 93, 108, 115, 127, 128, 170, 174, 190, 194
controversy, 64, 137, 139
convenience, 110
Conversi, Daniele, 29, 52n110
Cookson, Peter, 25, 51n93
cooperation, 13, 14, 24, 37, 61, 67, 69, 71, 72, 82, 87, 88, 103, 109, 110, 116, 117, 121, 122, 124, 131n25, 136, 139, 141, 143, 145, 152, 157, 166, 169, 172, 186, 190
coordination, 4, 68, 165
Cormier, Dave, 10
cornerstone, 1, 126
corollary, 24, 27, 35, 141
corporatization, 114, 130n16
counterbalance, 189
counterpart, 5, 72, 81, 90, 103, 107, 111, 119, 187–9
Cox, Robert, 20, 49n63

Crawford, Gordon, 15, 31, 32, 47n34, 47n35, 53n123, 91, 104n17, 104n18
creation, 26, 130n16, 157, 192–3
credibility, 84, 86, 100, 113
crisis, 14, 38, 123
criteria, 5, 41, 42, 175, 184
criticism, 27, 32, 185
critics, 165
cross border, 1, 3, 9, 11–13, 59, 71, 75, 87, 138, 156, 182, 183
crosscultural, 5, 172
crux, 23, 27, 32, 142
curricula, curriculum, 21, 22, 24, 25, 27, 29, 30, 33, 36, 39, 43, 64–5, 71, 73, 76n7, 91, 111, 117, 121, 127, 138, 141, 143–57, 160–1n60, 169, 184, 185, 191, 192

D
Dakar, Senegal, 179n25
Dale, Roger, 30, 36, 53n120
Damayanti, Ika, 158n7
Daniel, John, 15, 51n88, 52n110
Darmasiswa scholarships, 97, 188
Dasen, P.R., 53n122
Dayak ethnic group, 135
dean, 141, 145
debt, 54n136, 92, 120
decentralization, 61
defence, 41, 68, 78n36, 105n31, 121, 165, 178n7
definition, 9–13, 17, 18, 29, 163, 164, 168, 182
delivery, 4, 7n5, 9, 10, 12, 13, 16, 17, 24, 34, 39, 42, 71, 73, 86–8, 113, 116, 128, 136, 138–40, 142, 147, 156, 176, 181–3, 185, 193
de-mining, 67
demise, 35, 143
democracy, 29, 66, 105n31, 146

democratization, 121, 122
dentistry, 67, 164
Denzin, Norman, 7n13
dependence, 21, 23, 27, 31, 33, 44, 52n104, 82, 84, 89, 91, 92, 94, 103, 138, 155–7, 181, 187, 188, 193
DeRosa, Dean, 55n147
Dessoff, Alan, 7n7, 106n39
Deutscher Akademischer Austauschdienst (DAAD), 13
development, 1–3, 5, 6n4, 10, 13–15, 19, 22–4, 26–8, 31–3, 36, 38, 39, 43, 46n24, 57, 69, 71, 72, 78n37, 79n43, 89, 91, 93, 121–9, 131n28, 143, 154, 155, 157, 165, 166, 168, 170, 176, 178n7, 182, 187, 188, 190
De Wit, Hans, 51n94
Dhakidae, Daniel, 201
Dharmawan, Frederik, 199
Dhavan, Shah, 213
differential, 3, 22, 146
Diouf, Abdou, 168, 169, 179n25
director, 66, 72, 99, 109, 110, 117, 118, 149, 150
directorate, 12
disaster, 69, 166
disease, 100, 126
diversity, 144
dividends, 62
Djiwandono, Soedjati, 68, 164
dollar, 66, 93, 167
dominance, domination, 5, 18, 19, 21, 22, 27, 29, 36, 43, 89, 91, 151, 181
donations, 16
Donnans, Hastings, 53n116
donor, 15, 26, 27, 31–7, 43, 58, 68, 119, 122, 165, 187
Downes, Gerard, 179n20
Draxler, Alexandra, 179n28
Drysdale, Robert, 32, 53n128

E
earth, 69, 166
Easterlin, Richard, 46n22
Eckstein, Harry, 201
economists, 133n49
education, 1, 9–55, 57–79, 81–107, 136, 163–81
educationalists, 157, 192
Education for All (EFA), 2, 83
educator(s), 2, 10–13, 27, 41, 59, 64, 72, 73, 83, 85, 113, 120, 124, 126, 131n21, 138, 154, 156, 182, 183, 187, 188
Effendi, Sofian, 131n23
effort(s), 26, 46n24, 58, 84, 86, 108, 125, 144, 171, 173, 174, 185
Egege, Sandra, 54n143
Elbe, Stefan, 199
elementary, 114, 148, 192
elimination, 40, 41
elite, 32, 57, 64, 94, 139
Elliot, Julian, 2, 7n8, 21, 49n71, 54n144, 112, 129n6, 181
embargo, 119
embassy, 66, 68, 69, 78n29, 108, 159n35, 164, 166
emissaries, 96
employment, 36, 104n11, 126
empowerment, 19
Encyclopaedia, 54n136
endorsement, 75
enforcement, 32, 37, 38, 44
engagement, 21, 72
England, 87, 98
English Language Fellow Program (ELFP), 2, 101, 143, 144
enrolment(s), 57, 74
enterprise, 7n14, 62, 130n16
environmental, 126
equality, 5, 15, 34, 35, 107–33, 186
equity, 61
era, 1, 46n19, 61, 68, 123, 146, 165, 182

INDEX 221

eradicate, 126
establishment, 27, 39, 40, 67, 69, 115, 124, 144, 164, 166, 184
Etzioni, Amitai, 125, 132n44
European Action Scheme for the Mobility of University Students (ERASMUS), 13
evolution, 69, 166
examination, 30, 32, 35, 111, 112
expansion, 13, 14, 21, 23, 29, 31, 63, 64
expatriates, 21, 62, 67, 81, 88–94, 164, 187
expectation, 101, 108, 109, 168
expenditure, 65, 91, 103, 114, 187
expertise, 43, 44, 141, 181, 187
exploitation, 23, 34, 111
exploration, 107
exporter, 23, 39
ExxonMobil, 5, 15, 115, 117, 124

F
facilities, 115–17, 123
faculty, 92, 93, 96
Fadilah, Rangga, 130n10
Fahmi, Mohammad, 200
failure, 86, 95, 171, 172
Fairuz, 146
Fasimpaur, Karen, 45n8
Faure, Guy, 214
fee(s), 11, 40, 58, 62, 87, 101, 113, 131n21
Feith, Herbert, 158n2
Fetsch, Frank P., 200
fieldwork, 39, 40
Fischer, Karin, 77n21, 77n22
Fitriani, Evi, 159n21
Floyd, Robert, 130n11
fluency, 143
folktales, 148, 186, 192
football, 59

Foreign Direct Investment (FDI), 40
foreigners, 62, 73, 89, 91, 100, 186, 187
forum, 139
foundation(s), 1, 4, 5, 14, 63, 65, 74, 123, 141, 145, 172, 184, 191
Fox, Christina, 18, 19, 48n51
franchise, 41
Frank, Andre, 23, 50n86, 131n7
Frase, Peter, 113, 129n7
freedom, 94, 185
Free Trade Agreement (FTA), 55n147, 163
Friawan, Deni, 76n2, 76n6, 77n11, 130n18
friendship(s), 96
Fulbright Scholarship, 14
fundamentalism, 95
fundamentalists, 98
Furedi, Frank, 19, 49n57, 49n62

G
Gandhi Institute of Business and Technology, 70, 74, 140
Gargano, Terra, 21, 45n5, 49n64, 53n113, 53n114, 54n144
Gaughran, Audrey, 211
Gellner, Ernest, 52n110
General Agreement on Trade in Services (GATS), 1, 3, 12, 14, 16, 22, 23, 27, 35–7, 59–61, 76n7, 112, 114, 142, 146
generation(s), 148, 175, 186, 192
Geneva, Switzerland, 12
geopolitical, 96
geothermal, 69, 166
Gerring, John, 6, 8n15
Gidden, Anthony, 22
Giles, Sophie, 137, 158n5–8
globalization, 1, 14, 21, 139, 153
globe, 30

glossary, 129n9
goal(s), 2, 74, 83, 89, 125–8, 141, 153, 154
Gonzales, Alfonso, 54n136
Goodwin, Robin, 137, 158n5–8
governance, 68, 71, 78n37, 120, 121, 165, 178n7, 186
government(s), 2, 13, 58, 86, 108, 139, 165, 186
Gray, Clive, 130n11
Greece, 13
Green, Madeleine, 112, 129n8
Green, Mike or Michael, 68, 78n32, 78n37, 165, 177n2, 178n7
Griffith Institute for Higher Education, 54n143
Grotius, Hugo, 48n46
guidance, 137, 155, 173
guideline(s), 16, 101, 154, 185
Güruz, Kemal, 46n18, 46n23, 46n26, 46n27

H

Hadiniwata, Bob, 201
Hadiz, Vedi, 201
Hale, Claudia, 158n9
Hannah, Janet, 47n35, 105n31, 169, 170, 176, 179n29, 181
Hara, Abubakar, 201
Harden, Nathan, 11, 45n10–12
Hardihardaja, J., 58, 76n5
harmony, 137, 138, 156
Harnden, Toby, 210
Hart, L.A., 48n44
Harvard, 11, 32
Harvard Institute for International Development (HIID), 2
Hassan, Amris, 70, 167
Hauck, V., 179n30, 180n34
Hayden, Mary, 25, 51n94
Haz, Vice-Pres. Hamzah, 106n38, 185

Heath, Joseph, 52n106
Hein, Gordon, 201
Hellwig, Tineke, 210
Henkin, Louise, 35, 54n139
Herbert, Werlin, 201
Hermanto, Agus, 140
hierarchy, 136
Higher Education Leadership and Management (HELM), 92
Hindley, Donald, 132n29, 132n45
Hinduism, 135–7, 145, 147, 148, 156, 186, 192
Hinsley, Francis, 48n43
Hinz, Sarah, 179n22
historical, 1, 13, 19, 23, 31, 33, 88, 170
HIV, 126
Holland, 212
homogenization, 21–2, 24, 25, 27–31, 36, 44, 138–47, 156, 186, 191, 192
Hong Kong, 59
hostility, 97, 100, 101
Huang, Futao, 2, 18, 19, 21, 34, 45n5, 47n29, 49n65, 49n67, 50n72, 53n132, 54n144
human(s), 22, 26, 28–30, 32, 65, 68, 89, 91, 120, 123, 125, 126, 154, 165, 182
humanities, 58
Hume, Cameron, 6n4, 131n28
hunger, 126
Huntington, Samuel, 29, 52n108
hybrid, hybridization, 22, 24–6, 28–31, 35, 44, 54n141, 136, 147–55, 157, 186, 192–3

I

icons, 155
identification, 4, 174
ideology, 17
Idrus, Nirwan, 202

INDEX   223

ignorance, 101
illiteracy, 1, 26, 123, 126
imbalance, 168
immigration, 61, 62, 140
imperative, 20, 99
imperialism, imperialist, 5, 19, 22–4, 31–3, 50n77, 81, 85, 91, 94, 155, 156, 181, 187, 188, 193
implementation, 4, 114
implication, 4, 5, 17, 61, 75, 120, 149, 188
imprisonment, 73
improvement, 116, 123, 133n28
inability, 75
inadequacy, 26
incapacity, 26
inclusion, 25, 145, 146, 169, 184, 192
incoming, 136
inconsistency, 74, 140
incorporation, 137
independence, 91, 92, 122, 123, 125, 141, 144, 147, 148
India, 14, 26, 75, 86, 122, 135, 171, 175
indication, indicator, 6, 81, 89, 155, 157, 167, 185, 186, 193
indigenous, 135–8, 142, 143, 145, 147, 148, 156, 186, 192
Indonesia, 1, 13, 57, 81, 107–33, 135, 163, 181
Indonesia-US relationship, 66, 85, 102, 188
inequality, 15, 20, 35, 108, 119
infant, 54n136
influenza, 100
infrastructure, 2, 28, 40, 124, 131n28
initiation, 174
initiative, 1, 16, 22, 39, 66, 71, 83, 112, 121, 183, 190
insight, 18, 19, 175, 194
insistence, 41
inspection, 63

installation, 75
institution, 3–5, 9–12, 14–16, 21–3, 27, 30–2, 34–6, 38–44, 57–9, 61, 63, 64, 67, 68, 71–5, 82–5, 87, 89, 91, 100, 110, 113–15, 117, 122, 123, 125, 138–41, 145, 153, 164, 165, 167, 169, 172, 173, 176, 181–5, 187, 190, 191
institutionalise, 141
instrumental, 151, 170, 176, 184
integrate, integration, 18, 22, 169
integrity, 6, 63, 147, 156, 181
Intel, 115, 124
intellectual, 65, 186
interaction, 18, 20, 135, 136, 145, 147, 150, 152, 157, 185
interdependence, 3, 109, 149, 152, 157
interfaculty, 141
International Court of Justice (ICJ), 34
International Financial Institutions (IFIs), 120
internationalization, 24, 149
International Monetary Fund (IMF), 120
Internet, 10, 16, 42
internship, 12, 39, 40, 70
interpenetration, 151, 152, 157
interpretation, 4, 26, 30
intertwined, 19, 48n48
intervention, 41, 42, 184
interviewee, 153
introduction, 1–8, 17
intrusion, 41
invade, 99
invaluable, 153
investigation, 36
investment, 40, 61, 92, 105n31, 112, 114, 116, 127
investor, 112, 113
invitations, 2
involvement, 2, 27, 28, 43, 68, 89, 111, 125, 127, 149, 150, 165, 184

Iraq, 95, 98
Irwin, Rachel, 202
Ishengoma, J.M, 179n21
Islam, 135–8, 145, 147, 148, 153, 156, 186, 192
Islamist, 185
issue, 1, 6, 17, 18, 36, 62, 67, 75, 97, 101, 107, 113, 114, 116, 121, 123, 137, 157, 169, 173, 191, 192

J
Jakarta, 67, 97, 164, 183
Jandt, Fred, 158n10
Japan, 70, 84–6, 93, 171, 190
Javanese, 135–7, 151, 152
Jing, Gu Jian, 47n29, 54n144
Johnston, Marylyn, 160n57
Jones, L.P, 130n11
judiciary, 121
jurisdiction, 41, 42

K
Kaharingan, 135
Kahin, Audrey, 198
Kay, Lena, 132n37
Keats, Daphne, 46n25
Kelly, G.P, 15, 47n34
Keynes, Milton, 179n26
Khon Kaen University, 70
Kilby, Christopher, 53n129
King, Kenneth, 168, 179n24
Kivimaki, Timo, 105n32, 129n5, 130n30, 134n33
Kleden, Ignas, 203
Knight, Jane, 3, 7n11, 9, 25, 26, 41, 44n3, 44n4, 51n94, 51n95, 182
KOPERTIS, Coordination of Private Higher Education Institutions. *See* Kordinasi Perguruan Tinggi Swasta (KOPERTIS), Coordination of Private Higher Education Institutions (KOPERTIS)
Koran, 153
Korea, 85, 93, 171, 172, 190
Krasner, Stephen, 3, 34, 37, 38, 54n134, 54n146, 55n147, 55n151
Krause, Keith, 157n1
Kroef, Justus, 46n20
Kuan, Eric Koo Peng, 199
Kubo, A.E., 79n55
Kurikulum Tingkat Satuan Pendidikan (KTSP), Education Unit Level Curriculum, 64. *See also* Kurikulum Tingkat Satuan Pendidikan (KTSP), Education Unit Level Curriculum
Kutieleh, Salah, 54n143

L
Lane, Bernard, 158n13, 158n14, 158n17, 159n22
Larson, Deborah, 204
LDS. *See* less developed state (LDS)
Leadbeater, Maire, 68, 78n39, 165, 178n9
leader, leadership, 25, 68, 71, 119–24, 126, 128, 136, 154, 165, 175, 187, 190
learners, 9, 35, 83, 137
lecturer, 73, 98, 137, 139, 140, 153, 170
legislated, 59–65, 75, 184
Leifer, Michael, 77n23
Lembaga Ilmu Pengetahuan Indonesia (LIPI), Indonesian Institute of Sciences, 84
less developed state (LDS), 1, 3, 6, 13–21, 23, 24, 26–39, 42–4, 52n104, 54n136, 103, 111, 112, 125, 141, 147, 168, 181, 184, 186–8, 194

Leung, K, 158n6
liberalization, 112–14
liberty, 118, 128
Limkokwing University for Creative Technology, 70, 74, 140
Lincoln, Yvonna, 7n13
Lingard, Bob, 29, 30, 52n107, 53n114, 53n115, 54n142, 140, 159n27
Lipschutz, Ronald, 160n48, 160n59
literacy, 54n136, 123
literature, 1, 4, 16, 17, 104n10, 141, 144, 147, 148, 153, 164, 192
lobbies, 94
Loughlin, Martin, 54n137
Lum, Thomas, 67

M

Machan, Tibor, 129n1
machinery, 59
maintenance, 18, 24, 39, 42, 127, 149, 157, 177, 192
malaria, 126
Malaysia, 44n3, 139, 172, 194
Malik, Abdul, 6n1, 63, 76n1, 77n12, 134n43, 159n28
Maluku, 136
management, 64, 69, 82, 89–91, 116, 120, 124, 166
Marginson, Simon, 130n16, 55n153
marketplace, 30
Maroy, Christian, 54n142
Marut, Don, 104n15
Massachusetts, 32
Massachusetts Institute of Technology (MIT), 32
Massey University, 170
Massive Open Online Courses (MOOCs), 10, 11, 45n11
math, mathematics, 95, 146, 154
Maulia, Erwida, 76n4
maximise, 110

maximum, 62, 73, 140
McBurnie, Grant, 10, 41, 44n3, 45n5, 55n153
McClure, Maureen, 7n6
McNamara, Robert, 46n27
MDG. *See* Millennium Development Goals (MDG)
mechanism, 112, 113, 168, 193
medicine, 58
Megawati, 185
Meiji Restoration, 13
melange, 29
Memmi, 19
memorandum, 16. *See also* memorandum of agreement (MoA); memorandum of understanding (MoU)
memorandum of agreement (MoA), 16, 37
memorandum of understanding (MoU), 16, 37, 59, 82, 83, 87–9, 90, 93, 94, 96–8, 101, 104n10, 115, 117, 118, 128, 137, 144, 145, 149–53, 163, 170, 185
mergers, 10, 39
merit, 1, 57
method, 25, 32, 154, 194
Millennium Development Goals (MDG), 2, 125, 126
mimesis, 21
ministerial, 65, 73, 121
ministry, 4, 59, 61, 62, 69, 71, 73, 91, 131n21, 139, 146, 154, 165, 185
Ministry of National Education (MONE), 63, 115
mission, 122, 187, 190
MKDK, specialist basic subjects. *See* Mata Kuliah Dasar Keahlian (MKDK), specialist basic subjects
MKDP, supporting subjects. *See* Mata Kuliah Penunjang (MKDP), supporting subjects

MKDU, general basic subjects. *See* Mata Kuliah Dasar Umum (MKDU), general basic subjects
MoA. *See* memorandum of agreement (MoA)
mobility, 9, 10, 13–15, 17, 31, 34, 42, 182, 185, 186
modernity, 3
Moll, Luis, 18–20, 48n49, 49n59, 54n144
Monash University, 72, 139
MONE. *See* Ministry of National Education (MONE)
monetary, 121
Monkman, Karen, 49n61
MOOCs. *See* Massive Open Online Courses (MOOCs)
Mooney, Francis, 161n29
Moran, Louise, 181n27
Morgan, G., 168, 179n23
Morrow, Raymond, 18, 20, 48n47
mortality, 54n136, 126
motivation, 112
MoU. *See* memorandum of understanding (MoU)
movement, 9, 10, 12, 21, 39, 59, 71, 138, 156, 170, 182, 184
Mugridge, Ian, 181n27
Muller, Joachim, 46n28
multiculturalism, 153
multilateral, 120
multinational, 30
Munck, Ronaldo, 19, 49n57, 49n62, 50n85
mutuality, 122, 185
myriad, 35, 49n61

N
Nafisah, Nia, 160n7
Naidoo, Rajani, 3, 7n12, 18, 26, 27, 48n50, 52n103
Nanere, Marthin, 104n16
nanotechnology, 84
Nasional Kurikulum (KURNAS), national curriculum, 154
nationalism, nationalist, 104n14, 119
nationality, 41
Natsios, Andrew, 46n24
needy, 109
negotiation, 4–6, 15, 18, 37, 104n14, 110, 118–21, 125, 136, 138, 139, 151, 157, 164, 167, 168, 194
negotiator, 90, 91, 97, 107, 108, 142, 143, 149–51, 164, 169–5, 186, 192, 193
neighbour, 69, 100, 114, 166, 172, 173, 175
Neil, Michael, 179n26
nepotism, 101
Netherlands, 72, 88, 144. *See also* Holland
Netherlands Zendeliggenootschap, Dutch mission-based education, 72
neutrality, 51n88
New South Wales (NSW), Australia, 130n16
New York, USA, 126
New Zealand, 4, 5, 14, 67–71, 85–7, 93, 94, 98, 107, 163–7, 169–77, 183, 184, 189, 190, 193, 194
New Zealander, 164
Nguyen, Phuong-Mai, 2, 7n8, 21, 49n71, 50n72, 54n144, 112, 129n6, 181
Nitisastro, Widjoyo, 123
noble, 65
Noel, Brett, 160n9
non-normative, 6, 163–80
nonprofits, 73, 74, 79n49, 139, 140, 183, 185
non-state, 4, 15, 18, 20, 42, 43, 48n45, 49n61, 115, 116, 128, 182
non-Western, 3, 21, 112

norm, 109–11, 129n3, 186
normative, 6, 17, 28, 108, 163–80
Norwine, Jim, 54n136
Novotny, Daniel, 94, 99, 105n27, 106n35, 106n36, 106n38
Nsubuga-Kyobe, Apollo, 104n16
Nuh, Mohammad, 140
Nye, Joseph, 29, 52n108, 52n109

O
Obama, Barack (Pres), 66, 77n22, 97
obedience, 137, 138, 156
obstacle, 33, 101, 188
offshore, 4, 10, 16, 27, 42, 68, 69, 164, 166
Ohio, USA, 4
open educational resources (OER), 10
opponents, 76n7, 136
opposition, 36, 97, 100, 106n37
Oregon, USA, 96, 101
organization, 4, 12, 13, 82, 142, 152, 169, 183
orientation, 21
origin, 72, 182
O'Sullivan, Brendan, 113, 130n15
Otago University, 68, 164
outcome, 100, 121, 125, 146, 169, 175
outline, 5, 6, 43, 65, 73, 110, 112, 125, 126, 147, 164, 175, 186
outreach, 124
ownership, 112, 167, 170, 176

P
Paasi, Anssi, 55n155
Pacific, 66, 93, 96
Pakistan, 14, 98
Palestine, 94
Pancasila, state ideology of, 136
Pancawardhana (education based on Pancasila), 148. *See also* Pancasila, state ideology of

Pardoen, S., 206
parliament, 121, 140
participation, 58, 115, 123, 126, 145, 154, 184
partnership(s), 2, 5, 6, 10, 15, 20, 31, 43, 66, 67, 71–3, 82, 84, 90, 92, 94–7, 99, 102, 117, 120, 121, 124, 125, 128, 153, 154, 163, 164, 167–70, 175–7, 178n13, 183, 184, 187, 188, 190, 193–4
partnerships for enhanced engagement in research (PEER), 2, 124
Passasung, Nikolaus, 161n34
paternalism, 168
Pearson Commission Report, 46n27
pecuniary, 110
Pelita Harapan Foundation, 74
Pembaharuan, Suara, 160n53
Pennycook, Alastair, 3, 18, 22, 48n50, 50n74, 142, 181
Peraturan Pemerintah (PP), government regulation, 141, 150
perception, 21, 82, 84, 99, 145, 157, 194
Pereira, Ana, 12, 45n15, 45n16, 54n146
performance, 112, 124
periphery, 22
personnel, 73–5
perspective, 1, 3, 17–20, 24–8, 33, 35, 37, 43, 76n7, 100, 118, 152, 170, 172, 174, 182, 188
Pew Research Centre, 98
phenomenon, 1, 13, 45n11, 64
Pieterse, Jan, 24, 29, 51n90, 52n112, 147, 151, 160n45, 160n49
Pike, Graham, 48n53
pillars of service of higher education (Tri Darma Perguruan Tinggi), 65
polytechnic, 57, 121
Poortinga, Ype, 53n122
Portland, Oregon, USA, 4, 151
post-colonialism, 19, 52n104

postgraduate, 69, 87, 93, 166
post-secondary, 2–4, 10, 12–17, 23, 42, 46n29, 57–79, 92, 113, 114, 123, 131n21, 142, 164–7, 182, 184, 192
poverty, 1, 26, 32, 120, 123, 126, 168
PPP. *See* public-private partnership (PPP)
practitioners, 27, 43, 74
preference, 149, 152
preparation, 174
presence, 5, 9, 10, 12, 13, 15, 21, 28, 42, 57–79, 86, 87, 113, 115, 116, 139, 140, 145, 182, 183, 185
preservation, 19, 28, 41, 153, 186, 192
presidency, 2, 102, 185
president, 46n27, 63, 66, 69, 71, 78n27, 87, 88, 91, 93, 97, 113, 123, 166, 168
prestige, 29
primacy, 17, 28, 35
principle(s), 16, 31, 34, 35, 37, 73, 86, 109, 114, 121, 137, 163, 168, 169, 171, 172, 177, 185, 186, 194
priority, prioritising, 27, 64, 66, 73, 95, 116, 155, 157, 173
Private Training Establishment (PTE), 163
privatization, 64, 112, 113
probe, 105n29
productivity, 141
professors, 11, 110
profit-making, 70, 74, 140
program, 2–4, 9–11, 13–17, 37, 42, 43, 63, 64, 68–73, 75, 77n16, 83–8, 101, 114–17, 120–4, 128, 138, 139, 142–4, 148, 154, 156, 157, 163, 165, 166, 169–71, 174–7, 181–5, 190, 192–4
programmes to extend scholarships and training to achieve sustainable impacts (PRESTASI), 2, 124

prohibition, 148
promotion, 34, 38, 112, 174
proponents, 19, 139
proposals, 37, 174
proposition, 187
provider(s), 3–5, 10, 11, 15, 22, 23, 34, 36–9, 42–4, 59–61, 64, 70, 71, 74–6, 76n7, 77n16, 84, 89, 91, 92, 110–16, 118, 127, 128, 138–40, 142, 146, 175, 182–7
province, 146
provision(s), 2, 3, 9, 10, 14, 16, 31, 34, 59–64, 73, 107, 114–16, 128, 138, 174, 182, 183, 185
provost, 16
publication(s), 4, 184
public-private partnership (PPP), 4, 7n14, 83, 85, 115, 117, 124
Punten, hello, 153
Purwadi, 76n1
Putera, Eka, 136, 158n4

Q

Quacquarelli Symonds (QS), 58
qualification, 10, 11, 17, 38, 75, 76, 86, 101, 138
quantitative, 159n22
quotas, 94, 102, 190

R

Rais, Amien, 106n38
ratification, ratify, 16, 59
RCEP. *See* Regional Comprehensive Economic Partnership (RCEP)
realities, 107, 172
recipient, 3, 15, 21, 23, 26, 27, 31–6, 38, 39, 43, 44, 91, 93, 96, 181, 187
reciprocal, 85, 167, 168, 170–2, 193
reciprocity, 168, 185

recognition, 3, 34, 41, 42, 58, 85, 100, 113, 118, 122, 127, 185, 187
reconfiguration, 31
reconstruction, 43, 123
rector, 16, 63
reform, reformation, 120, 121, 123
Regel, Ompron, 141, 159n30
regime, 65
regional, 61, 67, 68, 117, 121, 131n25, 165
Regional Comprehensive Economic Partnership (RCEP), 163
regulatory, 72, 147, 156, 191
rehabilitate, 122
relationship, 2, 3, 5, 6, 15, 17–20, 23, 28–31, 33, 34, 37, 38, 43, 66–72, 81–91, 93–103, 107–12, 115, 116, 118–20, 122, 125–8, 129n2, 129n3, 131n25, 131n26, 137–9, 141, 144, 146, 147, 149–51, 154–7, 163–80, 183–94
relevance, 121, 124, 125
reliance, 83, 85, 103, 187, 188
relief, 124
removal, 14, 16, 38, 44, 114
renewable, 69, 93, 166
RENSTRA, 2, 129n4
repatriation, 41
repercussions, 102
requirement, 59, 112, 114, 170
researcher, 10, 82–5, 105n29, 143, 152, 153, 168, 175, 187, 188
resistance, 120
responsibility, 16, 31, 32, 59, 61, 63, 108, 117, 121, 122, 131n26
restriction, 61, 113, 141
retention, 44
revenue, 172
Rezasyah, Teuku, 124
rhetoric, 168
Rhoads, Robert, 50n81
Rhodes, Robert, 129n7

Rhoten, Diana, 50n76, 50n78, 53n113, 53n126, 54n141, 54n144, 104n17
Riady, Aileen, 74
Riady, John, 139, 158n18
Ricklefs, Merle Calvin, 159n36
Riker, David, 47n32
Rizal, Saiful, 130n20
Rizvi, Fazal, 25, 29, 30, 51n94, 52n107, 53n114, 53n115, 54n142, 142, 159n27
RMIT University, 72
Robertson, Susan, 30, 36, 53n120, 54n145
Rockefeller Foundation, 14, 123
Rowe, William, 51n89, 52n111, 54n141
royalties, 62
rubber, 189
Rudijanto, 158n15, 158n19, 159n22
Rukun, principle of avoiding conflict, 137
rupiah, 92
Russia, 26

S
Sabbatical, 12
safeguards, 61, 137, 184
Said, Edward, 23, 50n82, 50n85
Saito, Masaru, 46n22
sake, 98
salaries, 133n21
Salim, Emil, 123
Samoff, Joel, 22, 50n80
Sampoerna Foundation, 4
sanctioning, 114
Sanou, Sini, 54n141
Santos, Boaventura, 23, 50n81
Sasak ethnic group, 135
Satan, 98
Saud, Udin, 160n57
Sauve, Pierre, 12, 45n14, 54n146

SBY (Pres. Susilo Bambang Yudhoyono of Indonesia), 69, 166
Schelling, Vivian, 51n89, 53n111
scholar, 10, 12, 16, 19, 25, 28, 31, 34, 51n88, 98, 100, 104n10, 109, 152, 177, 182, 194
scholarship, 2, 13, 14, 25, 39, 40, 67, 69–71, 85, 91–3, 97, 99, 101, 116, 124, 164, 166, 170, 171, 173, 176, 177, 180n31, 183, 188, 193
schooling, 12
Schott, Jeffrey, 55n147
Schwarz, Adam, 78n36, 178n6
Schwindt, Erika, 25, 51n94
scientific, 13, 23, 65, 181
Scoop, 78n40, 178n10
Sebastian, Eugene, 72
secondary, 4, 12, 46n29, 60, 74, 114
security, 67, 78n36, 94, 99, 105n31, 138, 178n6
Segall, Marshall, 53n122
sekolah tinggi, advanced school, 57
Selvaratnam, Viswanathan, 18, 19, 21, 46n25, 49n66, 49n67, 50n72, 50n84, 50n85, 53n113
Semarang, 58
semester, 84
Senegal, 179n24
sensitivity, 24
Setiawan, Denny, 161n60
Shale, Douglas, 25, 51n93
Shin, Yashui, 133n49
Shoemake, Ann, 158n9
shortages, 72, 74, 75, 141
shortfall, 185
Silver, Charles, 78n26
Singapore, 33, 86, 104n13, 171, 175
Siqueira, Angela, 7n10, 22, 50n75, 50n83, 129n7, 142, 159n32, 160n42
situations, 10, 17, 26, 33, 37, 52n104, 118, 156, 182

skills, 2, 3, 24, 41, 65, 72, 74, 75, 83, 85, 86, 120, 124, 126, 143, 172, 181, 186, 188
Smith, James, 159n21
Soejatmiah, Sri, 159n31
solidarity, 31, 53n113
Sophists, 13
sovereignty, 1, 3–6, 9–55, 89, 103n2, 107, 110–19, 121, 127–9, 148, 155–9, 168, 182, 184–94
Soviet Union, 119
specialised, 90
specialist, 124
spheres, 30
Spilimbergo, Antonio, 29, 52n106
Sri Lanka, 14
stability, 1, 33, 180n31, 182
stabilization, 33
stakeholders, 16, 73, 79n49
standardization, 89
Stanford University, 6n1, 50n81, 51n96, 129n1, 133n60
statistics, 146, 154
status, 1, 26, 61, 63, 64, 78n39, 108, 123, 126, 178n9
Stellenbosch, South Africa, 179n21
Stoltz, Karl, 66, 78n25
strategic, 2, 14, 103, 121
strength, 85, 118
Stromquist, Nelly, 19, 49n61
structuralism, 19, 48n48
Subiandro, 135
subsidies, 58
Sudibyo, Bambang, 66, 77n24
Suharto, 1, 2, 61, 65, 68, 104n14, 123, 146, 165, 182
suicide, 137
Sukarno, 2, 104n14, 148
Sukma, Rizal, 209
Sulawesi, 136
Sumarlin, J.B., 123
Sumatra, 136

summarise, 38, 101
Sundanese, 152
superiority, 15, 82, 84
Suprapto, Parikesit, 112
Suprayitno, Totok, 66, 77n22
supremacy, 17, 35, 37, 48n46
Surabaya, 58
Surakhmad, Winarno, 113
survival, 137
sustainability, 69, 124, 126, 166, 178n19
Syarief, A.H., 210
Sydney, Australia, 51n88
symbiotic, 133n26
symmetrical, 167
sympathy, 94
syncretistic, 136
synthesis, 136
system, 3, 11, 19, 21, 22, 26, 27, 30, 35–7, 44, 57–65, 72, 74, 75, 76n7, 112, 136–9, 141, 142, 144, 147, 155, 156, 168, 182, 186, 191
systematic, 141
systemization, 142

T
Taiwan, 33
Tambah, Andreas, 139
TAPP. *See* The Aceh Polytechnic Program (TAPP)
taxpayers, 62
Taylor, David, 69, 70, 166, 167
teacher, 69, 83, 85, 121, 123, 126, 137, 138, 141, 144, 156, 166
technological, 15, 90, 172, 174
technology, 2, 5, 11, 58, 67, 71, 72, 81–7, 90, 91, 95, 116, 121, 122, 124, 136, 154, 181, 186
Teichler, Ulrich, 212
tension, 5, 20, 94, 95, 99, 101, 105n29

Terlouw, Cees, 2, 7n8, 21, 49n71, 54n144, 112, 129n6, 181
territorial, 24, 34, 35, 41, 119, 185, 189, 191
territoriality, 41
territory, 17, 36, 38, 115, 138, 145–7, 151, 156, 182, 184, 185, 191
terrorism, terrorist, 78n27, 95, 185, 189
tertiary, 12, 30, 58, 72–4, 114, 141, 163
textbooks, 141, 144, 148
Thailand, 70, 86, 171
The Aceh Polytechnic Program (TAPP), 132n38
theoretical, 3, 18, 20, 143, 194
theorists, 3, 18–24, 27–37, 43, 52n104, 91, 111, 157, 181, 182, 187
theory, 5, 19, 47n43, 52n104
thinkers, 137
Thompson, Hayden, 51n94
Thompson, Jeff, 25, 51n94
Thomson, Janice, 37, 55n148
threat, 1, 3, 23, 27, 30, 31, 33, 99, 118–20, 128, 142, 143, 149, 150, 152, 184, 189, 190, 192
Thummarukudy, Muralee, 45n8
Tiara Bangsa Anglo-Chinese School, 74
Tickner, Arlene, 55n149
Tikly, Leon, 3, 7n9, 18, 19, 22, 30–2, 36, 49n57, 49n62, 50n73, 50n76, 50n78, 50n79, 50n84, 53n113, 53n117, 53n126, 91, 104n17, 146, 160n44, 181
Tilak, Jandhyala, 26, 32, 52n99, 52n100, 53n127
Timor, 68, 69, 120, 165
TNE. *See* Transnational Education (TNE)
tolerance, 151, 152, 184
Tomlinson, John, 21, 49n68, 52n105, 140, 159n26
Tong-In, Wongsothorn, 76n5

Tooley, Michael, 48n43
topic, 110, 111, 127
Toraja, Tanah, 136
Torres, Carlos, 18–20, 34, 48n47, 48n51, 49n60, 49n62, 50n80, 50n81, 51n94, 52n113, 53n114, 53n133, 54n144
tradable, 139
tradition, 24, 30, 138, 147, 156
traditionalism, 136
Transnational Education (TNE), 1–6, 9–55, 65–72, 81–106, 111, 115, 116, 121, 127, 128, 138–140, 145, 155, 157, 164, 167, 181–9, 191, 193, 194
transnationalism, 19, 143, 147
transparency, 167, 168, 186
transportation, 123, 125
transposition, 168
Treacher, David, 69, 166
treasury, 63
treatment, 3, 22, 59, 60, 108, 142, 146, 186
treaty, 185
Triandis, H.C., 158n6, 158n7, 158n11, 161n61
tribal, 135
Tunja, Colombia, 175
Turner, Brandon, 47n32
twinning, 10, 11, 15, 17, 43, 138, 156, 182, 183

U

Umakoshi, Toru, 6n1, 132n43
UMI Dissertation Information Service, 201
underdevelopment, 31, 90
uneasiness, 137
unemployment, 89
unequal, 20, 110, 118, 129n3
unification, 144
uniformity, 29
uniqueness, 82, 84, 103
unitary, 73
United Nations Millennium Summit, 126
unity, 152
University of Airlangga, 58
University of Diponegoro, 4, 58
University of Gadjah Mada, 57, 58, 88
University of Padjajaran, 58
University of Slamet Riyadi, 70
University of Wellington, 171
unstructured, 141
unsustained, 175
US Agency for International Development (USAID), 2, 5, 6n3, 6n4, 7n6, 15, 32, 46n24, 67, 83, 85, 92, 97, 100, 103n1, 105n22, 120–4, 126, 128, 131n22, 131n24, 132n28, 132n36, 132n38, 132n40, 132n46, 133n51–3, 133n57, 133n61, 141, 142, 144, 154, 160n56, 187, 190
UUD (Indonesian Constitution), 145, 184, 191

V

validation, 39
Van der Kroef, Justus, 46n20
Van De Walle, Nicolas, 130n11
Van Heek, Marieke, 212
Vaughn, Bruce, 212
venture, 62
Verger, Anthony, 54n140
Victoria University, 85, 86, 174
Vietnam, 90
violation, 35
virtue, 136
visa(s), 41, 186
vision, 74, 75, 116, 131n25
visitor, 62, 140
vocational, 60, 75, 89, 91, 124

W

Waelchli, H., 213
Wales, 87, 105n27, 106n35
Walker, Melanie, 46n21
Walker, Neil, 54n137
Wang, Yibling, 76n5
Wanni, Nada, 179n22
Wardhana, Ali, 123
warrant, 38
Washington D.C., USA, 45n4, 45n14, 52n108, 55n147, 66, 67, 77n21, 122, 130n11, 190
Waters, Malcolm, 21, 49n69, 53n115
weakness, 105n32, 129n5, 143
Weinstein, Franklin, 89–92, 104n12, 104n13, 104n20
Welch, A.R., 76n1, 76n6
welding, 125
welfare, 4, 160n40
Westernization, 21, 29, 140, 141
Westgarth, Corrs Chamber, 72, 79n50
West Papua, 136
Wicaksono, Teguh, 76n2, 76n6, 77n11, 130n18
William, 51n89
Wilson, Frank, 178n18
Wilson, Thomas, 53n116
wisdom, 121, 148, 152, 186, 192
Wolfensohn, James, 47n33
workforce, 33, 123, 125
workshops, 16, 104n10, 143
World Trade Organization (WTO), 1, 3, 7n10, 12, 45n13, 45n15, 50n75, 59, 76n7, 113, 129n7, 130n15, 142, 159n32
writers, 22, 25, 37, 181
WTO. *See* World Trade Organization (WTO)

Y

Yakoboski, Paul, 44n4
Yesnowitz, Joshua, 6, 8n15
Yogyakarta, 57
youth, 97, 124, 188
Yudhi, Wahdi, 104n16
Yudhoyono, Susilo Bambang, 66, 69, 91, 97, 102, 166
Yugoslavia, 122

The manufacturer's authorised representative in the EU is Springer Nature Customer Service Centre GmbH, Europaplatz 3, 69115 Heidelberg, Germany. If you have any concerns regarding our products, please contact ProductSafety@springernature.com

Printed and bound by CPI Group (UK) Ltd, Croydon, CR0 4YY

23/03/2026

02076672-0009